Cognitive Science, Literature, and the Arts

Cognitive Science, Literature, and the Arts

A Guide for Humanists

Patrick Colm Hogan

ROUTLEDGE
NEW YORK AND LONDON

Published in 2003 by
Routledge
29 West 35th Street
New York, NY 10001
www.routledge-ny.com

Published in Great Britain by
Routledge
11 New Fetter Lane
London EC4P 4EE
www.routledge.co.uk

10   9   8   7   6   5   4   3   2   1

Cataloging-in-Publication Data is available from the Library of Congress

ISBN 0-415-94244-6 (hb)
ISBN 0-415-94245-4 (pb)

For my brother

CONTENTS

Acknowledgments

I owe my engagement with cognitive science first of all to my wife, Lalita Pandit, who began reading in the field well before I did and has been a constant source of support and encouragement. My further research was aided by a community of scholars with whom I was able to discuss and debate cognitive science and the arts at conferences in Santa Barbara, Jerusalem, Dartmouth, and elsewhere. This community included Jamshed Bharucha, Terence Deacon, Paul Hernadi, Steven Pinker, Alan Richardson, Elaine Scarry, Ellen Spolsky, Francis Steen, John Tooby, and Lisa Zunshine. I would like to give particular thanks to David Bordwell, Norman Holland, Keith Oatley, and Mark Turner—four path-breaking researchers, without whose work I could never have undertaken a book on cognition and literature, for there would have been no field to discuss. Lalita Pandit read several sections of the manuscript and gave suggestions that have improved the work immensely. Without the encouragement and support of William Germano and Matthew Byrnie at Routledge, this book probably would not have been written. I am also grateful to Henry Bashwiner and his colleagues at Routledge who handled the book's production. Finally, the Office of the Chancellor at the University of Connecticut provided me with a release from teaching duties in order to complete work on this book. The time was invaluable.

The Dustheap of History
Why Cognitive Science Now?

In the early 1990s, a committee for the American Comparative Literature Association argued that comparatists had better move from their narrow literary areas into the larger field of culture study or they would be left on the "dustheap of history" (Bernheimer, et al., 5). Literary study has been around for a very long time, not only in the West, but throughout much of the world; the likelihood that literary study will ever be left on the dustheap of history seems slim. Nonetheless, it is clearly shortsighted for literary researchers and other humanists to ignore important trends in other fields that bear directly on the arts. One such trend is culture study. Many anthropologists, sociologists, and historians have moved toward culture study in the past twenty years. They have developed methods and isolated topics that enrich literary and artistic analyses. Literary critics and theorists have responded by developing the study of culture still further, producing work that not only applies culturalist insights, but helps to reshape the field itself.

Yet, if many social scientists have embraced culturalism in recent years, still more linguists, psychologists, neurobiologists, philosophers, even many anthropologists and sociologists, have moved toward cognitivism. It is customary to refer to the development of cognitive science as "the cognitive revolution" (see, for example, Fodor, 3). The expression is not mere rhetoric. Cognitivist methods, topics, and principles have come to dominate what are arguably the most intellectually exciting academic fields today. The astounding proliferation of programs in the field is testimony to the meteoric rise of cognitive science (see, for example, Dawson, 4–5).

Mark Turner saw the trend more than a decade ago. In *Reading Minds*, he made the almost Foucaultian prediction that "The coming age will be known and remembered, I believe, as the age in which the human mind was discovered. I can think of no equal intellectual achievement" (vii). However, Turner does not draw Foucaultian conclusions from this. Rather, he calls for "a reframing of the study of English so that it comes to be seen as inseparable from the discovery of mind, participating and even leading the way in that discovery" (vii). The discovery to which Turner refers is, of course, cognitive science. Turner goes on to argue that cognitive science will ultimately "require the study" of literature as a crucial product and activity of the human mind. In the past three or four years, cognitive scientists have come increasingly to recognize the truth of Turner's claim. Neurobiologists, cognitive anthropologists, evolutionary psychologists, and computer scientists have taken up literature and art, investigating their structures and purposes, in order to integrate them into an ongoing research program in cognition. Critics and theorists from the arts and humanities have increasingly turned to cognitive science as well. Some of this work goes back two decades. But it is only within the past three or four years that the cognitive study of literature and art has become widespread, passing beyond a limited circle of researchers to a wide range of readers and writers, across a wide range of disciplines. In a recent interview, Steven Pinker maintained that the "growing" list of "scholars and critics" drawing on cognitive science is part of a general trend. He concludes that "We may be seeing a coming together of the humanities and the science of human nature" (Brockman, 6).

The general convergence is important, to be sure. But to my mind, the crucial phrase in Turner's call for literary cognitivism is the one that envisions literary study as "leading the way" in "the discovery of mind" (vii). Turner overstates the case here. I doubt that it is either possible or desirable for literary critics to be the dominant figures in an area that encompasses such a wide range of technical scientific fields, such as neuropharmacology. Norman Holland probably speaks for all of us when he explains that "I cannot write intelligently about cholecystokinin" (*The Brain* 13). The important point is that humanists should not think of themselves as simply applying cognitive science to literature, taking up what scientists have taught us in order to glean a few interpretive insights—or, worse still, to generate the next set of books and articles for tenure and promotion, based simply on the novelty of the approach. It is crucial for humanists and scientists to recognize that the arts should not be some marginal area to which cognitive discoveries are imported after they are made elsewhere. Arts are central to our lives. We think of our attention to arts as peripheral for isolable cognitive reasons. Specifically, we have a prototype for attention to the arts. That prototype overstresses distinctive features. So, when we think of "attention to the arts," we think of, say, a trip to the ballet or to an art museum. We don't think of watching TV. But watching TV, reading novels, reading stories, going to movies, listening to pop music—these are all "attention to the arts." For most of us, attention to the arts takes up far more of our free time than, say, sex or eating, which all cognitivists recognize as pretty central human activities. For many people, attention to the arts even takes up more time than personal interactions. Moreover, many of our personal interactions include features (e.g., story telling) that are closely related to the arts. In short, the arts are not marginal for understanding the human mind. They are not even one somewhat significant area. They are absolutely central. Put differently, if you have a theory of the human mind that does not explain the arts, you have a very poor theory of the human mind. Indeed, I would go so far as to say that literary study is likely to survive anything, though it will be impoverished (not to mention boring) if it ignores important intellectual developments. However, cognitive science cannot afford to ignore literature and the arts. If cognitive science fails to address this crucial part of our everyday lives, then cognitive science will be left on the dustheap of history.

In connection with this, I believe that Turner is correct that humanists must at least be among the leaders in the cognitive revolution. Literature and the arts pose specific problems for cognitive study; they raise specific issues; they present specific challenges. Humanists who have studied the arts intensively for a long period are in the best position to address these problems, issues, and challenges. A neurobiologist who turns briefly to literature as a side issue is unlikely to do it justice. Of course, humanists have the converse problem. They need to achieve familiarity with cognitive methods and principles. Some writers have proposed collaboration between humanists and scientists (e.g., coauthorship) as a solution to this problem. That is certainly one possibility. However, it is not always practicable. Moreover, even collaboration requires that both parties know quite a bit about both areas.

All this leads to my reasons for undertaking the present volume. The purpose of this book is to provide adequate background for readers to participate in and contribute to a research program in cognitive science and the arts, either individually or collaboratively. The book is aimed primarily at humanists in the sense that I do not give detailed explanations of basic literary history or film technique. I do, however, devote a chapter to introducing the basic principles of cognitive architecture. On the other hand, I believe cognitive scientists will benefit from the treatment of literature, film, music, and painting.[1] They may even find the discussion of cognitive architecture to contain one or two points of interest.

In keeping with its main purpose, this book is not intended as an overview of all the work in the field. Rather, it is a selection of topics and principles designed to allow a reader to take up, understand, develop, and critique other work in cognition, literature, and the arts, and to pursue such work on his or her own. Cognitive science is a vast field. Cognitive theorists might refer to engineering principles, recent debates in the philosophy of language, or research in pharmacology. But most of this is simply not currently relevant for research in the arts. Thus I have sought to define the basic concepts, outline the basic methods, and explore some exemplary instances of cognitive work as these bear on the study of the arts. In connection with this, I also do not try to survey all individual books and essays on cognition and the arts. Instead, I concentrate on one or two theorists or one or two approaches in each chapter. Again, my aim is to introduce the basic ideas of cognitive science and to discuss some of the most important research and theorization in cognition and the arts. It would make no sense to try to cover everything, just as it would make no sense for a guide to psychoanalysis and the arts to try to cover every book and article in the field, even every important book and article.

On the other hand, there is one significant difference between a psychoanalytic guide of this sort and a cognitive guide. The psychoanalytic study of the arts extends back over a century and has been a topic of deep interest to psychoanalysts since Freud himself. Research in cognition and the arts has developed more recently and, for the most part, less systematically. In consequence, some potentially important areas remain largely unexplored. For this reason, the following pages not only present a critical analysis of significant and influential research that has been done in the field. They also explore in a preliminary way some problems and issues that have received too little attention. In other words, the following chapters not only look to past research and theorization. They also point to future possibilities.

The organization of the book is fairly straightforward. The first chapter gives a taste of a cognitive scientific analysis, an illustration of the way a cognitive approach to art may work itself out in a particular case. Specifically, this chapter treats the way a listener cognitively processes music. The discussion is framed by a traditional quandary in aesthetics: Why are we engaged by certain pieces of music while being bored or irritated by others? The second chapter moves from the particular to the general, presenting an overview of cognitive theory. It begins with a broad discussion of what defines the field methodologically and turns from there to summaries of the two major "schools" of cognitivism—representational and connectionist. This chapter examines a range of essential, technical concepts from schemas, prototypes, and working memory (in representationalism) to connection strengths and activation thresholds (in connectionism). The next four chapters are organized around a simple division among author or creator (one chapter), text (two chapters), and reader or viewer (one chapter). In each case, I take up some specific issue that has been important in cognitive study. The third chapter (on the author) examines cognitive research on creativity, isolating some principles of basic creativity (which characterizes most remembered works in any given tradition) and some principles of "radical" creativity (which is associated with works that change the direction of a tradition). This chapter particularly emphasizes the work of Howard Gardner, on the one hand, and the "creative cognition" theorists, on the other. The following chapter examines metaphor, probably the most widely discussed literary topic in cognitive science. It concentrates on the influential theory of conceptual metaphor put forth by George Lakoff and Mark Turner, but also considers alternative views, primarily that of Andrew Ortony and Amos Tversky. The chapter concludes with a discussion of Mark Turner's more recent theory of "conceptual blending," integrating Turner's account with standard principles of representationalism. Chapter 5 takes up some of David Bordwell's ideas to consider the ways in which the viewer cognitively reconstructs the story from the "discourse" or presentation of that story in film. The second part of this chapter turns to the topic of literary universals, treating my own work on universal story structures. Chapter 6, drawing primarily on Keith Oatley's writings, focuses on emotive response to literature as a specifically cognitive phenomenon. It addresses two sources of emotive response—first, the work's narrative structure; second, the reader's individual memories. Chapter 7 reconsiders literary emotion through recent work in neurobiology—a crucial component of cognitive science today. This chapter sets out to reply to another traditional quandary of aesthetics: Why are we moved by the experiences of characters whom we know to be fictional? In the concluding chapter, I turn to evolutionary psychology, the most common system used to explain the development of cognitive and neurocognitive structures and processes. On the one hand, evolutionary study is clearly crucial for understanding human cognition. On the other hand, the field has been marred by methodological laxity. This chapter considers some problems with evolutionary psychology today and suggests some possibilities for its future development.

When appropriate, chapters include an illustrative application of the theory to a particular work. Chapter 1 (music) and chapter 3 (creativity) treat John Coltrane's "My Favorite Things." Chapters 3 (creativity) and 6 (emotional response) consider Pablo Picasso's *Les Demoiselles d'Avignon*. Chapters 2 (connectionism), 4 (conceptual blending), and 5 (story structure), and 7 (emotion and the brain) examine aspects of Shakespeare's *King Lear*. Chapters 4 (metaphor) and 5 (story structure) take up Percy Shelley's "Triumph of Life." Chapters 5 (narrative reconstruction) and 6 (emotional response) consider James Cameron's *Titanic*. There are also briefer references to other works (by John Ford, Anita Desai, Arnold Schoenberg, James Joyce, and others). I have chosen different media, with different modes of composition and production, and different levels of popular reception, in order to give the analyses greater breadth of cultural application.[2]

Predicting the future is not something that anyone does well. I have no special talent in the area. However, all the signs seem to be that cognitive science will become increasingly important over the next few years—across the biological sciences, the social sciences, and the humanities. Like anything else, this could be done well or it could be done badly. Humanists can contribute to the positive development of cognitive science in at least three ways. Most obviously, they can apply and extend cognitive theories in the arts. Second, they can use the arts to challenge cognitive theories and ideas. Again, literary study and related forms of scholarship and analysis can not only benefit from cognitive study. They can contribute to, and even radically alter, research programs in cognitive science. Literature and the arts raise issues about cognition that are not raised in the experimental research. They pose potential problems. They suggest counterexamples. Ultimately, they allow the possibility of more encompassing, more illuminating, and more valid theories of the human mind. Finally, humanists can engage in the sort of political analysis and criticism that is necessary for any discipline. There is nothing uniquely humanistic about this. Political analysis and criticism are part of being human, not of being a humanist. But, historically, humanists have had a particular interest in the political implications and consequences of theories. I have not always agreed with common views on these issues in the humanities. However, awareness of political issues and engagement with those issues has been deeply important in literary study over the past several decades. Given the clear social consequences of many topics treated by cognitive science—especially in the area of evolutionary psychology—such awareness and engagement should be deeply important in this field as well.

CHAPTER 1

"My Favorite Things"
Thinking Jazz

What happens when we listen to music? It is clearly not just a matter of experiencing sequences of sound, for we count some sequences as music and other sequences as noise. This, then, leads us to an apparently prior question: What happens when we distinguish music from noise? In fact, the two questions are inseparable, and they are largely cognitive questions. In the past, a number of theorists have proposed answers to both questions, and to related questions in other arts. Though no response has proven definitive, perhaps the most suggestive and promising responses have come from theorists who were precursors of cognitivism. The best example of this sort is that paragon of modern epistemology, Immanuel Kant. Kant, arguably the greatest philosopher of the modern period, set out an account of the human mind that anticipates cognitivism in many particulars. As Cynthia Freeland put it, he is one of the major "antecedents of the current enterprise of cognitive science" (65; see also Holland *The Brain* 10). His influential treatment of aesthetics clearly includes many important insights and many points of direct relevance for cognitive research in the field. Yet his development of those insights is often obscure. That obscurity may, to some extent, be dissipated by recent cognitive developments.

Specifically, it has been a commonplace since Kant that a feeling of aesthetical pleasure results when we can form the chaos of sensation into some unity—but only when that forming is not habitual. Music is a standard instance. As to unification, W. Jay Dowling (a prominent cognitive theorist of music) actually defines "listening to music" as "perceiving pattern invariants in musical events" (126). To hear a melody, then, is to hear a structure. Of course, this is only in part a matter of the sounds themselves. A melody may be so complex that we do not recognize or "hear" it. The "melody," in this case, strikes us as a random sequence of sounds, thus as noise. At the same time, perceiving patterns does not guarantee a positive aesthetic judgment. After all, merely hearing a melody does not mean that we enjoy it. Some patterns are just too simple. Though most of us have some intuitive sense of the relation between aesthetic experience and nonhabitual pattern-recognition, it has been very difficult to develop the point further. Indeed, even pattern-recognition alone has not been easy to explain. Kant maintained that the mental faculty of imagination synthesizes the set of incoming sensations before they are subsumed under categories of understanding. But it is difficult to say just what this synthesis involves, and just what it means for something to be conformable to the understanding.

Bring the Noise

Intuitively, we might further specify the Kantian idea by distinguishing two aspects of our experience of sound:

1. The intrinsic quality of the sound. Any note on a tuned piano strikes us as musical. A pot dropping to the floor, or a note on an untuned piano, strikes us as unmusical. Our experience and judgment in these cases seem to be based largely on the physics of sound (i.e., the physics of sound as it bears on human ears and brains; for an informative treatment of this topic, see chapter 2 and 100–105 of Jourdain).
2. The structural organization or patterning of different sounds. This aspect is more obviously psychological—and, indeed, cognitive.

In connection with these two aspects of our experience, there are three broad types of displeasure that we experience in relation to sounds that we listen to as music (in contrast with sounds that just happen in the background, that we listen to for information, etc.). The first, of course, concerns intrinsic quality of the sound. We simply find some sounds displeasing. On the other hand, displeasing sounds may have isolable internal structures and they may occur in structured sequences. As such, we may incorporate them in contexts where the displeasure contributes to pleasing effects. In these cases, we refer to the noise as "dissonance." Indeed, in these cases we do not feel that it is noise at all. We hear it as part of a larger, organized whole.

This leads us to the second sort of displeasure. It occurs when we are unable to recognize structural organization. We know that what we are hearing is not random sound—that is why we listen to it. (Random series of sounds occur in ordinary life all the time and we are unperturbed by them, except when they are both obtrusive and intrinsically unpleasurable.) But we hear it as random, thus as noise. This leads to frustration, sometimes even anger—as in those famous incidents when disgruntled patrons marched out of the concert hall cursing Beethoven, Stravinsky, John Cage, or whatever new and innovative composer they have just heard premier an experimental work. On the other hand, sometimes this frustration may lead, not to anger, but to boredom. Sometimes after a short period of annoyance, the frustration dissipates and all the classic features of boredom appear—wandering attention, fidgeting, drowsiness, and so on.

The final type of dissatisfaction is the reverse of this. We have just been discussing music that is too hard. We also experience displeasure when listening to music that is too easy. Here the problem is evidently that there is no challenge whatsoever in synthesizing the relevant unity. Needless to say, judgments of both excessive difficulty and excessive simplicity vary from person to person, and for different ages. Some people take great joy in "Raindrops Keep Falling on My Head," while others find it insufferable. The same point could be made about, say, Arnold Schoenberg's *Second Quartet,* if for the opposite reason. Children seem able to listen endlessly to "I Love You; You Love Me," sung by Barney the Dinosaur, while adults are frequently intolerant of its repetition. In the case of excessively simple music, the sequence of response seems to be almost the exact opposite of that in the case of excessively difficult music. Specifically, we begin with boredom, then become frustrated and even angry. (A few years ago, when the "I Love You" song was at the height of its popularity, a number of adult comedy shows had skits involving violence against Barney the Dinosaur, explicitly as comic punishment for his singing.)

Again, Kant and others give us some basic sense of what is going on here. When we find music too hard, we are unable to isolate patterns. When we find it too easy, that isolation has become habitual. But why is either of these a problem, and why do these problems give rise to the specific patterns just described? Cognitive science gives us a way of beginning to explain these phenomena in much greater detail.

To consider these issues, we need first to note a basic fact about our cognitive make-up. Perceptual novelty produces stimulation and draws attentional focus. Our brains become more active when faced with novel stimuli. Specifically, brain arousal is a function of the transmission of electrochemical impulses among brain cells. This transmission involves *axons,* or fibers extending out from the cells, and chemical *neurotransmitters.* As LeDoux explains, "In the presence of novel or otherwise significant stimuli the axon terminals release neurotransmitters and 'arouse' cortical cells, making them especially receptive to incoming signals" (Emotional 289).

With a low degree of stimulation, our attention wanders; we are dreamy and unfocused. Sleep is, for the most part, a period of low arousal in the *cortex* or outer layer of the brain. Our sense of boredom is, first of all, a matter of low cortical stimulation in a situation where dozing off is inappropriate and where attentional focus is important. Thus we become bored when listening to someone go on and on with the same sort of information. Jones is always complaining. Smith is always obsessing. Yah-dah, yah-dah, yah-dah. The displeasure here is not the result of low cortical stimulation alone. Rather, it is the result of conflict between the level of cortical stimulation and the need for attentional focus. The sameness of the person's speech leads to low cortical stimulation. But the context demands that we pay attention to the details of that speech. Boredom is what follows. If we experience low cortical stimulation when we lie down to sleep, that does not produce boredom because the necessity for attentional focus and engagement is absent. The situation is the same with boring music as with boring speech. The Barney song or "Raindrops Keep Falling On My Head" strikes us as the same thing over and over. The sameness leads to low cortical stimulation. If we can just doze off, that is not a problem. However, if that is not an option, the low cortical stimulation and the necessity of attentional focus, engagement, and so on, lead to boredom.

The precise opposite is the case with difficult music. Someone who cannot listen to Schoenberg—someone who cannot synthesize the stream of incoming sound—will experience continual cortical arousal because he/she will experience continual novelty. Initially, cortical stimulation is a positive experience. But, as in so much else, excessive cortical stimulation really is too much of a good thing. One cup of coffee wakes you up and gets you thinking. A dozen cups give you the jitters and makes it impossible for you to concentrate. As Anderson points out, "optimal" arousal is not at all the same thing as "maximal" arousal (117). Michael Ellis notes that something experienced as "absolutely novel" leads to "aversively high arousal" (qtd. in Anderson 118). That is not all. Excessive arousal is linked with a particular sort of cognitive frustration as well. Our inability to synthesize the incoming sequence of sounds makes us feel "lost." We cannot "follow along." This is referred to as *cognitive disorientation*. All cognitive processes are goal-oriented. We set out to understand situations and events and respond to them in relation to aims. We think through the situations and events in a series of steps, keeping track of where we have been and where we wish to end up. Cognitive disorientation occurs when we find ourselves unable to pursue any consistent cognitive process that leads from past and ongoing experiences to future goals. Any time we find ourselves interrupted or blocked in this process, we become frustrated. In keeping with this, a continually novel experience is a continually frustrating experience. What makes the experience continually novel is that we cannot connect preceding experiences with current experiences and with consistent future goals. For example, in continually novel music, we cannot develop expectations about where the melody will lead and how it will resolve. Anger is the result of prolonged or intense frustration of this sort.

This gives us a plausible explanation for boredom with Barney and anger at Arnold Schoenberg. But how do we explain the second stage of each response, the shift from boredom to frustration/anger in one case and from frustration/anger to boredom in the other? It is actually very easy to explain boredom with difficult music. As the novelty continues, it becomes hard to focus one's attention. As our attention becomes distracted, we find it increasingly difficult to concentrate on the novel sounds. That conflict between spontaneous attention and required attention (e.g., in a concert hall) is a central feature of boredom. But why does our attentional focus drift? It does so because, as the music continues, our experience of the novel sounds and sequences is increasingly an experience, not of novelty, but of sameness.

Here, we need to introduce one aspect of cognitive synthesis, a process called *encoding*. We encode any incoming stream of sensations when we provide those sensations with structure. We do not experience the world as it is in itself. We experience a structured version of the world. Certain details, certain properties, certain relations enter our minds while others do not. Technically, some details and the like are encoded, while others are not. When we say that we cannot follow a complex piece of music, we are not saying that we do not encode it at all. We do not encode the sound of a dog whistle—but that means we just don't hear it, not that we find it excessively complex. Rather, when we find a piece of music overly difficult, we find our encoding inadequate. It doesn't give us enough information to work with. The music is "cognitively opaque," as Lerdahl puts it (231).

Lerdahl distinguishes between two sorts of "musical grammar," the *compositional grammar* and the *listening grammar*. The former is the set of rules that the composer follows consciously or unconsciously in producing the piece—the principles through which he/she patterns the work. The latter is the set of rules that the listener follows (most often unconsciously) in hearing the piece. In many works there is a "gap" between the two (234). In part, this is a matter of encoding. Sometimes our encoding of the music is too crude for us even to approximate the compositional grammar. As a result, we cannot experience the sequence of sound events as a structured piece of music.

Consider, for example, the avant-garde jazz musician, Cecil Taylor. Though I enjoy his ensemble work, I find his solo piano performances very difficult to listen to. Taylor is known for technically virtuoso performances in which his fingers fly up and down the keyboard at a tremendous rate.

Unfortunately, I can't say anything more about Taylor's solos, because that is all I encode—broad contours of movement up and down the keyboard at a tremendous rate. In Lerdahl's terms, I do not hear the "musical surface" or sequence of sound events in such a way as to organize it into a "hierarchy of notes" (239)—for example, a tonal hierarchy in which one note is the tonic or resolving note, another is the tone that leads us to the tonic, and so on. Indeed, a tonal hierarchy—a structure which centers on a resolving note—is the most basic way of cognitively organizing music cross-culturally. Among other things, the tonal hierarchy of, say, the diatonic scale (the standard scale in western music), establishes "a unique 'vector of relations' for each pitch . . . so that the listener can orient himself unambiguously in relation to the other pitches" (247).

This reference to tonality leads to a slight refinement of the preliminary definition of music that we drew from Dowling. Our distinction between music and noise is not a matter of synthesizing the incoming sounds at all (in music) versus not synthesizing them (in noise), perceiving patterns (in music) versus not perceiving patterns (in noise). Rather, it is a matter of synthesizing sounds *in a certain way,* perceiving *certain types* of patterns. We will turn to the details of this below. For now, it is important to note that I clearly do synthesize or unify streams of noise as well as music. I hear the sound of a clattering pot as the sound of a clattering pot, not an unsynthesizable array. I also synthesize Cecil Taylor's solo piano performance. However, I synthesize it in a simple and repetitive form. Structurally, I hear it as the same thing, over and over again.

Thus, in the case of difficult music, I begin with a sense of continual novelty. This leads to excessive stimulation, cognitive disorientation, and frustration, as described. But, as the piece continues, I increasingly hear the music as repetition, thus not as novelty at all. Lacking new experiences, cortical stimulation spontaneously dissipates. The continual sameness of the experience of the music leads to low cortical stimulation with concomitant wandering attention (in a situation where attentional focus is required). The result is boredom. Thus, a sequence of responses that appears bizarre and contradictory—first anger, then boredom—becomes perfectly comprehensible in a cognitive context.

What about the sequence with simple music? This too makes sense when considered in terms of cognitive structures and processes. First, we need to clarify just what the response to banal music is. I do not believe that anger arises directly from boredom. Rather, our usual reaction, after the boredom stage, is something like, "That song is driving me crazy." This sense of "being driven crazy" is what leads to anger and it seems to apply particularly to music that is repeated continuously. People do not, in general, have this reaction when a banal tune is played for the first time. For example, I suspect that anger toward the Barney song did not begin on first hearing, even for those who disliked it very much right from the start. Anger, in this case, seems to require repetition.

To explain this, I need to introduce a few theoretical ideas. If indeed the shift from boredom to anger is the result of repeated exposure, then it must have something to do with memory. Cognitive scientists distinguish several types of memory. The structure closest to the ordinary language meaning of "memory" is *long-term memory,* a complex system of words, facts, and personal experiences, that are permanently stored in our minds. Items in long-term memory may be *activated* by a *probe.* A probe is some idea or perception that in some way matches with a particular memory. For example, part of long term memory is a set of words and associated meanings. These are called *lexical entries.* The word "dog" would serve as a probe that would match with the heading of a lexical entry (*dog*) and thereby activate the meaning ("barking, hairy quadruped, often a pet," or whatever). Suppose I hear someone say, "I am going to buy a dog." Part of what happens in understanding this sentence is that the utterance of the word "dog" serves as a probe that activates the meaning of "dog." Activation, in this context, means bringing that meaning into *working memory.* Working memory is a system that allows me to synthesize information from different sorts of input. Thus it allows me to put together the meanings in the sentence, "I am going to buy a dog," relating these to my current visual perception of Jones, who has his index finger extended in the direction of the pet store, and so on. Working memory has a number of components, including a *rehearsal loop* that repeatedly cycles information, keeping it active. This rehearsal loop has a specifiably limited capacity of five to nine units (e.g., five to nine words) or roughly two seconds (see Gathercole, 20).

When we hear a melody, part of that melody, as encoded, is stored in long term memory. Think, for example, of the song "My Favorite Things" or "Twinkle, Twinkle, Little Star." Most Americans can hum at least parts of those songs because they are stored in long-term memory. The title serves as a probe to activate these memories and allow the humming. As one hears a song over and over, it becomes more fully encoded, which is to say, more information is brought into working memory on each hearing. Along with this, the song is more fully stored in long term memory. Moreover, long-term memory is not like a dictionary. It does not have a fixed formal principle of organization (such as alphabetization, where words beginning with "a" are on top and those beginning with "z" are on the bottom). Rather, memories are organized largely on the basis of their frequency of access. More commonly activated items are "on top" and thus easier to access. For example, it is in general easier to access the lexical entry for 'closet' than for 'armoire.' It is also easier to access a personal memory we have repeatedly discussed, and harder to access a memory we have hardly ever discussed. So, as we hear a song over and over, it becomes easier to access that song. Put differently, more things serve as a probe for the song. A random word that happens to be in the lyrics of the song may activate the song for us simply because the song is so readily accessible.

But what does this have to do with our frustration/anger over the Barney song? Here, we need to return to working memory. When we activate a tune in long term memory, phrases from the tune begin to enter working memory. When we remember a tune very well, each phrase that cycles through working memory serves as a probe for the next phrase in that same song. The tendency of working memory to cyclic repetition combined with the exaggerated accessibility of a simple and frequently repeated tune gives rise to a situation in which the song is likely to cycle repeatedly through working memory. When this continues for a long time, we refer to it as "having a song stuck in your head." This cycling inhibits our capacity to think through problems of real concern to us, since our limited rehearsal memory is used up with the tune—a tune that, to make matters worse, we find unappealing anyway. This leads directly to frustration, and thereby to anger. This is at least part of the reason why boredom can give way to annoyance when an overly simple tune is repeated many times. Note that these same factors make it very difficult to ignore a repetitive song. Parents cannot just treat the Barney song as mere background. Hearing only a little will activate the long-term memory. Then you can be stuck with "I love you; you love me" like some taunting demon in your head for the rest of the day.

But, again, all this is based on a division between works that we synthesize and works that we do not synthesize. Thus far, we have treated that distinction as a sort of black box. Something goes on in our minds that allows us to synthesize some works, but not others, and that makes the synthesis of some too easy. Cognitive science is not silent about what that "something" is. The process of synthesis largely takes place in working memory. It involves inputs from long-term memory and from our senses—or, rather, from some sort of sensory processors. I should say a few words about sensory processors and long-term memory before treating the centerpiece, working memory.

An Ear for Music

From time to time, we all find a piece of music too difficult to synthesize. But some people have this experience more than others. Some have it almost all the time. When speaking of people who seem unable to make sense of any music, other than the very simplest and most repetitive, we say that they do not have an ear for music. Most of the time, our problems with complex music occur in working memory. However, when we are speaking of people who really cannot enjoy any music at all, the problem may indeed be located in the ear, or at least in sensory processing for sound.

Specifically, we all have some sort of processing units for our senses. Again, we do not simply hear all sound vibrations as they are in themselves, like some sort of ideal magnetophone. Rather, we are sensitive to some aspects of sound and some relations between sounds, while we are relatively insensitive to others, and we simply do not experience some aspects and relations at all. For example, in terms of speech sounds, we are sensitive to such intuitively comprehensible things as whether or not a speaker uses his/her vocal chords in saying something. And we are sensitive to such strange matters as whether he/she issues a little puff of air in uttering a particular consonant. (You may not know it, but you distinguish such sounds automatically all the time.) Language developed out of the sound features to which we are sensitive, perhaps making us more sensitive to them in turn. It is similarly the case that we are particularly sensitive to certain properties and relations of sound outside of speech. We have particular sorts of sensitivity to alterations in volume and pitch, to specific relations among simultaneous sounds, and so on.

We may think of various sensory processing systems as delivering sense data to working memory. However, they do not deliver "raw" data. Rather, these systems do at least three things, three things that constitute *encoding* (a process I have already mentioned, but have not fully spelled out). First, they *select* features from the stream of sensory experience. In other words, they do not process everything. Second, they *segment* the stream, breaking it into sequences that can be utilized in working memory and cycled through the rehearsal loop. Third, they partially *structure* the segments.

Take the "phonological processor." When someone speaks to us, we do not simply hear a stream of all the sounds he/she makes. As phonetic analyses indicate, that would be quite a mess. Our working memory would quickly overload and we would suffer cognitive disorientation every time someone greeted us and asked "How are you doing?" The phonological processor takes a complex and partially disordered mess of sound, but turns over a modified and limited packet of information to working memory. For example, the phonological processor will give us the information that a "t" does or does not have a little puff of air (in technical terms, is or is not "aspirated"). But there is plenty of information that it won't give us.

Our general auditory processor, indeed all perceptual processors, operate similarly. Thus, in listening to music, our working memory receives a set of sounds that have been selected, partially segmented, and partially structured by our auditory processor.[1]

With respect to music, segmentation involves at least a rhythmic component and a pitch sequence component.[2] (For simplicity, I will mostly leave harmony aside in what follows.) In pitch sequence, we may distinguish five levels of (hierarchical) structure: overall melody, themes (which compose the melody), phrases (which compose the themes), motifs (short, extramelodic sequences interspersed in phrases), and individual notes. Consider "My Favorite Things." Overall melody and individual notes should be clear enough. As I am using the terms, "My Favorite Things" has two themes. In the Rodgers and Hammerstein original, the first theme ('A') is repeated three times, then the second theme ('B') enters. The reader should be able to recall the two themes on the basis of the first and final verses, which begin with reference to raindrops and dog bites, respectively. '*Phrase*' is an ambiguous term. I am using it to refer to any structural unit of a theme. In a song such as "My Favorite Things," the first level of phrases is easy to isolate as it coincides with the lines of the verses. Thus there are three phrases in melody A. The first phrase (A1) is sung to the opening line about raindrops. It is repeated on the following line about copper kettles. The second phrase (A2) is sung on the third line (about packages). And the third phrase (A3) is sung on "These are a few of my favorite things." Constituents of these phrases may also be considered phrases, or subphrases. For clarity, I will most often refer to segments of phrases in terms of the standard rhythmic units—measures. Finally, motifs are sequences that exist outside the melody and may be inserted into the melody, usually as a variation. These include jazz "riffs." We will consider motifs in more detail below. These levels are marked only partially by the auditory processor. (As we will see, there are further levels of encoding later on, in working memory.)

Again, the incoming stream must be encoded not only for pitch sequence, but for rhythm. The fundamental rhythmic organization involves marking both individual beats and cycles of beats. In other words, it marks where each beat occurs and it marks where any recurrent sequence of beats begins—which is to say, it marks measures. We are good at marking rhythms in any context. But in songs the isolation of rhythmic pattern is facilitated by the words. As Howard Gardiner has pointed out, our earliest sense of musical rhythm is tied to speech rhythm: "Initially, the child's sensitivity to rhythm derives strictly from the placement of accents in the surface lyrics of the song" (154). Though we learn to separate the two, we are always inclined to use speech rhythm to guide our sense of musical rhythm. Rodgers and Hammerstein's original song helps us to encode the rhythm from the opening verse. The music is in waltz tempo. For the most part, each syllable of the first verse marks one beat. Moreover, the first line is in dactyls—stressed syllable, unstressed syllable, unstressed syllable. Thus each measure begins with a stressed syllable and is followed by two unstressed syllables, directly in keeping with waltz tempo. (The only exception comes in the last measure, which has just one unstressed syllable after the stressed syllable.) This makes the rhythm particularly easy to encode.

It is probably worth noting that encoding should not be confused with labeling. To encode the incoming stream of sound in this rhythm—segmenting each three beats as a unit—is not the same as self-consciously recognizing that this is a waltz tempo. One cannot accurately label the piece as being in 3/4 time unless one has encoded it this way. However, encoding does not at all guarantee correct labeling. We do have to acquire or at least develop the ability to encode various rhythms. But this occurs spontaneously and at a young age (by about five; see Gardner 154). Labeling, in contrast, is usually the result of explicit instruction occurring in school.

In discussing the organization of beats into measures with a particular, repeated pattern, we have moved from segmentation into the structure-assigning aspect of encoding. Clearly, the assignment of structure is important with respect to pitch as well. Specifically, the auditory processor has to encode the incoming stream of segmented sound (thus individual notes) for relative pitch. It has to indicate which notes are the same, which are higher or lower (and by how much), and so on. For instance, the opening of "My Favorite Things" would not be encoded as a series of identical tones, or as a series of tones that differ in unspecified ways. Conversely, for most people, the notes would not be encoded as absolute pitches (say, middle E, B, B, F#), but, again, as *relative* pitches. Thus, for most of us, the start of "My Favorite Things" would be encoded as (roughly) a middle-range opening note, ascent by a perfect fifth, repetition of the second note, descent by a perfect fourth, and so on. Finally, here as elsewhere, the assignment of structure does not simply copy nor even merely select facts (in this case, preexisting pitch relations). In part, it actually shapes our experience. For example, Dowling points out that "quarter-steps appear to be encoded as neighbouring half-steps, while the half-steps appear to be encoded accurately" (123). The smallest difference between consecutive pitches in a diatonic system (such as the standard system in the West) is the half-step. Encoding assimilates actual sound relations to those allowed by the system. In cases where the real-world sound relations do not fit the system, the real relations are, so to speak, "rounded off" by the auditory processor (or a subsequent, related processor) in order to fit the system.

In the Long Term

Working memory thus receives a complexly encoded stream of sound from the auditory processor. This stream includes clustered sequences of notes marked with relative pitch relations as well as cyclical sequences of beats. Though it is much tidier than the initial mess of sensation, this is still fairly disordered stuff. A lot more happens before we hear these sounds as music. This leads us to long-term memory.

First of all, elements of the incoming stream serve as probes to activate structures—more technically, *schemas*—from long-term memory. These structures are then used by working memory to organize the pitch and rhythm sequences still further. There are numerous schemas in long-term memory that help guide our assignment of structure to the incoming stream of sound. One particularly important set of schemas bears on the determination of the scale position of the notes. One of the first things working memory does is apply a schema that determines which note is the tonic or tonal center. Based on this, further schemas determine the relative scale positions of the other notes—not merely their relative pitch (which is already given), but their place and function in the scale (as leading tone, nonscale grace note, or whatever). How does this happen? Most of us have schemas in long-term memory that represent particularly common note and chord sequences. (Depending on experience, we will have more or fewer schemas of this sort.)[3] Any piece of music is likely to activate some of these schemas. More exactly, a piece of music *primes* these schemas, which is to say, it makes them ready for access. Then particular, encoded features of the stream of sound activate particular schemas from the primed set. As Lerdahl puts it, "the listener has at his disposal a number of hierarchical organizations possessing certain formal properties and . . . unconsciously attempts to assign" these to the music. For example, it seems that we determine the tonal center of a piece largely through two means. In the simplest case, we isolate the most frequently repeated pitch (i.e., we use a frequency schema). In the more complex case, we match particular intervals to pitch-interval schemas. Thus, the presentation of, say, a C-major chord then a G-major chord tends to trigger a I/V schema (i.e., a schema in which the chords are based on the tonic, or resolving tone, and the dominant, the fifth scale tone above the tonic). The addition of a D-minor chord may trigger the schema for a standard jazz chord sequence of I/II/V (II being the supertonic or second scale note).[4]

The tonal center of "My Favorite Things" is easy to isolate in both ways. In the first theme, the tonic (E) is repeated fifteen times (sixteen times in Coltrane's version). Moreover, the dominant (B), often the second most common note in a piece, is repeated nine times (ten times in Coltrane's version), and the supertonic (F#) is repeated seven times. No other note is repeated more than four times; most occur only twice. This is important because we do not identify the tonal center in isolation. We identify it in relation to other scale notes, in terms of both relative frequency and relative pitch. The dominant is almost always particularly important. The supertonic is often important (depending on the schemas involved). In Coltrane's version, the piano accompaniment is about 80 percent I and II chords (E and F#). In addition, the improvisations stress E and B (tonic and dominant). All this makes the schematization of scale relatively straightforward. But it is still schematization. Being the tonic is not, after all, some directly perceivable property of a particular tone (in this case, E).

Another function of long-term memory involves supplying *motifs*. As I indicated earlier, by "motif," I refer to any extramelodic sequence of notes or any extramelodic way of generating sequences of notes that may be integrated into a phrase as elaboration, ornamentation, or whatever. A simple example of a motif is a trill. A musician might trill a sustained note in order to make it less straightforward. More interesting cases of motifs are the complex "riffs" that we associate with particular jazz musicians. Within the general set of motifs, we may distinguish rhythmic and melodic motifs. A performer integrates motifs into a piece through working memory. For that reason, motifs are usually shorter than the two seconds of rehearsal memory. Among other things, motifs allow jazz musicians to develop improvisations with fluency as the execution of a motif requires minimal cognitive processing. Sloboda notes that "Many aspects of skill become partly automated, and not open to conscious introspection" ('Preface' xiii). Along the same lines, Pressing refers to "The change from *controlled* processing to *automatic* motor processing...a stage at which it has become possible to completely dispense with conscious monitoring of motor programmes, so that the hands appear to have a life of their own driven by the musical constraints of the situation" (139). Clarke makes a related point, referring to what he calls "events." We find "a number of events contained within the performer's repertoire" (8). An improvisation consists in "selections from this...repertoire" (9). Along the same lines, Weisberg discusses the use of "formulas" by Charlie Parker: "Charlie Parker (1920–1955), who is recognized as the greatest improviser in modern jazz... was legendary for playing fluently at incredible speed.... He was also recognized for never repeating himself. Perhaps surprisingly, given Parker's reputation, Owens (1995) has reported that Parker can be characterized as a 'formulaic' improviser. Over his career, Parker acquired a large repertoire of formulas—patterns of notes, ranging from two- or three-note clusters to strings encompassing perhaps a dozen notes—which he used in his solos" (237).

All these writers are referring, in their different terminologies, to what I call "motifs." On the other hand, my usage is somewhat broader than theirs. In my usage, motifs may be employed self-consciously; they may be varied; they may be more or less seamlessly integrated into a melody (in part through variation). Moreover, while many motifs preexist a particular improvisation, others are generated, then repeated and varied, in the course of an improvisation.[5]

Motifs are important not only for performers. They bear on a listener's cognitive processing of music as well. When a motif occurs in the course of a piece of music (e.g., when we hear a trill or a recognizable Coltrane riff), we may schematize and store that motif in long-term memory or perhaps some sort of temporary memory buffer. When that motif recurs later in the piece, it triggers the memory. The two instances are linked in working memory. As a result, the motif is stored again, probably in a more fully elaborated and more stable form. This recurrence contributes directly to our sense that the piece is patterned. Insofar as this carries over from one piece to another, it also contributes to our recognition of a particular musician's style—our sense that the body of his/her work is patterned. Moreover, the best musicians do not simply insert a motif as an isolated sequence. They adapt it to the piece, shape it to a phrase so that it in effect becomes part of that phrase. Take the example of the trill. When a saxophone player introduces a trill into a phrase, he/she begins with a note already present and structurally important in the phrase. Moreover, he/she may vary the speed, direction, or interval of the trill, depending on context.[6] The trill is not simply the repetition of a prefabricated musical sequence. It is the use of a technique in the context of a particular piece. In this way, the trill becomes part of the phrase in question. Indeed, when a phrase incorporates a trill, the subsequent recurrence of the trill may serve as a probe to reactivate the memory of the whole phrase, even without the restatement of that phrase in its entirety. This further enhances our sense of patterning.

But to get a sense of why this enhances our sense of patterning or, more generally, how all this works to produce a coherent musical experience, we need to examine working memory in greater detail.

Hard Work with Working Memory

The task of working memory is first of all to integrate all the incoming material. This begins with the incoming stream of sound. Again, the structures encoded by the auditory processor serve as probes in long-term memory. Activated schemas from long-term memory enter into working memory. These serve to further select, segment, and structure the incoming stream. In other words, they encode it more completely. Most obviously, they serve to encode the sounds, beyond their relative pitch relations, into their scale relations—at least defining the tonal center.

Working memory also employs schemas from long-term memory to isolate themes and phrases that constitute those themes. This is, first of all, a type of segmentation. It extends and, in a sense, completes the partial segmentation that occurred in the auditory processor. Once the themes and their constituent phrases have been isolated, then working memory can proceed with one of its most important tasks in our experience of music, perhaps especially jazz music—the mapping of variations. Specifically, working memory assigns incoming phrases to one of three categories. The first category comprises the basic phrases that are the main constituents of themes. (I will refer to these as "thematic phrases.") These phrases are stored in some sort of memory buffer for schema-based comparison with subsequent incoming phrases. If a new incoming phrase has the right sort of relation to a stored phrase, then it is assigned to the second category—variations on previous thematic phrases. (We will discuss some of these "right relations" below.) Finally, some incoming sequences, such as unintegrated motifs, are assigned to the third category, nonthematic phrases. Though relatively rare in written music, these are common in improvisatory music, especially improvisatory music that sounds formulaic. These nonthematic phrases prominently include the motifs used by jazz musicians to fill out their improvisations. On the other hand, not all motifs are categorized as nonthematic. Indeed, the expert handling of motifs by a skilled jazz musician usually leads the listener to categorize those motifs as variations on thematic phrases.

This process of identifying thematic phrases and variations is simplified in the case of Coltrane's "My Favorite Things" as the themes and basic phrases are already in the listener's long-term memory. They only have to be recalled, not discovered. As Dowling explains, even "untrained listeners distinguish alterations to melodies stored in long-term memory" (124). In any case, with the thematic phrases stored, any incoming sequence of sounds may serve as a probe. If such a sequence activates one of the thematic phrases, then that thematic phrase is sent through rehearsal memory and there is a further level of structural attribution as the incoming sequence is mapped onto the thematic phrase. Moreover, it is very easy to activate thematic phrases stored in memory as they are already primed by the context of the entire piece. For this reason, we tend to hear incoming sequences as variations on thematic phrases, even when the relation between the two is fairly distant. As Lerdahl explains, "At global levels parallelism becomes the overriding grouping principle: listeners try to hear parallel passages in parallel places in the overall structure" (240).

More exactly, in Coltrane's "My Favorite Things," each phrase is four measures long. In Coltrane's performance, each measure lasts one second. In consequence, the unit that cycles through working memory is probably a semiphrase (i.e., a half phrase of two measures). This is a particularly apt unit in this case because it reflects a structural division within many of the phrases themselves. Consider the first phrase, A1, connected with the opening line about raindrops. The first measure begins with the tonic, E, moving up to the dominant, B. The second measure begins on the supertonic, F#, moving down to E. The second semiphrase begins with the B, moving up to E. The final measure begins with F# and moves down to E (EBB/F# EE// BEE/F#E).

If we treat the first semiphrase as the initial statement, we see that the second semiphrase is, in effect, a variation on the first. Working memory presumably cycles the first semiphrase through rehearsal memory while mapping it onto the incoming sounds of the second. The result is that the second semiphrase is (or at least may be) categorized as a variation of the first. The opening measure of the variation (roughly) reverses the opening measure of the statement (EBB becomes BEE). The second measure of the variation simply ties together the second and third notes from the statement. In other words, F#EE becomes F#E, where the E note in the variation is held for two beats (while each E in the initial statement had been held for one beat). The second measure of the variation is, in this way, a simplification of the second measure of the statement. Similar points could be made about A2.

In contrast, A3 does not break after the second measure. It works as a single unit. On the other hand, the melodic structure is much simpler. The music and lyrics of A3 are as follows:

B   C D/E   F# G //A B   A   / F#   (E B)

These are a/ few of my// favorite/ things

The first eight notes of the phrase are the scale tones, ascending from the dominant, B. The next two notes descend from the dominant in a very simplified inversion of the ascent, reducing it from eight notes to three (counting the higher B with both the ascent and the descent). Coltrane adds two notes to his rendition of the second phrase, E and B (here included in parentheses).[7] This addition fills out the descent. It remains a simplified version of the ascent, but now the simplification includes the three crucial notes—tonic, dominant, and supertonic (E, B, and F#), along with the subdominant (A) which is the fourth most important note in this theme.

It is difficult to say just how listeners store these phrases. Indeed, different listeners almost certainly store them somewhat differently. Moreover, details of storage change for any given listener each time he/she hears the song. Nonetheless, it is clear that each phrase is segmented or separated out from the others. Moreover, its structure is defined and stored in some buffer. In some cases, that structure may be stored as an initial sequence, then a rule for generating a variation. Thus A1 may be stored as the first semiphrase, with some sort of annotation for inversion and simplification. A3 may be stored simply as an ascending scale sequence, followed by a simplified descent.

In speaking of reversal and simplification here, I am speaking of schematic or rule-governed ways of generating variations. Clearly these apply not only within, but across phrases. Indeed, the only way we can produce or recognize a variation is by way of some schematic or rule-governed transformation of a prior thematic phrase. Specifically, as a jazz musician is improvising on one or another thematic phrase (e.g., A1 of "My Favorite Things"), he/she will produce variations by activating *procedural schemas* (schematically organized procedures or actions) and applying these to the thematic phrases. These procedural schemas include the standard variations isolated by musicologists (e.g., inversion). When listeners hear these variations, they in effect apply the same procedural schemas in reverse. In other words, they map an incoming variation onto a stored thematic phrase by way of the same procedural schema used by the performer, thereby relating, say, EBB to BEE just as the performer did.

Boredom Revisited

In short, we isolate and store complexly encoded thematic phrases. Once these are stored, incoming sequences serve as probes to trigger one or another phrase. If no phrases are triggered, then the incoming sequence is categorized as novel, and temporarily stored itself. If one of the thematic phrases is activated, then the thematic phrase cycles through rehearsal memory and the incoming phrase is structured by working memory as a variation on that thematic phrase. This structuring is a function of mapping the variation onto the thematic phrase via schemas for variation (inversion, simplification, and so on).

Here we may return to boredom and cognitive disorientation. Boredom occurs when the incoming sequences serve as probes that activate stored phrases that are virtually identical with the incoming stream (perhaps precisely identical in terms of encoded features), thus lacking novelty. We do, of course, tolerate a certain degree of repetition. We are willing to accept parts of musical pieces that simply activate and repeat stored sequences. But there is a limit to our tolerance. I suspect that there is some time sequence here and that it is related to spontaneous dissipation of cortical arousal. In other words, cortical arousal declines when it is not sustained by novel inputs. It seems likely that our willingness to accept repetitive inputs is related directly to this decline. (We will return to this point below.)

As to cognitive disorientation, it seems that this occurs when we are consistently unable to map the incoming stream of sounds onto one or another thematic phrase. This may occur because the relation of theme and variation is too complex, the procedural schema is unknown, or our memory of the thematic phrase has decayed. More extreme forms of disorientation occur when we are not able to schematize the incoming stream in terms of scale. The most extreme forms of disorientation occur when even the auditory processor cannot encode the sound in terms of notes and rhythmic cycles. The first sort of disorientation occurs in very complex tonal music, such as is to be found in late Romanticism. Obvious instances of the second sort would include modernist experimentalism, such as twelve-tone music. Cases of the third would include postmodern experimentalism, where the music can appear to be a random sequence of noises, as in some of Stockhausen's compositions.

Of course, here too, things are not that simple. Perhaps most obviously, many of us enjoy atonal and postmodern avant-garde music—including some pieces (by, for example, John Cage or David Tudor) that actually are randomly generated sounds. In part, this appears to result from our ability to hear these sounds also as encoded sequences and variations, though the sequences might lack a tonal center and may not even divide into discrete notes. With tonal music, too, the situation is more complex. After all, we do not immediately become confused by the introduction of new sequences that do not map onto earlier thematic phrases. We allow for interpolations, even interpolations that are not developed further in the course of the piece. Again, we seem to have a category for nonthematic phrases—and we may tolerate or even enjoy quite a few of these in, say, a particular jazz improvisation. More importantly, we not only allow for but expect the introduction of new themes. Even in such a straightforward tune as the Rodgers and Hammerstein "My Favorite Things," there is a second theme (theme "B," which enters with the line about dog bites). However, the crucial point in these cases is that there is a limit to our tolerance of interpolations and new themes. And there are cognitive reasons for this. This limit too is probably related to the spontaneous dissipation time for cognitive arousal, as well as the storage capacity of our short-term memory buffers.

It is clear that there is still work to be done in accounting for our experience of music. However, it is no less clear that cognitive science greatly extends our understanding beyond basic Kantian insights, mapping out our experience of musical tone, scale, rhythm, variation, and so on, in great detail. Moreover, cognitive science allows us to relate the fine-grained analysis of cognitive processes in music to broader issues, such as optimal cortical arousal. In doing this, it gives us a more comprehensive and more illuminating account of why we respond to music the way we do. It even makes sense of our seemingly senseless changes in attitude—from boredom to frustration/anger, in the case of overly simple music; from frustration/anger to boredom in the case of overly complex music. Moreover, we have arrived at these results with only the barest background in cognitive theory. To develop these ideas, to understand their consequences in music and elsewhere, and to address other important topics in cognition and the arts, we need to discuss the general methods of cognitive science and we need to outline its basic theoretical principles far more systematically. That is the purpose of the following chapter.

Before going on to this, however, we should more thoroughly consider one particular case. I have been using "My Favorite Things" as an example throughout this chapter, focusing primarily on the basic melody. Coltrane's version of this tune is particularly interesting in the present context. It potentially involves all three types of disorientation. Coltrane plays sequences of notes that seem to deviate irreconcilably from the initial thematic phrases. Moreover, he manipulates tones above the ordinary range of the instrument to produce screeching waves of sound that cannot be encoded easily for scale—or even readily segmented for notes. At the same time, the basic melody is so familiar and trite that it simultaneously risks banality and boredom. Yet this piece has appealed to a wide range of listeners with a wide range of musical tastes. Coltrane has managed to make a piece of music that is not too disorienting to be popular, and not so straightforwardly structured as to be boring even for avant-garde listeners. In a recent article, Pascal Zachary explains the unique status of the piece. He notes that the 1960 recording "was both wholly absorbing and exhaustingly demanding." He goes on to explain that "What is astonishing about Coltrane's handling of this Rodgers and Hammerstein showtune is that he fuses avant-garde and pop so deliciously." He concludes that Coltrane had a unique "ability to satisfy an audience's craving for both the familiar and the unknown" (29). Coltrane himself said that "'Favorite Things' is my favorite piece of all those I have recorded. I don't think I would like to do it over in any way, whereas all the other discs I've made could be improved in some details" (qtd. in Porter *John Coltrane* 184). I will end with a few brief comments on how he managed this feat—which is, again, a cognitive feat.[8]

Thinking "My Favorite Things"

In "My Favorite Things" and elsewhere, John Coltrane showed the local precision and global rigor of organization that one expects only from composers who are producing completely written works. His precision and rigor led to the remarkable success of this piece. In chapter 5, I will consider Coltrane's innovations, the way he broke with common practices, thus the way "My Favorite Things" takes part in the avant-garde. Here, I will just assume this aspect of the work. The question I wish to examine in this section, then, is not why he appealed to the avant-garde listener (i.e., how he avoided banality). Rather, I wish to consider how he appealed to the ordinary listener, how he helped to assure cognitive orientation even within a work that has complex, nonstandard structures.[9]

The most obvious reason for this has to do with Coltrane's choice of theme. "My Favorite Things" is widely known, easily recognizable. It is, again, stored in the long-term memories of most listeners. This eliminates the potential problem of losing track of a thematic phrase. Even if Coltrane does not play a particular thematic phrase for a long time, it is always there in long-term memory. There is no chance that the thematic phrases will decay in the course of the piece. Moreover, this presence in long term memory allows Coltrane much more freedom in playing variations on these phrases. Indeed, even Coltrane's simplest statements of the themes are variations relative to the Rodgers and Hammerstein original. Another obvious technique used by Coltrane is his continual return to straightforward, easily identifiable restatements of the theme. These restatements are variations on the original, which helps prevent banality. However, they are unmistakable versions of those thematic phrases. Orientation is also facilitated by the other instruments. Porter remarks on the "repetitive patterns of the piano and bass" with their "simplified . . . structure" (*John Coltrane* 183) and Scott Anderson, notes the "use of E and B—tonic and dominant—as pedal points," which is to say, sustained notes in the lowest register (see Randel 617). At the very least, almost no one is likely to be so disoriented as to be unable to identify the tonic and the dominant.

But all this is fairly ordinary. What is most remarkable about Coltrane's performance are his two long solos. Each is 136 measures long, thus two minutes and sixteen seconds (see Scott Anderson's timings for 7:27–9:43 and 10:00–12:16). McCoy Tyner's long piano solo is only one measure longer. These two Coltrane solos (and, to a lesser extent, the Tyner solo) are the points where the listener would most likely become disoriented. Coltrane works against this by several means. First, he sticks to the four measure phrase, adding a second level of structure in which he pairs phrases. The result is a sense of cycling every eight measures (thus eight seconds or four circuits of rehearsal memory; the ease with which we perform this cycling is presumably related to the buffer capacities of working memory). At least in the first long solo, these cycles are routinely marked by a concluding return to some sort of tonal resolution or partial resolution—typically on the dominant B, rather than the tonic E, however.[10]

Coltrane also makes use of standard variations. In this regard, "My Favorite Things" is particularly well-suited to Coltrane's improvisatory style. Specifically, much of each solo is a series of ascents and descents, which are partially scalar, though they include chromatic elements. Since A3 is a phrase of scalar ascent and descent, these improvisations are very likely to activate A3 and we are very likely to map them onto A3. This necessarily gives the solos a sense of coherence and orientation. Of course, A3 is not the only phrase that Coltrane varies. He takes up A1 and A2 as well. Indeed, even the most complex parts of "My Favorite Things" tend to alternate between such partially scalar sequences—which we are likely to hear as variations on A3—and more obviously distinctive variations on the other phrases, or on phrase-integrated motifs.

This is not to say that there are no passages a listener might be unable to schematize. At least in my listening, however, the passages that lack any sense of familiarity never extend for more than thirty measures (thus thirty seconds). To judge this, I simply took Coan's transcription and circled the passages where I felt a sense of recurrence or isolable pattern. In doing this, I was not straining to make connections. I simply marked my experience of patterning, my experiential sense of a return to familiarity. It seems that this timing is not accidental, but relates to some aspect of cognition. Research by Cook indicates that listeners sustain a sense of tonal continuity, and thus respond to tonal closure, for sequences of thirty seconds in duration. However, when tested with fifty-five second sequences, the sense of tonal continuity had dissipated and listeners no longer responded to tonal closure (73–5; Cook did not test for sequences between thirty and fifty-five seconds). Clarke and Krumhansl found that listeners' segmentation of music followed the "same criteria" at "different levels of structure, from the musical surface to higher-level grouping involving durations of 30–50 seconds" (Cook 72). This suggests that there is some cognitive significance to this particular duration. Perhaps this is the time it takes for cortical arousal to dissipate. Or perhaps some component of working memory operates at time spans within this range. This is clearly a point for further research. In any case, this duration seems to be of central importance to a listener's sense of cognitive orientation or disorientation. A listener's sense of unfamiliarity in "My Favorite Things" would turn to disorientation if extended beyond this range. Here too, then, Coltrane's practice is exemplary, and his success quite understandable from a cognitive point of view—that is, assuming my experiential sense of patterning is not entirely idiosyncratic.

Coltrane also uses a number of rhythmic schemas for producing a sense of both coherence and variation. Some are fairly straightforward, such as mimicking the rhythms of a particular phrase (e.g., A1) while using notes other than those in the original phrase (see, for example, Coan 114, stave eleven, measures one and two, and 109, stave two, measures four and five; on our cognitive capacity for processing this sort of variation, see Jourdain 8). One of Coltrane's—and, in this case, Tyner's—most interesting schemas of this sort involves the use of speech rhythms. As we noted above, Howard Gardner's research indicates that our first sense of musical rhythm is bound up with our sense of speech rhythm. There is no reason to believe that we ever lose the tendency to link the two. In fact, we almost certainly rely on such a connection in many cases. I believe that Coltrane, and Tyner, draw on a speech rhythm/musical rhythm parallel in structuring their improvisations, and that we as listeners do so as well. Specifically, the most memorable words in "My Favorite Things" are the words that give us the title—"favorite things." It becomes much easier for us to hear many segments of this piece as unified because, whatever the melodic sequence, the rhythmic sequence mimics that of "favorite things," with the simple variation that sometimes "favorite" has three syllables and sometimes it has two. In other words, given the prominence of this phrase, its ready accessibility to working memory, any close approximation to its rhythmic contour (or other distinctive properties) is likely to activate the phrase and lead us to map it onto the incoming sequence. The result is that we implicitly hear many sequences (especially some repeated chord sequences in the piano) as melodic variations on a single rhythmic motif. If this seems far-fetched, I should note that Coltrane used this mimicking of speech rhythm quite overtly elsewhere in his work—even in cases where he was not improvising on a song that already connected musical rhythms with speech rhythms through lyrics. It was, in other words, a significant procedural schema for him. The most famous instance of this is *A Love Supreme,* perhaps Coltrane's masterpiece. In that work, he explicitly uses the rhythmic pattern of the title phrase and, indeed, its pitch contour. This is signaled eventually by Coltrane actually chanting the phrase. Porter goes so far as to see this as the primary organizational principle of the entire work. As he puts it, "Virtually the whole piece is based on the little 'A Love Supreme' motive chanted by Coltrane (overdubbed as two voices) at the end of Part One" ("John Coltrane" 442).[11]

In sum, Coltrane's "My Favorite Things" astutely combines common and unusual variations, motifs distinctively linked with thematic phrases, a cyclical improvisatory structure, a simplified harmonic accompaniment, a strong emphasis on the tonic and dominant, as well as other "cognition friendly" techniques. This produces a work that allows for encoding and variation mapping, but in unexpected ways. At those points where encoding and variation mapping are blocked, the blockage is limited in duration so that our capacities are not overloaded and cortical arousal does not dissipate.

Of course, some listeners will have either the disorientation problem or the boredom problem. Nothing pleases everybody. The point is that Coltrane's "My Favorite Things" has been developed in such a way that it fits human cognitive structure remarkably well and thus minimizes the likelihood of either. This has resulted in a work that appeals to both popular and avant-garde audiences—according to Zachary, "perhaps the last time in jazz history that the cutting edge met pop culture and both triumphed" (29).

CHAPTER 2

Is It Cognitive Science Yet?
Some Basic Principles

Having considered a specific case of cognitive scientific analysis, we should now examine the broader theoretical principles that underlie that analysis and define cognitive science as a research program. Most basically, cognitive science is an interdisciplinary form of study aimed at understanding human cognition. It grew out of post-Behaviorist psychology, linguistics (especially Chomskyan linguistics), computer science, and, later on, neurobiology, though it now has connections with virtually every discipline in the modern university. Cognitive science includes a range of schools and tendencies that often seem to have little to do with one another. Nonetheless, there are common methodological principles shared by all or at least most cognitive scientists. I will begin by setting out some of these common principles, before turning to a more detailed look at the two most prominent schools of cognitive science today—representationalism and connectionism.

How to Think Cognitively: Three Stages of Analysis and Understanding

Michael Dawson points out that work in cognitive science almost always involves three components that can be listed as a series of steps in addressing a cognitive problem. For example, the problem might be: How do we listen to and enjoy a piece of music? Or how do we understand a metaphor? Or how do we produce stories? Given such a problem, different cognitive scientists may come to different conclusions. However, they will most often approach the problem in similar ways.

According to Dawson, the first step in thinking as a cognitive scientist involves formulating the problem in terms of *information processing*. As we saw in the last chapter, a cognitive account of music addresses such issues as selection, segmentation, and structuration of perceptual inputs. Simply thinking in these terms shows that we are addressing music as a problem of information processing. In this case, we are asking just what information enters working memory from perception and how it does so.

Of course, as this reference to selection, et cetera indicates, we do not receive "pure" environmental information in our minds. Our cognitive apparatuses shape and organize that information. This leads us to the second stage or component of cognitive scientific analysis—defining the precise *cognitive architecture* we will be using to examine the problem. "Cognitive architecture" is just the way cognitive scientists refer to what makes up the human mind. In this second stage, we need to formulate all our analyses not only in terms of information processing, but in terms of a well-specified cognitive architecture.

There are three broad components to any cognitive architecture: structures, processes, and contents. *Structures* are the general organizational principles of the mind. For example, the distinction between working memory and long-term memory is a structural distinction. Structures define the relations into which processes and contents can enter. Indeed, they allow processes and contents to exist at all. *Contents* are most often understood as representations or symbols.[1] Thus my idea of a cat or my internal lexical entry for "cat" is a mental content. Contents have specific locations in structures. Thus my internal lexical entry for *cat* is located within my internal lexicon, which is itself part of (i.e., a substructure of) my long-term memory system. Moreover, the lexical link between *cat* and, say, *dog* is a link that is allowed by cognitive structure. Cognitive structure defines the possible ways in which contents—in this case, lexical entries—may be connected with one another. *Processes* are operations that run on contents. These, too, are structurally constrained, for a process functions within a cognitive structure or across cognitive structures. For example, mapping an incoming sequence of notes onto a thematic (musical) phrase is a process. But of course working memory itself—with its restrictions on what sort of information its components can carry (e.g., auditory, but not olfactory, information in the rehearsal loop) and how much (e.g., about two seconds in the rehearsal loop)—is a structure.

There are three main sorts of cognitive architecture used by cognitive scientists—representational, connectionist, and neurobiological. Many cognitivists also make reference to "folk psychological" theory. While everyone accepts neurobiological accounts, all other architectures are controversial. Moreover, they are routinely seen as mutually exclusive. In my view, they are not contradictory, but complementary. They are better thought of as levels of analysis and theorization (comparable to physics, chemistry, and biology) than as alternatives in a single plain.

Before going on to treat these different architectures, however, we need to articulate the third and final component of a standard cognitive scientific account. Again, we must first define and examine our problem in terms of information processing. Second, we must articulate our analysis in terms of cognitive architecture only. Finally, we must develop our analyses as *algo-* *rithmic sequences*. The basic idea here is that any cognitive scientific analysis should consist in a set of steps that is fully explicit in moving from inputs of the (information processing) problem to outputs. This sequence of steps should make reference only to structures, processes, and contents available within the cognitive architecture. Finally, each step should be derived from the preceding step by the application of some specified process of the cognitive architecture. Put differently, insofar as the cognitive architecture may be implemented on a computer, the solution to the problem should be a program that would run on the computer and would produce the right outputs given the relevant inputs. Indeed, a good heuristic procedure for testing the adequacy of a solution to a problem in cognitive science is designing a program that will yield the right results given the proper input.[2]

Returning to the varieties of cognitive architecture, I would distinguish four distinct levels of cognitive theorization and analysis. These levels may be set out on a scale of relative intentionality or physicality. One end of the spectrum is defined by a sort of pure intentionalism. This level is concerned with our subjective experience as such. It focuses on "what it is like to be" a person (to borrow a phrase from Thomas Nagel). At the intentional level, we talk about how we feel, what we would like to accomplish, what we believe, and so on. The opposite end of the spectrum is neurophysiology. This is purely objectal (i.e., concerning objects), purely concrete and material. At this level, we do not talk about what we want or how we like to do something. We talk instead about neurons and synapses. In between, we have representationalism, which is nearer to the intentional end of the spectrum, and connectionism, which is nearer to the neurophysiological end. Here, one might ask if there is any purpose to these distinct levels. I believe there is.

Consider intentionalism. In my view, we do really have subjective experience. That subjective experience is not eliminable. No matter how much some writers may discuss the explanatory capacities of neurophysiological accounts, they never touch on "what it is like to be" a world-experiencing, self-conscious subjectivity. Indeed, eliminative physicalism (the view that there are only physical entities and nothing mentalistic per se) does not seem to be a logically coherent position. The much disparaged tradition of Cartesian doubt does suggest that one thing we cannot coherently deny is the existence of subjective experience.[3]

On the other hand, the nature of our minds is such that we understand by objectifying. Even with respect to our subjective experience, we reflect on it, making it an object of consciousness, in order to comprehend it—a point emphasized by Phenomenological philosophers. Thus scientific inquiry into the nature of cognition requires some degree of objectification. The "folk psychology" of beliefs, aims, character, habit, and so on, provides the beginning of systematic objectification. Moreover, it provides many principles we count as almost definitive of mind. But there is a problem with folk psychology. Simply put, it is not a science. It is a set of pragmatic ideas, which are only partially explicit, and which have been developed over a period of time in order to deal with daily life. Thus it does not define a cognitive architecture systematically and precisely. Here, representationalism enters.

Representationalism covers a range of theories. However, all share a connection with intentionalism and folk psychology. Thus Jerry Fodor—a prominent representationalist philosopher—writes that "Psychological explanation," including that in cognitive science, "is intentional through and through." Indeed, for this reason, Fodor opposes "the putatively purely extensional idiom of neuroscience" (7), which is to say, the purely objectal and material account of mind that some neurobiologists advocate, an account that eschews anything having to do with intent or folk psychology. Fodor goes on to explain that "Laws about causal relations among beliefs, desire, and actions are the paradigms" (7) for psychological explanation. (By "causal relations" here, he simply means that, in ordinary folk psychology, we say that Jones went to the store *because* he wanted—or had a desire for—bread and believed he had none at home. Thus his action stands in a causal relation with the desire and the belief.) Fodor even explains representations (the fundamental contents of representationalist architecture) in relation to this level of subjectivity, writing that "'Mental representations' are the primitive bearers of intentional content" (7).

One may think of the initial impulse of representationalism as a rigorous systematization of folk psychology.[4] This includes a thorough objectification that is explicit about cognitive architecture. Moreover, rather than relying on informal experiential data, and rather than keeping the theory in a relatively constant state for millennia, representationalism takes up experimental method. In other words, folk psychologists (i.e., all of us, when we are speaking informally) simply presume the validity of a (vague and implicit) folk psychological theory and use it to explain events of everyday occurrence, changing contents in specific cases, but not structures or processes. Representationalists set out to design particular empirical studies that will provide evidence for or against the positing of particular structures and processes, as well as contents.

The benefit of intentionalism is that it is intuitively comprehensible. The deficit is that it is inadequately objectal—and, when objectified in folk psychology, overly simple. Representationalism sets out to preserve the basic intuitive comprehensibility of intentionalism and the related folk psychology of "memory," "knowledge," "expectation," and so on, while altering the excessive simplification and lack of objectification. At the other end of the spectrum, the brain has the opposite problem. It is so objectal that talk about the brain tends to lose any intuitive connection with intention or subjective experience. At the same time, the brain is so complex that it is very difficult to talk about it at all, except in fairly general terms. One can discuss the ways that a particular hemisphere operates in the preservation and recall of memories. However, it is (currently) impossible to discuss, in concrete neurological terms, why Jones did a particular thing at a particular time—which is just the sort of thing intentionalism and folk psychology are good at doing. The complexity of the brain is so staggering that tracing paths for particular thoughts and actions is not something we can do.

To a certain extent, the function of connectionism is to resolve the difficulties of neurobiology. Most importantly, connectionism creates a structure closely related to that of the brain, but much simpler. Though still complex, a connectionist "neural network" can be modeled by a computer and, for any given set of inputs, its outputs may be generated by the computer. The network can be manipulated in such a way that, for any given inputs, it will produce the same outputs as the human brain. The advantage of the network is that the sequence from input to output is more comprehensible—even though the network operates on the same general principles as the brain, using the same sort of architecture. Moreover, in setting up the neural network, we can directly assign particular ideas or experiences to particular units or nodes (the connectionist equivalent of neurons). In this way, we may easily relate our analyses to intention.

In short, connectionist architecture parallels neurobiological architecture. However, it simplifies that architecture, allowing us to discuss particular cognitive problems in terms of brainlike units without actually entering into the full complexity of the brain. Thus, while representationalism renders intentionalism more objectal or bodylike, connectionism moves in the opposite direction, making the brain more mindlike. Moreover, while representationalism makes folk psychology more complex, connectionism simplifies neurobiology.

Finally, it is important to add one further type of theoretical account that is not a level of cognitive architecture per se, but is involved in explaining cognitive architectures at every level—evolution. Within cognitive science, the standard cognitive architectures are used to explain particular occurrences and general patterns in human cognition. However, the question invariably arises as to why we have precisely these cognitive architectures. Thus there is a "metalevel" issue here. The structures and processes that explain human thought and action are themselves phenomena requiring explanation. Within cognitive science, these metalevel explanations are virtually always evolutionary explanations.

In sum, we have four different varieties or levels of cognitivist account with four different sorts of architecture, and one metalevel theory that operates to explain the different architectures:

> subjective/intentional experience (plus folk psychology)
> representationalism
> connectionism
> neurobiology
> metalevel: evolution

In the rest of this chapter, I will set out some of the most commonly accepted basic principles of representionalism and connectionism, as these bear on treatments of literature and the arts. (I will consider neurobiology and evolution in chapters 7 and 8 respectively.)

Representationalism on the Mind (Part One): Working Memory and Processes of Encoding

Representationalism comprises a wide range of structures and processes. Indeed, it comprises a wide range of views on structures and processes, including disagreements on some aspects of basic architecture. One cannot possibly cover all these in part of one chapter. Because of its importance to literary and artistic study, and because of its centrality to representationalist theories, I will focus in particular on memory. Memory is one of the most widely researched and theorized topics in cognitive science. Moreover, along with perception, it is perhaps the most important area across different subfields within cognitive study. This is unsurprising, given its crucial place in every aspect of human thought and action—including our creation of and response to literature and the arts. In treating representational architecture, then, I will begin with the structure and processes of working memory, treating some mainstream (though by no means undisputed) views on these topics. I will also consider some aspects of perception, insofar as these bear on working memory. In the next section, I will take up the structures and processes of long-term memory.

To give some intuitive idea of working memory, we might say that it is what we are keeping in mind right now, along with whatever we are "holding in the back of our mind." It is, in a sense, everything that is cognitively active at the present time. This is not confined to what we are conscious of, but extends to a range of things that are, so to speak, part of our current train of thought. Technically, working memory is a set of specialized subsystems overseen or coordinated by a "central executive to control the system as a whole" (Johnson-Laird 156). This *central executive* is roughly our self as an experiencing, goal directed, decision-making agency. LeDoux explains working memory as "a temporary storage mechanism that allows several pieces of information to be held in mind at the same time and compared, contrasted, and otherwise interrelated" (*Emotional* 270). For example, as we saw in chapter 1, it allows for the assignment of structure and the mapping of structures, as from thematic phrase to variation.

More exactly, working memory may be seen as bounded by perceptual systems, on the one hand, and long-term memory systems, on the other. If we, so to speak, move with some sensory input, such as a stream of music, the first part of working memory we encounter might be a sensory input buffer (see figure 1). A buffer is a temporary storage unit that does not retain anything of its contents once they leave. In other words, a buffer does not involve extended storage of information, only "temporary holding" of information. Moreover, a buffer does not have "rehearsal" capacity. Information enters, is held briefly, then dumped. It does not continue to cycle through. In effect, the buffer allows our perception to stretch over a timeless point of "now" and experience a sensory present that is very brief. Thus it produces segmentation and internal unification (e.g., the segmentation and internal

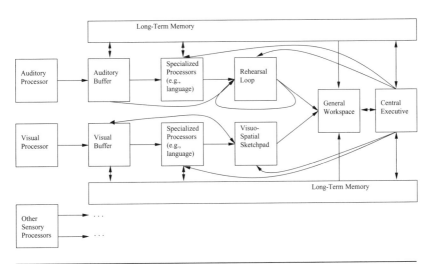

Fig. 1. A simplified model of sensory processing in working memory. Single headed arrows indicate that information passes in one direction. Double headed arrows indicate that information passes in both directions. The spatial processor has been left out of this figure.

unification of musical notes or perhaps short phrases). Johnson-Laird explains that we have "a sensory memory for a visual image that persists for about a quarter of a second." In hearing, we "retain a brief 'echo.'" More generally, "Each sense must have its own memory system whose contents are continuously replaced by new incoming information and cannot be rehearsed" (149). There is some disagreement on the number and nature of these buffers. For example, LeDoux posits a series of buffers that retain their information longer than indicated by Johnson-Laird: "each sensory system has one or more temporary buffers. These aid in perception, allowing the system to compare what it is seeing or hearing now to what it saw or heard a moment ago. There are also temporary buffers associated with aspects of language use (these help you keep the first part of a sentence in mind until you've heard the last part so that the whole thing can be understood). The specialized memory buffers work in parallel, independent of one another" (*Emotional* 270–1).

I will assume that there is an auditory buffer, a visual buffer, and so on. These receive information from the basic sensory processors. They serve to further segment this information, as just noted. This segmentation may be understood as produced by the holding capacity of the buffer plus its one function, which is matching with long-term memory. (Perhaps this function should be separated off into a preprocessor connected with the buffer, so that the buffer is purely a storage device. For our purposes, however, the distinction is inconsequential.) Specifically, these units quickly link incoming information with long term memory in a simple matching function. This matching function serves to encode the information further. For example, a glimpse of a face may get matched with my long term memory of Doe (cf. LeDoux *Synaptic* 191). The glimpse contains relatively unstructured and diffuse information (e.g., patches of light and dark that may be contingent matters of lighting or matters of skin tone and hair color). The holding capacity of the buffer (about a quarter of a second, according to Johnson-Laird) has partially segmented the glimpse. Further encoding results from the match with the memory of Doe. That memory serves to select out certain bits of information from the glimpse and structure them in such a way that I in effect "see" this hazy patch "as" Doe. This is the sort of thing that happens when you are moving through a crowd and suddenly turn back, thinking you saw a friend, only to realize that it is someone completely different—perhaps someone who does not even particularly resemble your friend, except in a very rough, crude way.

The fact that we turn in a certain direction to find someone indicates that something else happens with this information in addition to matching. It is sent simultaneously to a spatial processor in which it is related to other perceptions in terms of basic spatial relations. Speaking of the brain, LeDoux refers to these two operations—the sensory buffer with its matching function (or associated matching processor) and the spatial processor—as the "'what' and 'where'...pathways...The 'what' pathway is involved in object recognition, and the 'where' pathway in figuring out the spatial location" (*Synaptic* 181). LeDoux is speaking specifically of vision, but the same point seems to hold for sound.[5] (There is presumably some sort of bodily mapping for touch.)

From here, the information may go to a specialized processor. The matching function determines this. For example, if an incoming sound stream is matched with speech sounds, then it will be sent for language processing. Whether sent to a specialized processor or not, the new information arrives at what we would ordinarily consider our "minds." As LeDoux points out, consciousness is largely a matter of one segment of working memory—the "work space." In addition to the central executive, the work space has two well-established, specialized components, as well as a general space where information from various structures may be brought together and synthesized. As to the specialized components, we have, first, a rehearsal loop for temporally ordered sequences (such as bits of music). Second, we have something comparable for spatially ordered complexes. These appear to be specialized for two senses, hearing and sight. The *auditory rehearsal loop* allows us to keep about two seconds of auditory material cycling through memory. This is a part of working memory that bears crucially on our ability to map themes and variations in music. Parallel to this, we have a *visuo-spatial sketchpad*. This allows us to organize different spatial perceptions into unified items and complexes of related items. It is crucial for viewing paintings or films. For example, suppose you see a person from the side, then you see the person from the front, perhaps through two shots in a film. You synthesize the two into some sort of unity. This is a function of the visuo-spatial sketchpad. The sketchpad also enables us to engage in certain sorts of imaginative activity. For example, imagine a cup with a handle. Now, slowly turn the cup, so that the handle is on the opposite side. You can engage in this sort of imagination, which is in some ways rather strange. You do it through the visuo-spatial sketchpad. Thus the sketchpad has some functions of what literary critics call "imagination."

Finally, we have the *general workspace* and the *central executive*. The executive may be understood as orienting the various operations of working memory to larger systemic goals and integrating information in ways that bear on those goals. For example, it brings together information from the auditory rehearsal loop and the visuo-spatial sketchpad as well as "information received from short-term buffers" and "long-term memories that are also activated" (LeDoux *Emotional* 273). Clearly, we synthesize sights, sounds, smells, and so on. We do not keep these separated in sense-defined boxes.[6] We also place these experiences in spatial relations that are not confined to one sense at a time (e.g., we recognize a sound and a visual image as spatially related). All this occurs in the general workspace. Moreover, we do not synthesize this information randomly or in a single, fixed manner, but in ways that bear on currently active goals. For example, we synthesize ambient sounds and sights one way when trying to cross the street and another way when sitting at a street-side café. Finally, as this indicates, such integration involves hierarchical organization, the activation of further information from long-term memory, and a range of other executive operations.

This leads us from *structures* of working memory to *processes* of working memory. Here we might return to the start again, following the path of some sensory input, such as a stream of music. Sensory buffers receive information from perceptual systems, information which these systems draw from physical experiences of light, sound, and so on. As we saw in chapter 1, perceptual systems do not simply transmit a replica of the real world. Rather, perceptual systems run certain processes on the initial sensory inputs. Most obviously, they *select* just what gets passed on to working memory. Moreover, there is necessarily some degree of *segmentation* and *structuring* of inputs at the perceptual level. In other words, perceptual systems *encode* sensory experiences, thereby producing information from those experiences. Again, we only encode certain information from the environment. Properties and relations that we do not encode are simply not available for use by working memory. If we do not encode something, then for us it simply does not exist.

Selection is probably easiest to recognize. First, there are simply some things that our perceptual systems cannot register. We cannot hear certain pitches. From our point of view, those pitches do not exist. They are never passed on by the auditory system to working memory. Moreover, out of all the things we could in principle perceive, we do not "notice" everything. Noticing, in this sense, appears to be governed by two criteria, one coming from us, the other coming from the world. As Johnson-Laird explains, "the human cognitive system selects just certain impinging information for further processing" in "two different ways: one depends on deliberate decisions emanating from the central executive, and the other reflects the automatic 'attention-grabbing' effects of certain classes of events" (156). The former would include whatever we are focusing our attention on at a given time. The latter (i.e., attention-grabbing events) would include such things as sudden loud sounds and rapid motion nearby in the visual field.

As indicated in the preceding chapter, not all selection occurs in the perceptual processors. The stream of information entering working memory from, say, the auditory processor is already selective. However, only part of that information is selected for further processing and retention. Recall that information in buffers leaves no trace unless it is re-stored in another buffer or entered into long-term memory. Johnson-Laird's two modes of selection reappear here. The attentional focus of the central executive serves to select some information. This is why one reads a novel or poem so differently when one reads it to teach in a general education class, to analyze for professional publication, to critique politically, and so on. In each case, one encodes the work differently, in part due to selection. Even at this level, however, selection is not solely a function of goals provided by the central executive. Some information is selected due to its high saliency. In working memory, that high saliency is not a simple function of perceptual information passed on by our perceptual systems (i.e., it is not confined to such things as loud noises). This is because many "attention grabbing" effects of events are not merely perceptual, but involve long-term memory as well. For example, we "filter out" background conversation at a party—until someone nearby mentions our name (LeDoux *Synaptic,* 191). That bit of information is selected and taken up by the central executive. In cases such as this, it seems clear that a fairly broad range of information is passed on by perceptual systems, only some of which is subsequently selected for further processing in working memory. In short, selection operates recurrently in cognitive processing and it follows some version of Johnson-Laird's two criteria at each level.

The mention of hearing one's name leads nicely to *segmentation.* It seems that hearing "Pat Hogan" is an easy thing. The name is said and I just hear it. But actually things are more complicated. Again, there is some preliminary sound segmentation in the auditory processor. For example, a single voice must be segmented out from other sounds. In this case, the sounds are identified as linguistic and sent through specialized language processors. This involves, among other things, the segmentation of speech sounds and word units. All this is required for a sound event even to be matchable with my name, as stored in long-term memory, and thus to be "attention grabbing" at this level. Segmentation also occurs in the isolation of notes, phrases, and so on, in music (as discussed in chapter 1), the spontaneous recognition of rhythm in metered poetry (as when we unself-consciously "pick up" recurrent rhythmic units of both feet and lines), etc.

Finally, *structuration* occurs when the relations among selected and segmented bits of information are defined by reference to some system. We have already given the example of steps in a diatonic scale. Tones that have less than a quarter-step difference are heard as the same. Those with more than a quarter-step difference but less than a three-quarters-step difference are heard as a half-step apart. This may occur in the auditory processor or subsequently. The assignment of tonal structure per se almost certainly occurs in working memory as it presumably requires some sort of matching with long-term memory. Indeed, matching with items in long-term memory usually has a structuring function. In other words, it is not simply a matter of recognizing identity. For example, I might hear a sound sequence, "Bah . . . ogn" muddled up with a lot of noise. I end up "hearing" "Pat Hogan" because my name, which is prominent in long-term memory and thus easy to activate as a "match," provides a structure for the fragmentary sounds.

Needless to say, structuration (like other aspects of encoding) does not stop with such small-scale units as names—nor do other aspects of encoding. As we already know from chapter 1, a central process in working memory is the assignment of structure to increasingly large complexes. Structuration of musical inputs does not end with the isolation of the tonic. It goes on to the definition of thematic phrases and the mapping of variations. Structuration of linguistic inputs does not stop with phonology, but goes on to morphology and syntax. Here, as elsewhere, structuration can occur in different ways. For at least some types of structural assignment, such as syntax, we need specialized processing units. Other types of structural assignment, such as the mapping of variations onto themes in music, appear to be done by the central executive in the general workspace.

Whether or not it involves specialized processors, the recursive generation of increasingly inclusive structures is a crucial process in working memory. We may think of it as a series of re-encodings with two components. One is the formation of multielement units. (This is a matter of selection and segmentation.) The other is the assignment of hierarchical relations among the elements or subunits of these units. (This is a matter of structuration.) A large (hierarchically structured) complex of (hierarchically structured) subunits is referred to as a *model*. Whenever we try to deal with any aspect of the world in any way, we necessarily form a model of that aspect of the world. Indeed, "model" is not so much a theoretical concept as a practical one. Models are differentiated from other units of information because of their use.

There are many sorts of model. For a moment, I would like to concentrate on one in particular. If the complex of hierarchically structured units concerns the environment in which we are acting, it is called a "situation model." It is not the actual world, but what we what we take the world to be—which is to say, what is represented in our mind through the layers of encodings (i.e., selections, segmentations, and structurations) just outlined. This complex guides our responses to and actions in the world. Though the model is open to alteration, it also focuses our attention and gives structure to ambiguous information (i.e., it serves a further encoding function). In Piagetian terms, it does *accommodate* itself to experience (i.e., it changes as new information enters), but it also *assimilates* that experience to itself (i.e., it selects, segments, and structures the information). Moreover, it does not do this once and for all, but through an ongoing process of encoding, action/observation, and re-encoding, a process sometimes referred to as a *feedback loop.*[7]

Take a simple example. I walk into a room where I have never been. I look to the left and see three people. I recognize them as the people I am meeting. I see them sitting on two sofas, with a place for me. I walk over, say hello, and sit down. This simple sequence involves highly complex cognitive activity. In looking at the sofas, I have to put them together as units. Though the people are visually no less continuous with the sofas than are parts of the sofas themselves, I have to distinguish the people as separate units. I have to assign structural relations to the persons, sofas, the floor. I have to locate spaces where I can walk, approximate distance relative to where I am standing, and so on. My complex idea of the entire hierarchy of nested structures is a situation model. It tacitly guides my actions when I walk over, turn my back to the sofa, and sit down. I gauge how quickly to sit, where to relax my muscles, and so on, by tacit reference to the situation model. At the same time, that situation model is continually being revised by new (encoded) information from my attentional focus and the changing perspective that results from action (e.g., walking closer to the sofa).

We could understand the development of such a situation model in roughly the following terms. First, I open a general (or underspecified) category in the workspace. In this case, the category might be "a room," perhaps with some sort of distinguishing designation (e.g., "HBL 127"). This gives a very broad structure to my expectations and actions already. Along with current goals, it guides my attention and provides structure for incoming information. In the workspace, then, I use the structure provided by the category "a room" as a grid through which I can assign relations (e.g., spatial relations) to items in the room. Of course, I am synthesizing and assigning structure to those items as well, also by way of broad categories, such as "sofa" (based on encoded information from sensory processors). Thus we have elements assigned to hierarchical structures, which are themselves treated as elements for further hierarchical structures, and so on—all guided, at each stage, by goals of the central executive, as well as the salience of the inputs themselves.

Needless to say, these points apply no less to literary experience than to entering a room. Imagine that I am reading the following passage (from J. M. Coetzee's *Waiting for the Barbarians*): "We sit in the best room of the inn with a flask between us and a bowl of nuts" (1). Here too working memory opens up a category in the workspace, perhaps the category *novel.* We draw on general principles of the category to provide an initial orientation (thus a guide for encoding information). These principles include such subsidiary categories as *character.* We open a *character* category for each person mentioned. We form the nonhuman objects by reference to relevant categories as well, and—this time drawing on the visuo-spatial sketchpad—we outline the structure of the room. Even in this simple sentence, there is a great deal to puzzle out in the workspace, and much of it we probably just ignore on a first reading. For example, many readers may forget almost immediately about the bowl of nuts. In other words, at some stage that information may not be selected for further processing. After all, for most readers, nuts would not be important for central executive goals and they would have low saliency. (Contrast a situation in which a reader was given the task of analyzing food imagery before he/she began the novel.) In short, when reading literature, we go through the same sort of complex, recurrent processes of encoding that we do in ordinary life, relying on the same cognitive architecture and generating the same sorts of situation models in working memory. (We will consider this issue in detail when we discuss the viewer's cognition of film in chapter 5.)

Representationalism on the Mind (Part Two): Long-Term Memory and the Mental Lexicon

Up to this point, I have spoken of *long-term memory* as if it were a single cognitive structure. The first thing to say here is that long-term memory comprises two or three separate systems, or perhaps subsystems. Everyone seems to agree that "experiences and knowledge" must be separated off from "skills" (Johnson-Laird 156). Some writers, such as Schacter, argue in addition that experiences and knowledge should be separated from one another, the former placed in a special *episodic* memory (Schacter 17, 134–5). The evidence for such distinctions is strong. On the other hand, however many systems there are, they are clearly and closely interrelated, with ready access from one system to related items in other systems (e.g., from knowledge about bicycles to memories of bicycles and skills at riding bicycles).

For our purposes, a particularly crucial part of long term memory is the *mental lexicon* (sometimes referred to as *semantic memory*). The mental lexicon is not very much like a printed dictionary. It is not a list of words followed by definitions. Rather, it is a system of circuits that spread throughout long-term memory, encompassing a wide range of information. Ideas about lions, beliefs about lions, common attitudes toward lions, visual images of lions—these are all linked to one another and to the word "lion." That circuit or complex is the *lexical entry* for "lion." The same point holds for particulars such as "HBL 127." It too is part of a circuit encompassing beliefs, images, and so forth. Thus, the mental lexicon comprises the entire knowledge portion of long-term memory (which is, again, distinct from, but closely interrelated with, episodic memory and skills memory).

One important difference between the mental lexicon and a printed dictionary is that lexical entries–like all aspects of long-term memory–are *content addressable.* In other words, we can access a word from a meaning, a meaning from a referent, the rest of a meaning from part of a meaning, and so on. We do not have to begin with the sound shape, "dog," then go to the meaning. We first see a dog, then think of the word "dog." We can begin with the meaning, or part of the meaning—or simply part of what is included in the mental lexicon, even if we would not ordinarily refer to it as *the meaning.* Thus it is very easy for us to get from "pet" to "dog." We may not be sure that a particular pet is a dog, but if we learn that Bobby wants a pet, "dog" will be one of the first words that comes to our lips and the idea of a dog will be one of the first ideas that comes into our head.

Moreover, lexical entries are accessible from other lexical entries whenever the two are *linked.* Unlike a dictionary, the mental lexicon leads us from *cat* to *dog* and from *soup* to *sandwich.* Lexical entries may be linked with one another in a number of different ways. For example, two entries may be connected by complementarity, as in the link between *male* and *female.* Other connections might include synonymy and scalar relations (e.g., *hot* is linked with *warm* in the scale of temperature). Moreover, entries may be subsumed under more abstract entries (e.g., *robin* is subsumed under *bird*). When entries share a superordinate category and a single type of relation (e.g., "temperature" and the scalar relation), they form a domain. For instance, the domain of temperature includes the entries for *hot, warm, cool,* and so on. Any lexical relation may generate a domain, including mere sequence. Thus *Monday, Tuesday,* and so on, define the domain *days of the week.* (As this example suggests, the lexical entry for a domain may or may not have a one-word label.) I isolate domains for particular attention because they are of central importance to metaphor. Specifically, it is common for one, relatively concrete domain, to be used to conceptualize another more abstract or amorphous domain. Thus we commonly understand emotional intensity by reference to the scalar domain of temperature, as in "Jones has warm feelings for Smith, but Smith gave Jones a cool reception." The point is consequential in the study of literature, for much literary metaphor is an extension and complication of this common domain mapping.

As the case of domains suggests, lexical entries have not only external relations, but internal structures. Internally, lexical entries may be thought of, first of all, as hierarchized lists of features. Features are any semantic elements that refer to properties or relations of relevant objects. (*Object* here includes anything that can be the referent of a lexical item—not only such material things as dogs, but fantasies, epochs, virtues, and so on.) Thus the entry for soup might include such features as *liquid, edible,* and *goes well with a sandwich.* These features are hierarchized in the sense that some are marked as more important than others. In the case just mentioned, *liquid* is more important than *goes well with a sandwich.* Thus we would be very strongly disinclined to call something *soup* if it is a gas. In contrast, the fact that something does not go well with a sandwich would not really convince us that it is not a soup. We could think of the more important features—the more definitional features—as being higher on the feature lists and the less important features as being lower on the lists.[8]

Not all feature lists are of the same sort. We have just been considering the main, descriptive part of a lexical entry. This includes all the "definitional" and "empirical" or dictionary and encyclopedia information, all the features that we assume apply to the relevant objects (e.g., soups). In addition to this, lexical entries include distinctive feature lists for ideals, norms, common beliefs, and so on. For example, my lexical entry for *Irish* includes such features as *prone to drink* and *gabby*. But it does not include them in the main, descriptive entry. Rather, they are part of the feature list *common beliefs about*.

On the other hand, to speak of lexical entries solely in terms of features and lists of features is not correct. Features are usually not important on their own. Rather, they are important in the various structured complexes of which they are a part. There are three types of lexical feature complex that play a crucial role in cognitive science: *schemas, prototypes,* and *exemplars* (or, as I will call them, *exempla*). We should consider each in turn.

When we think of definitions, we think of necessary and sufficient conditions. These are the sorts of definition that scientists strive to achieve. However, they are relatively rare in the mental lexicon. The structure that comes closest to definitions is the schema. There are two sorts of schemas. The first are representational schemas, often called simply *schemas*. The second are procedural schemas. *Representational schemas* are, roughly, the feature lists just mentioned. However, in addition to being ordered in terms of importance, features in a schema are structured into *default hierarchies* as well. Default hierarchies provide features that we assume apply unless we are given information to the contrary. Moreover, default hierarchies usually include *specified alternatives* to the default. For example, our lexical entry for *man* has a default feature of *two arms*. Alternatives to the default would most often be specified as *born without an arm/both arms* and *lost an arm/both arms*. Thus, unless we are given evidence to the contrary, we assume someone who is a man has two arms. If we find out that a particular man does not have two arms, we shift to one of the specified alternatives (e.g., we do not assume he has three or more arms).

When a schema does not concern an object, but a situation in which we take action, then it is more commonly referred to as a *script* (see, for example, Herman's distinction between schemas and scripts in understanding narrative).[9] A script too is organized into a hierarchy with defaults and alternatives. But the basic ordering principle is temporal, and the items in the hierarchy organize actions (rather than naming properties and relations). A standard example is going into a restaurant. We have a script that tells us to look for various indicators that will allow us to determine if we seat ourselves or wait for a hostess. If we wait for a hostess, we prepare to answer the questions, "How many?" and "Smoking or nonsmoking?" We wait a certain amount of time for menus. If we do not receive them, we look for someone with the telltale properties of an employee, and so on. Each of these steps in the restaurant script involves its own subscripts (the seating subscript, the hostess subscript). We have scripts of this sort for virtually every kind of social interaction. A student taking a class has a script which includes subscripts for asking questions and taking tests. A person in a singles bar has a script and subscripts. People going to a movie at a theater, mailing a letter, walking into the office—all follow scripts. Scripts are important not only in guiding our own action, but in understanding other people's actions and reports of actions, including those reports that appear in literature. As Herman has stressed, we simply could not understand literary works without a broad range of scripts. Suppose I read the following sentences: "Would she be at home? It was a chance. I found a booth. Fumbled for a quarter. 444-3993. Was that it? I waited for the ring." I would not be able to make any sense out of this passage without a script for making a telephone call.

The final sort of schema (after representational schemas/scripts) is one that "runs" in the course of any given action we undertake. These *procedural schemas* constitute the skills of *skills memory* (equivalently, *procedural memory*). Procedural schemas are what allow us to do things such as follow scripts. Their components, which are also hierarchized (presumably with defaults and alternatives), are in effect nonconscious instructions to execute particular physical or mental actions. A common example is playing a musical instrument or riding a bicycle. When I am first learning to ride a bicycle, I have to make self-conscious decisions to lean in a certain way in order to correct imbalances, to hold my hands in a particular manner, to grab the brakes, and so on. While some of this remains self-conscious, a great deal eventually disappears from conscious consideration. It is incorporated into procedural schemas as I gain the skill of riding a bicycle. Jazz improvisation gives another good example. Initially, I self-consciously try to play certain variations or motifs. For example, at a certain point, I may have to keep trying to play a series of alternating sixteenth and eighth notes in a fast tempo. After a while, the necessary movements become incorporated into a procedural schema. At that point, when I decide to play the sequence, the schema runs on its own and I play the notes without thinking of them one by one.

The second type of lexical complex (after schemas) is, again, the *prototype*. Prototypes are, basically, standard cases. Initially, they may be thought of as schemas in which all the defaults are in place. For example, the prototypical man has two arms, two legs, and so on. But prototypes are more than that. At the very least, prototypes add "average" properties to defaults. Average properties in this case derive from instances of the relevant category (e.g., men), but they do not do so scientifically. In other words, our prototypical man is in part an average man. But our implicit calculation of the "average" here does not follow statistical principles. Most importantly, the averaging is "weighted" by saliency. The prototypical man for any given person will involve average properties, not of all men, but of men who are highly salient in that person's experience. Saliency here has several aspects. Two merit particular emphasis. One is simply a matter of experiential idiosyncrasies. Someone living in Norway is likely to envision the prototypical man as having blond hair. Someone living in Nigeria is likely to envision the prototypical man as having black hair. The point is not confined to real life. Fiction too contributes to prototypes. An American who sees many television programs with young, blonde women is likely to have a prototype for women that is younger and blonder than the average woman.

Perhaps more interestingly, the weighting of averages is also bound up with *contrast effects*. In other words, the saliency of particular instances of one category is in part a function of their contrast with instances of some opposed category. For example, being a man is, in part, a matter of not being a woman, and vice versa. For this reason, "manly" men will be more salient in defining the prototype for a man. As a result, the prototypical man will incorporate characteristics that are more highly contrastive with the prototypical woman than would result from simple averaging. Thus, if a square jaw is associated with men and not women, then the prototypical man will have a squarer jaw than will the actual statistically average man. A striking example of this is "diet food" (see Kahneman and Miller 143). Studies show that lettuce is widely considered the most prototypical diet food, in part because it has no calories whatsoever. However, if one were to average the calories in diet foods, one would clearly come up with a number far above zero. The prominence of lettuce is the result of the contrast effect.

The final lexical complex is the particular case. Lexical entries include not only schemas and prototypes, but also instances. (Or, if they do not include instances, they are connected with such instances in episodic memory.) Thus the entry for *man* includes (or is linked to) representations of particular men. The entry for *bird* includes representations of particular birds. These are commonly referred to as *exemplars*. However, there is a problem with this term, and indeed with the concept. "Exemplar" is used ambiguously to refer to instances of a category in general and highly prototypical instances of a category. In the first sense, a particular ostrich would be an exemplar of the category *bird*. In the second sense, however, it would not be an exemplar, because ostriches—unlike, say, robins—are not at all prototypical birds. In order to avoid this ambiguity, I have proposed that we use *exemplum* (pl., *exempla*) for instances in general, confining "exemplar" to prototypical instances. I will follow this usage in the following pages, though the reader should know that it is not standard in the field.

All the terms we have just considered apply not only to men, birds, and other things in nature. They apply also to artifacts, such as dramas, symphonies, and portraits. And they apply in very consequential ways. We tacitly define genres by feature hierarchies, usually with no clear point at which features shift from definitional to empirically likely. We have contrastive prototypes for literary periods, prototypes that guide us in understanding and evaluating particular works and broader tendencies. When we write literary or art criticism, we rely on scripts; indeed, literary theory could be understood in part as a set of diverse scripts for producing literary analyses. Moreover, not only is our thought about literature pervaded by these lexical structures, so too is the production of literature. Thus, for example, when authors set out to write in a particular genre, they themselves draw on feature hierarchies and contrastive prototypes, as well as salient exemplars.[10] Authors also follow scripts. Both authors and readers rely on procedural schemas, including schemas particular to literature (e.g., schemas regarding certain sorts of narrative inference). In short, the particular nature and varieties of lexical structures have significant implications for a wide range of issues in literature and the arts. We will consider some of these issues in the following chapters.

Finally, I should say a few words about lexical processes. The most obvious lexical process is full activation or access. This is simply a version of activating elements in long-term memory, which we have already discussed. When we access a particular lexical entry, we bring it into working memory. Thus when I hear "Have a seat on the sofa," I access the lexical entry for *sofa*, which then enters into working memory. With the representational information of *sofa* in my working memory, I am in a position to identify where I am being invited to sit. A more subtle lexical process is *priming*. Whenever I activate one lexical entry, linked lexical entries are partially activated. They are not actually brought into the workplace and subjected to operations in working memory. However, they are more readily accessible, more easily activated, than entries that are simply latent in long-term memory. For example, a common experiment involves having test subjects read sequences of letters projected onto a screen, then press a "word" or "nonword" button, depending on whether on not they recognize the letters as forming a word. Thus, faced with *dog,* they would press the "word" button, but faced with *glarb,* they would press the "nonword" button. Testers time each response. Presumably, identifying a word involves finding the word in one's mental lexicon (i.e., matching it with an item in long term memory). One finds *dog*, but not *glarb*. If words were always accessible or inaccessible to the same degree, then it should always take the same amount of time to identify, say, *river* as a word. But, in fact, it takes longer to identify *river* when it follows *dog* than when it follows *bank* or *boat*. The prior term (*bank* or *boat*) serves to "prime" the lexical entry for *river*, along with other related entries. As we will see, the point has significant consequences for our understanding of the suggestiveness and emotive impact of literary works. It also provides an apt transition to connectionism, for connectionism relies heavily on just this sort of *spreading activation*.

Making the Connectionist Circuit

Connectionism developed after representationalism, and partially in response to it, though in some ways it involves a return to much older approaches to the human mind—specifically, associationist psychology. At the same time, connectionism is, as already mentioned, a sort of abstraction from and simplification of brain processes. Specifically, the main structural units of neurobiological architecture are *neurons*. Neurons include a cell body and two sorts of appendages, *axons* and *dendrites*. Axons lead out from neurons; dendrites lead into neurons. Neurons send electrical impulses out to other neurons through axons and receive them through dendrites (see LeDoux *Synaptic*, 2, for a brief explanation and illustration). As LeDoux explains, a *synapse* is the "point at which the sending and receiving elements of neurons meet" (*Synaptic* 42). As this suggests, the main processes of neurobiological architecture are the transferal and inhibition of electrical activation. Needless to say, these processes are not confined to pairs of neurons, but proceed through larger sequences or *circuits* (groups of neurons "linked together by synaptic connections" [LeDoux *Synaptic* 49]).

Connectionism involves a fairly sparse architecture directly parallel with that of neurobiology. This architecture includes a structure of units or nodes, connections of various strengths among nodes, and processes for transferring and inhibiting activation between nodes. Honeck explains the basic premise of connectionism in the following way: "connectionism...is essentially the idea that the mind is a brain that creates knowledge by building connections between nodes in a vast network. Inputs...to the network activate some nodes, inhibit others, and over time begin to produce a stable pattern of response across the network. The system's knowledge is...the pattern of connections. The strength of the knowledge is reflected in the weight of the connections" (264).

Pinker notes that the model for connectionism comes not only from the human brain, but from the computer as well. He points out that "both computers and brains represent concepts as *patterns* of activity over *sets* of units.

A simple example is the lowly bite, which represents an alphanumeric character in your computer. The representation of the letter B is 01000010, where the digits (bits) correspond to tiny pieces of silicon laid out in a row. The second and seventh pieces are charged . . . the other pieces are uncharged" (*How* 101). Suppose a reader sees the word *tall*. In a representational account, the letter *t* activates some item in long-term memory, some part of the lexicon. This lexical entry for *t* contains a guide to pronunciation, including a default and specified alternatives. Thus *t* would issue in a series of instructions (a procedural schema) which would lead the reader to pronounce an unvoiced alveolar stop (the usual or default *t* sound, as in *Tom*), unless one of the alternatives is triggered. For example, the lexicon might list *tion* as an exception to the usual pronunciation of *t*. In contrast, a connectionist account would say that the visual stimulation produced by the letter *t* would lead to a particular pattern of unit activation—say, 11000001, with the first, second, and last units charged and the others not charged. This pattern of activation would spread throughout the network producing other patterns, including the pattern of pronunciation that we describe as unvoiced alveolar stop.

Another name for a connectionist network is a "*parallel distributed processing*" or PDP network. "*Parallel*" refers to the fact that, in a connectionist system, multiple processes are carried on simultaneously. As described above, a representationalist account of reading *t* is "serial." In other words, it proceeds one step at a time. First, we isolate the relevant lexical entry. Then we check for exceptions. If there are exceptions (e.g., *tion*), we return to the input to see if the exception applies. If it does not apply (e.g., if the word is *tall*), then we proceed with the normal pronunciation. In contrast, a connectionist account involves many processes going on at the same time, such that the final result does not derive from a single-track procedure, but rather is the most prominent or most repeated result of a range of processes. Since these processes occur simultaneously, they are referred to as "parallel" (again, as opposed to "serial"). Connectionist processing is also "*distributed*" because it is not "localized." In other words, the contents in a connectionist system are not single, discrete representations, but patterns of activation "distributed" across units. This is true in two senses. First, suppose that we are dealing with sets of eight units. Knowledge of the normal pronunciation of *t* is distributed across those eight units as a particular set of activations. Knowledge of exceptions is also distributed across units as particular sets of activations. Second, any set of units continually activates other units, so that the information is spread throughout—or "distributed across"—the entire network via these transfers of activation.

Connectionists argue that both features (i.e., parallelism and distribution) provide advantages to PDP networks over earlier models because the brain operates in a parallel and distributed manner. In fact, this is not quite accurate. First of all, the brain is not entirely distributed. Some functions really are localized. For this reason, PDP networks require some degree of localization in order to imitate the way the human brain works. Thus Colin Martindale has argued that the connectionist network "should be partitioned into modules devoted to specific tasks, such as reading, speech perception, and semantic memory" (250). Moreover, just as a connectionist network does not have to be entirely distributed (i.e., it may be modularized), there is really no reason that a representational system has to be localized, at least not in the brain. Within a representational account, pronouncing *t* is, in fact, one thing. Insofar as we imagine the lexicon spatially, we think of it as located in one place. But that "one place" in the mind does not have to be one place in the brain. (We will return to this point in the final chapter.) Put differently, there is no reason why a single "space" at the representational level cannot be a distributed set of spaces at another (connectionist or neurobiological) level.

Parallel processing is probably more broadly advantageous than distributed processing, for it captures aspects of human thought that are much more difficult to account for serially. Suppose, for example, that you are asked to state the first U.S. vice president that comes to mind. You might immediately say "Dick Cheney," because he is the current VP. Or you might say "Al Gore." Or you might say, "Oh, there was that pretty, stupid guy who couldn't spell." Or you might say someone else. In a traditional representationalist account, you would respond to this question by activating your lexical entry for "vice president," then scan the entry for names, presumably stopping at the first name you come to. In a connectionist account, however, the activation pattern for "vice president" would spread throughout the network. This activation pattern would, in turn, activate other patterns to which it was connected, which would activate other patterns, and so on. Simultaneously, it would inhibit certain activation patterns. For example, the vice president pattern—or, for simplicity of illustration, we might say the vice president node—would probably pass on activation to the Dick Cheney node and the Al Gore node, but it would perhaps inhibit the president node. Eventually, the activations and inhibitions would balance one another (eventually here means in milliseconds). At that point, there will probably be one node that has the highest level of activation. That node gives the name that you mention.

This seems to put connectionism and representationalism—or, more properly, parallel processing and serial processing—on a par. But there are strange twists here and, at least in some cases, they appear to favor parallel processing. Suppose we are asked to write down the name of the first vice president that comes to mind. Suppose Jones writes down "Dick Cheney" and I write down "Al Gore." We announce our answers and Jones says, "Yeah, I thought of him too." This probably does not mean that Jones self-consciously chose "Dick Cheney" over "Al Gore" as her answer. After all, the instruction was to write the first name that came to mind. It also probably does not mean that Al Gore occurred to her much later. The suggestion of the statement is that Al Gore was somehow in the running, that Jones might have thought of him first, but that she didn't. Indeed, Jones may never have explicitly formulated Al Gore as a possibility, even after writing down "Dick Cheney." Nonetheless, Jones may have the distinct sense that she "thought of" Gore. In contrast, suppose Smith writes down "George Bush." I might say, "Oh, I forgot about him," indicating that he was not in the running. A serial processing account does not have any obvious way of explaining this sense that some vice presidents were "in the running" and others were not. However, a parallel processing account does. Specifically, in a parallel processing account, a number of vice president nodes would have been activated. Indeed, those different vice president nodes are part of what is being processed in parallel. If Jones writes "Dick Cheney," that means that the Cheney node had the highest activation level when the system reached equilibrium. However, if Gore was "in the running," then the Gore node also had some degree of activation, though it did not draw attentional focus. In contrast, when I say that I forgot about George Bush, that means that the George Bush node had no activation—or a sub-"threshold" activation—when the system achieved equilibrium. The situation becomes even stranger when Doe says, "Spiro Agnew" and both Jones and I have the sense that we neither thought of him nor forgot about him.

A connectionist account could explain this situation in several ways. One approach might say that various nodes maintain a sort of "background" activation depending on daily life. As long as Dick Cheney is the current vice president, we continually hear about him in his capacity as vice president. This may give the Dick Cheney node a higher level of constant activation than, say, the Spiro Agnew node. If a particular unit has a higher resting activation rate, then it will begin with an advantage over other units. If the Cheney and Agnew units are given the same input of activation, the Cheney node will reach a higher total activation because it begins with a higher level of activation. This makes a particular difference given the standard connectionist principle that there is an *activation or firing threshold* that distinguishes an active from a latent—or a firing from a nonfiring—node. In other words, by a connectionist account, one node transmits its activation to another node if and only if its own level of activation has passed a certain minimal degree. Suppose, in our example, that the input to all the vice president nodes is 1 and the activation threshold is 1.5. Suppose also that the Cheney node has a background activation of 1, but the Agnew node has 0. Then, given the input, the Agnew node will not surpass the activation threshold, but the Cheney node will. Since Al Gore was recently a candidate for president, since he remains a topic of jokes in late night television and appears occasionally on the television or in interviews, his node too would have a higher level of constant activation than Agnew, though probably a lower level than that of Cheney. On the other hand, suppose that I had just watched a C-SPAN broadcast of a talk by Gore. Then, at least temporarily, the Gore node might have a more highly activated background level than the Cheney node in my *neural net* or grid of nodes. Jones did not see this talk. Thus, for Jones, Cheney has the higher background activation level. In consequence, I am more likely to come up with Gore and Jones is more likely to come up with Cheney, though for each of us both nodes would have some degree of activation and thus be "in the running." Consider the case of Jones. Perhaps, for Jones, the Gore node has a constant activation of 0.5. The input activation gives the Cheney node an activation of 2 and the Gore node an activation of 1.5. Since the Cheney node is highest, it draws attentional focus. However, the Gore node fires also (thus Jones's sense that she "thought of" Gore), while the Agnew node had some activation (0.5), but did not fire (thus Jones's sense that she neither thought of nor forgot about Agnew).

But what about George Bush? He is even more prominent than Gore, so the level of background activation for his node should be higher than that for Gore. Here we may need to take *inhibition* into account. Connectionism allows not only activation to pass from one node to another, but also inhibition. Suppose it is the case that there is an inhibitory connection between the vice president node and the president nodes. In other words, suppose that the neural network operates in such a way that activating vice president nodes serves to partially inhibit or lower the activation of president nodes. In more commonsense terms, when trying to think of vice presidents, we may try to put presidents out of our minds. Since George Bush was president, his node might for that reason have an inhibitory connection coming from the vice president node. In some cases, the inhibiting effects of the president node may be so great that the George Bush node ends up with an activation level that is not only below the firing threshold, but is actually zero or below zero. (In representational terms, it is not only not activated, it is not even primed.) This may account for my sense that I "forgot about" Bush. Indeed, in a case such as this, I might equally have said, "Oh, I forgot that he was vice president." But, of course, the information was still there in long-term memory for I immediately recognize "George Bush" as a correct answer. It seems plausible to explain my forgetting, then, as a result of inhibition.

To recapitulate, one could think of the process in terms of figure 2. Again, for simplicity, suppose the vice presidents and the vice president category are represented by single units. The vice president input (i.e., the initial instruction to name a vice president) feeds activation to a general vice president

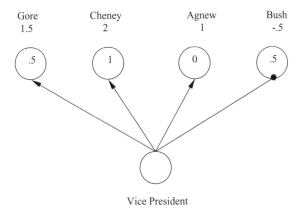

Fig. 2. A simplified connectionist account of vice president activations, using background activation and inhibitory connections. Excitatory connections are indicated by an arrow. The inhibitory connection is indicated by a line with a blunt end. Background activation is printed within the nodes. The resulting activation for each node appears below its name.

category node, which in turn communicates activation to vice president person nodes—Al Gore, Dick Cheney, Spiro Agnew, and so on. Now suppose that Spiro Agnew has 0 background activation, Al Gore has 0.5, and Dick Cheney has 1. The communication of activation from the vice president category node would distribute activation of +1 to all these units in parallel. This yields Agnew 1, Gore 1.5, and Cheney 2. If, say, 1.5 is the firing threshold, then only Agnew fails to reach activation. Cheney is the highest—hence what Jones writes down. But what about Bush? This process should yield an activation of 1.5 for Bush, the same as Gore. Here, we may posit an *inhibition* of activation from the vice president input to all president nodes. Suppose that this inhibition has a value of −1. This is transmitted to the Bush node, rather than the activation, yielding a total activation of −.5.[11] The result is our sense that we "forgot" Bush, "thought of" Gore (without making him the object of attentional focus or self-consciously deciding between him and Cheney), and neither forgot nor thought of Agnew. (Of course, a genuine connectionist analysis of this would be much more complex. I have simplified the account for purposes of illustration.)

But here one might reasonably ask—why would there be an inhibition in cases such as this? How would it arise in the first place? Generally, inhibition may be explained as the result of prior feedback. Initially, the vice president node would activate the president nodes, for presidents and vice presidents would be linked together in complex circuits. But this would routinely yield wrong responses to problems about vice presidents (e.g., "Clinton" would be a wrong answer for the instruction "Name a vice president"). Connectionist architecture includes specific procedures for correcting errors such as this through the alteration of nodal connections. These procedures are called *learning rules*. One of these is the *Delta Learning Rule*, by which falsity reacts back on the initial connections, adjusting them for a superior final output. In the case we are considering, the Delta rule may have operated to establish inhibitory connections between the vice president node and president nodes. Or perhaps we should not posit a general inhibition here. Perhaps the inhibition is confined to vice presidents who became president. These would be the cases where errors are most likely, and thus the cases where the Delta rule would be most applicable. At least for a time right after the relevant election (e.g., Bush's election as president), there would be many occasions for a false activation of the vice president node in relation to the new president and vice versa (e.g., there would be many occasions on which one might accidentally refer to President Bush as "the Vice President"). Through the Delta rule, this would lead to an inhibitory relation between the vice president node and the Bush node.

This is not the only way a connectionist could account for the preceding data. A connectionist might rely, rather, on *strength of connection*. In the connectionist view, not all nodes are equally bonded. Some have very strong links; others are only weakly related. If two nodes are very strongly connected, then the activation of one might be increased when it passes to the second. If they are less strongly connected, then the activation of one might be passed on to the second, but in a reduced form. For example, a connection strength of 1.5 would take an input of 1 and pass it on as 1.5 while a connection strength of 0.5 would take an activation of 1 and pass it on as 0.5. In these terms, the strength of connection between the vice president node and the Cheney node may be higher than that between the vice president node and the Agnew node. This would make sense given that the vice president node is now repeatedly associated with Cheney (in news broadcasts referring to "Vice President Dick Cheney," and so on), whereas it is hardly ever associated with Agnew, except in some occasional historical program. Thus we would expect the Dick Cheney node to receive the highest level of activation from the vice president node. On the other hand, we would also expect the Al Gore node to have a high connection strength with the vice president node since Al Gore is routinely introduced as "former Vice President Al Gore." Thus we would expect a high level of activation to be passed to the Al Gore node from the vice president node. This would put both "in the running," with the Gore node being most active in some cases for contingent, individual reasons.

Strength of connection may also be used to explain why George Bush may not be "in the running." Since becoming president, Bush is never introduced

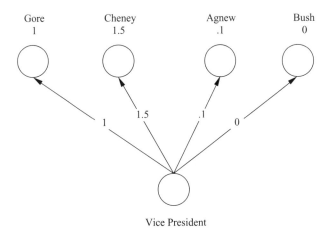

Fig. 3. A simplified connectionist account of vice president activations, using different connection strengths. Connection strengths are printed on the arrows.

as "former Vice President George Bush," but always as "President" or, now, "former President." We do not need to posit any sort of inhibition to account for Bush not being in the running for at least some people. As references to "vice president" are repeatedly associated with Dick Cheney and Al Gore, but virtually never with George Bush, the strength of the connection between the vice president node and the George Bush node, once strong, would gradually weaken to the point that it is probably now very slight for many people. To account for the difference between Agnew and Bush through connection strengths, we might say that the connection strength between the vice president node and the Agnew node is very low, but that between the vice president node and the Bush node is now zero. (See figure 3.)

It is worth pausing for a moment over the idea that the strength of connection between the Bush node and the vice president node decreases as Bush is referred to as "President" or "former President," while Gore and Cheney are referred to as "Vice President" or "Former Vice President." Here as elsewhere the alteration in connections is due to a learning rule, in this case the *Hebb Learning Rule*, probably the most important such rule in connectionism. Named after the psychologist, Donald Hebb, this is a simple rule governing connection strengths. It says that when two connected units are simultaneously active, then the connection between them is strengthened. When one is active and the other is not, the connection between them is weakened.[12] Thus every time I refer to "Vice President Dick Cheney," both the "vice president" node and the "Dick Cheney" node are activated.

This simultaneous activation increases the connection strength between the nodes. It simultaneously reduces the connection strength between the vice president node and the Gore, Bush, Agnew, and other nodes. As years go by and Bush is never referred to as vice president, whereas Gore and Cheney are referred to as vice president, the connection strengths for Gore and Cheney will increase while that for Bush will decrease.

What about Bush versus Agnew? Neither the Bush node nor the Agnew node is likely to be activated simultaneously with the vice president node. In other words, when someone refers to a vice president, it is far more likely to be Gore or Cheney than Agnew or Bush. In this way, Agnew and Bush are roughly equal. However, virtually all activations of the Agnew node are likely to activate the vice president node. For example, every reference to Agnew is likely to include reference to the fact that he was vice president. In contrast, the vast majority of references to Bush are likely to make no reference to his vice presidency. Thus the vast majority of activations of the Bush node will not involve simultaneous activation of the vice president node. As a result, by the Hebb rule, the connection between the vice president node and the Bush node is likely to undergo many more instances of weakening than the Agnew node. Specifically, the Bush/vice president connection will be weakened almost every time Bush is mentioned, while the Agnew/vice president connection will be strengthened virtually every time Agnew is mentioned (while both will be weakened at comparable rates with mentions of the vice presidency).

In any case, however we analyze the details of the connectionist account here, activation or inhibition passes to the Cheney, Gore, Bush and other nodes simultaneously. All these sequences are processed in parallel. The result—Dick Cheney, Al Gore, whatever—occurs only when all processing stops and the system reaches equilibrium. This is different from a serial system in which possible solutions are addressed one by one and processing presumably stops when the first adequate solution is reached.[13]

Though often seen as offering an advantage for connectionism over representationalism, there is no reason why representationalism cannot incorporate parallel processing. Classical formulations of representationalism are serial, but that is only because serial processing is the easiest to formulate initially. We generally tend to think about processes as serial operations. Thus we would expect early formulations of any theory in this area to adopt a serial approach without really considering a parallel processing alternative— though priming, a standard process in representational architecture, does operate in parallel. In any case, it is easy enough to incorporate at least some features of parallel processing into representationalism, indicating again that these are not mutually contradictory alternatives.

In conclusion, we might look at a more artistic example than the "name a vice president" game—specifically, a literary metaphor. Whether integrated

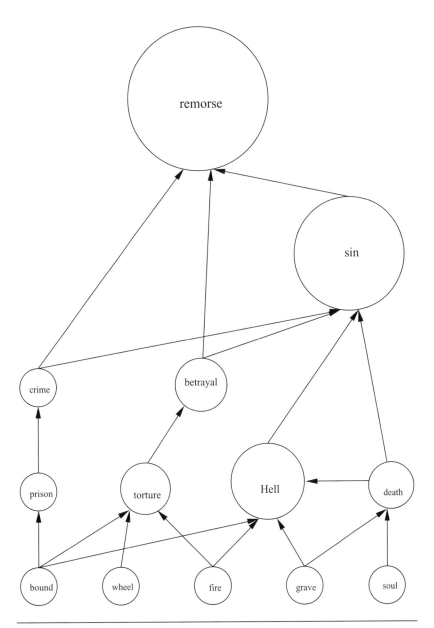

Fig. 4. A partial, simplified version of a connectionist model for a metaphorical passage in *King Lear*, insofar as it bears on Lear himself: "You do me wrong to take me out o' the grave. / Thou art a soul in bliss; but I am bound / Upon a wheel of fire" (IV. vii. 51–53). The size of the nodes loosely suggests the relative degree of activation as a function of inputs. A fuller account would need to treat the contrast between Cordelia's soul and Lear's soul.

with representationalism or not, connectionist architecture allows us to clarify and render more precise our account of complex literary processes. It is not at all confined to artificial and simplified examples, such as that of Bush and Agnew. Consider, for example, a well-known passage from *King Lear*. When Lear wakes from his madness to see Cordelia, he tells her, "You do me wrong to take me out o' the grave./Thou art a soul in bliss; but I am bound/Upon a wheel of fire" (IV. vii. 51–3). We understand that Lear is saying that he is being tortured, not only by the actions and attitudes of Goneril and Regan, but more importantly by his own remorse for the way he treated Cordelia. He is also saying that he is in Hell, thus suffering terrible pain, as punishment for his sins, prominently the abuse and banishment of Cordelia. The Hell meaning is more salient, but the torture meaning is clear as well, and both feed into the feeling of remorse. A representational approach that uses serial processing would account for this response via the scanning of lexical items. Thus we would activate meanings of "bind," "wheel," "fire," and so on. We would synthesize these. We might then scan for entries containing both "bind" and "fire." This could perhaps lead us to the entries for "Hell" and "torture." Ultimately, we might be able to account for the data this way. However, a parallel processing approach has clear advantages. A PDP account would go something like this. Lear mentions being in the grave and he refers to Cordelia as a soul in bliss. This all serves to activate "death," "afterlife," "Heaven," and "Hell." Terms such as "bound" and "fire" send further activation to "Hell," giving it a high degree of activation. "Bound" may also activate "prison," and "wheel" may activate "torture," as may "fire." "Prison" and "Hell" would, in turn, activate nodes for crime and sin. "Torture" may activate a node for crimes of betrayal in particular, as torture is linked with treason, espionage, and heresy rather than, say, theft and murder. All this then contributes to the overwhelming sense of remorse communicated by the passage, for these various circuits ultimately converge on remorse and related nodes (see figure 4). Here as elsewhere, the connectionist approach captures important features of our experience that are not readily captured in a serial, representational account.[14]

Cognitive science is a tremendously complex, varied, and theoretically rich field. I do not pretend to have done more than scratch the surface in this chapter. However, I have introduced a number of the most important concepts and set out the methodological principles that define cognitive science. This will provide a foundation for the following chapters, where we will draw on these concepts and principles, adding to them and modifying them in our examinations of literature, film, music, and painting.

CHAPTER 3

The Author
Maestros and Geniuses

In the past decade or so, creativity has become an important topic of research in cognitive science, commonly under the rubric of "creative cognition." As Finke explains, "the goal" of creative cognition study "is to use the methods of cognitive science to understand how creative ideas are generated, to explore the mental processes and structures that underlie creative thinking, and to identify the various properties of those structures that promote creative exploration and discovery" (303). Before one begins to address these issues, however, one might wish to ask about the definition of creativity itself. A standard definition is given by Sternberg and Lubart: "Creativity is the ability to produce work that is both novel (i.e., original, unexpected) and appropriate (i.e., useful, adaptive concerning task constraints)" (3). Creative work is not only innovative, but also good in its kind. Standing on one's head in the classroom may be highly innovative. It would not thereby constitute creative teaching.

This definition of creativity may seem dull, almost banal. After all, doesn't it apply not only to Mozart, but to a clever idea about how to seat people at a wedding? Yes, it does. But this is a good thing. A fundamental tenet of most work in creative cognition is that both the novelty and the appropriateness of creative work result from standard cognitive principles and processes. There is no great cognitive leap from ordinary mortals to artists. Artists think in just the same way as everyone else for, after all, their minds are structured in the same way. In explaining artistic creation, one necessarily relies on the very same cognitive architecture as when explaining run-of-the-mill human thought. As Ward, Smith, and Finke put it, "the hallmark of *normative* human cognition is its generative capacity to move beyond discrete stored experiences." In keeping with this, "creative accomplishments, from the most mundane to the most extraordinary, are based on those ordinary mental processes" (189). Differences in individual creativity "are understandable in terms of variations in the use of specifiable processes or combinations of processes, the intensity of application of such processes, the richness or flexibility of stored cognitive structures to which the processes are applied, the capacity of memory systems (such as working memory), and other known and observable fundamental cognitive principles." In short, "Creative cognition explicitly rejects the notion that extraordinary forms of creativity are the products of minds that operate according to principles that are fundamentally different than those associated with normative cognition" (191). In another place, Smith, Ward, and Finke phrase the general point more succinctly: "the systematic implementation of ordinary cognitive processes can give rise to creative discoveries" (Preface vii).

Robert Weisberg has been one of the writers most insistent on this continuity between ordinary acts, on the one hand, and great art or great science, on the other. As Sternberg and Lubart summarize, "Weisberg... proposes that creativity involves essentially ordinary cognitive processes, yielding extraordinary products" (8). Indeed, Weisberg argues that greater creativity is to a considerable extent simply a matter of greater knowledge. What he does not say is that this knowledge should be diverse, though this is precisely what his studies suggest. For example, he mentions the case of an engineer solving a problem in physiology (247). Weisberg points out that the engineer had more knowledge than other people who had approached the problem and failed. But the crucial point is that he had more knowledge in different areas. This is precisely the conclusion reached by Martindale, who explains that "to maximize creativity, one's best bet is to have knowledge about a wide variety of things. A number of studies have shown that creative people have a very wide range of interests" ("Creativity" 252). Thus creative cognition researchers do not deny any difference between great writers, painters, mathematicians, physicists, and everyone else. But they try to explain the great difference in output by relatively small differences in cognitive structures (e.g., a slightly greater capacity in working memory), processes (e.g., slightly broader priming), and contents (e.g., a slightly greater variety of schemas, prototypes, etc., drawn from a slightly wider range of fields). The cognitive difference between Einstein and an indifferent professor of Physics may be very small, though its consequences are vast.

On the other hand, as the reference to "writers, painters, mathematicians, physicists" may suggest, certain sorts of continuity may be overemphasized by creative cognition theorists. I do not mean that creativity is discontinuous with ordinary cognition. However, not all things that are called "creative" may be cognitively identical. The creativity of Schoenberg or John Coltrane may not be the same as that of Niels Bohr or Max Planck. Each may well be continuous with ordinary cognition. But each may be continuous with different aspects of ordinary cognition. This returns us to the problem of definitions. Perhaps it was a mistake to begin with the notion of "creativity." After all, creativity is a concept from folk psychology and, as such, it may not be suited to scientific study. More technically, creativity may not have "cognitive reality." In other words, it may not name a single, unified phenomenon at the level of cognitive processes.

Reading research in creative cognition, a humanist is likely to be struck by the fact that much of the work focuses on sorts of creativity that do not seem to bear any relation to art. For example, in one study, "students were asked to generate various means for increasing the number of European tourists to the United States" (Runco and Sakamoto 64). It is simply not clear that studies of this sort tell us anything about painting or music. Other research does treat art, but much of this does not clearly distinguish composing a symphony from making some scientific discovery. Thus many writers in the field act as if finding a solution to structure of benzine is creative in just the way that *Les Demoiselles d'Avignon* is creative. Perhaps that is the case, but it is not self-evident. Moreover, the background and ordinary practices of cognitive scientists lead them more often than not to favor scientific discoveries as models for creativity and thus to assimilate all other cases to Darwin's discovery of evolution or Watson and Crick's work on DNA. It is no doubt the case that there are important insights to be achieved by this approach. Nonetheless, it does not seem that all creativity is discovery in the scientific sense. The general point at least is recognized by some writers. For example, Smith, Ward, and Finke write that, "Creative cognition, like noncreative cognition, is by its very nature diverse and affected by many processes. To understand creativity, we must begin to assess those processes in creative contexts. An overarching theory of creativity is no more likely to be found than a unified theory that could explain all cognitive phenomena. Instead, it might be better to pursue more focused theories that can inform us about the role of specific processes in creative functioning" ("Principles" 334).

On the other hand, despite this potential problem with the practices and primary models of creative cognition theory, the basic premise of this approach seems indisputable. How else could creativity operate other than through ordinary cognitive processes? Insofar as creativity is a cognitive phenomenon—and clearly it is at least in part cognitive—it must be a function of ordinary human cognitive architecture. Indeed, creative cognition theorists are entirely right when they stress that creativity is everywhere in our ordinary lives—not only in clever decisions about wedding arrangements, but in every sentence we speak, as Chomsky has famously emphasized (e.g., "the normal use of language is constantly innovative" [*Language and Problems of Knowledge* 5]). Moreover, despite the scientific focus of much research in the field, there is work on cognition and creativity that bears directly on the arts—prominently the studies done by Howard Gardner, but including work by other researchers as well. Finally, even work that does not bear directly on the arts is not wholly irrelevant. At the very least, it may provide a starting point for further research. In the following pages, I will consider some of the strengths and weaknesses of creative cognition theory, elaborating and extending those aspects of the theory that seem particularly promising.

Knowledge, Networks, and Innovation

The definition cited earlier makes reference to two aspects of creativity—innovation and aptness. Innovation, of course, refers to what is different about a creative work. In part, aptness refers to what is the same, what is carried over from earlier ideas and practices. It is also a commonplace among writers in creative cognition that creativity involves both a break with the past in certain respects and continuity with the past in other respects. The point applies more obviously to science than to art. A creative hypothesis about the structure of DNA must not only be innovative, thus novel; it must also be continuous with what we already know about DNA, about biology more generally, and so on. The necessity of continuity is less self-evident in the arts. On the other hand, there clearly is such continuity. At the very least, there is a negative continuity. A new style necessarily relies on our understanding that it is *not* the earlier style. For example, atonal music presupposes our contrasting it with tonal music. A piece of atonal music would not have the same force or function if all music were atonal. Moreover, as a matter of fact, the continuities are deeper anyway. For example, Schoenberg often wrote in traditional musical forms, with traditional instrumentation. His radical development of twelve-tone composition relied on traditional techniques of variation, such as inversion. More generally, Schoenberg did not appear from nowhere, but descended from Wagner, Mahler, and other composers. Similarly, Matisse developed the Fauvist style out of earlier post-Impressionists, and so on.

But how do we understand this continuity in cognitive terms? Among other things, work in creative cognition indicates that continuity implies *mastery*. Indeed, this mastery has been quantified in Gardner's "10-year rule." As Feldman explains, this is "the finding that it takes a minimum of 10 years to move from novice to master in any of the domains so far studied" (173). Scientific and artistic work seem comparable in this respect.

Studies by Gardner and others indicate that it takes about a decade for painters, composers, biologists, and mathematicians to produce their first great works. In each case, they need ten years to master the field so that they have enough comprehension to innovate appropriately or successfully.

Gardner's account of how one achieves mastery of a field—then takes that mastery and moves to creativity—is, of course, more complex than the mere statement of a decade-long apprenticeship suggests. Moreover, it treats details of artistic creation, as distinct from scientific work. We will discuss Gardner's views more fully below. However, for the moment it is important to stress one implication of Gardner's work—that mastery involves the acquisition of a set of schemas (for Gardner's discussion of schemas, see *Art, Mind, and Brain* 175–8 and 362–8). Thus a particle physicist acquires a series of schemas regarding the structure and motion of atoms, protons, and so on, as well as schemas regarding experimental procedure, the operation of complex devices (such as accelerators), and other things. A painter acquires a set of schemas regarding figures, perspective, light, as well as the use of particular brushes, the mixing of colors, and so on. Matisse, for example, acquired a series of schemas that included naturalist, impressionist, and pointillist techniques.

For Gardner, creativity involves varying these schemas. The schemas, then, constitute the continuity. The variations, of course, constitute the innovation.

But is that really enough? The most ordinary, quotidian sorts of creativity involve variation on schemas. What if we are interested in the greater creativity of memorable work in art and science? Here, the precise type of variation is important. Creative cognition theorists tend to consider only certain, specifiable sorts of innovation to be extensive enough to count as significantly creative. Take a standard example from creative cognition theory. Suppose we are trying to figure out the structure of DNA. Suppose further that we start out thinking that the structure might be spherical. We discover that this does not work. The obvious thing to do now is to try some other ellipsoid—probably one of the "spheroids," ellipsoids that are close to spheres. There are two of these, the "oblate" and the "prolate" spheroid. The former has a "squashed" appearance (similar to the earth), while the latter has a "squeezed" and pointy appearance. These too turn out to be incorrect. Thus they fail the creativity definition by being inappropriate. But suppose one turned out to be correct. That too would not be a good case of creativity for creative cognition researchers. It would be creative in the sense that it would involve movement away from a default value. In other words, it would involve schemas and variations. However, that movement or variation is so slight that it would be no more creative than ordinary thought (as when we come up with a new way to drive to work, so that we can avoid a traffic jam).

In other words, it would not simply be continuous with quotidian creativity. It would be an instance of quotidian creativity. The shift from spherical to oblate spheroid is just the sort of shift we all engage in, unreflectively, every day. In contrast, the discovery that the structure of DNA is a double helix does count as creative—not only because it is correct, but because it is innovative in a nonquotidian way.

What, then, distinguishes banal from extraordinary creativity in this view? A number of writers say that it is a matter of *proximate versus remote associations*. When faced with a problem, we immediately consider possible solutions that are closely associated with the problem and/or its initial (failed) solution. Cognitively, ellipsoids are closely linked, with spheres being a sort of default in ordinary thought. Thus, once we try to explain DNA in terms of a spherical model, we are likely to shift to these proximate associations, trying oblate and prolate spheroids, for these are the most closely linked to spheres in our associative network. However, according to the creative cognition view, genuinely creative solutions to a problem can be found only by moving away from these proximate associations to more cognitively distant possibilities. This captures something we all know about firsthand. Everyone has had the experience of trying to figure out some problem, going over and over the details, trying solution after solution, but failing to come up with anything. Then we stop thinking about the problem and suddenly, out of the blue, the solution occurs to us—a solution that is simple but which differs in some crucial way from all the solutions we had tried earlier. The discussion of remote associations is in part an attempt to explain just this. The idea is that, in the first stage, we are stuck in a set of proximate associations. We obsessively go over these proximate associations, finding that none of them works. When we turn away from the problem, there is at least the possibility that some more distantly associated concept will arise.

In connection with this, one repeated empirical finding about creativity is its association with "defocused attention." According to this research, less creative people focus their attention quite narrowly when engaging in creative tasks. More creative people allow their attention broader scope. They are more freely associative. In some ways, this finding is trivial. A great deal of quantitative research on creativity—"psychometric" research, as it is called—concerns such readily quantifiable matters as number of word associations given by subjects. Thus, in some ways, the research may be seen as testing free association at least as much as it is testing creativity. (For an overview of psychometric work, see Plucker and Renzulli.) It should hardly come as a surprise that defocused attention yields a broader range of word associations. Nonetheless, this research does fit with the plausible idea that creative solutions to problems involve accessing remote associations. Attentional focus is, to a great extent, a matter of sharply constraining one's sphere of cognitive interest. Attentional focus is therefore likely to restrict access to remote associations, even for people with a broad range of associations. Conversely, defocused attention should make remote associations more accessible relative to proximate associations. In other words, proximate and remote associations should not be as sharply distinguished when one's attention is defocused.

Though the primary examples in this research are scientific, the general point about remote associations bears on literary work as well. Hackneyed metaphors or imagery clearly rely on proximate associations, while novel metaphors and imagery draw on remote associations. A Hallmark card or a television romance might be confined to standard images and vocabulary. Love may be linked with roses, moonlight, walks by the seashore, and so on. The themes of such a work might include, say, the unworthiness of the lover. A creative work shifts to more distant connections. Take Pablo Neruda's "The Insect." Instead of the moonlight walk by the shore, Neruda begins with a different sort of movement, a "journey" passing through "hills" from his beloved's hips to her feet. Instead of the ritual proclamation of the unworthiness of the lover, Neruda explains that he is "smaller than an insect." In place of the traditional comparison of the beloved's skin to lilies, ivory, and so on, Neruda finds her "the color of oats." Though, outside a cognitive framework, one might not think of the point this way, these are remote associations, for they are both distant from the usual images (thus innovative) and, at the same time, still associated with these standard images (thus continuous). More exactly, suppose Neruda is trying to describe the color of his beloved's skin. Due to the poetic tradition, he is likely to come up with such images as ivory and lilies. These are immediate or proximate associations. "Oats" is a related image, but clearly more distant, less readily accessible, more remote. Note also that it is still apt. In other words, it satisfies both criteria for creativity given above. In fact, it probably conveys the color of the beloved's skin more accurately than ivory or lilies. At the same time, the fact that it is a food brings a degree of sensual intimacy into the image that is entirely in keeping with Neruda's purposes, and very different from the other alternatives.

In contrast, we might consider another remote association—whitewash. In the proper context, this could be appropriate. But in Neruda's poem, as written, it is not. The color is (presumably) less accurate. The sensual suggestion of taste is lacking. Though equally innovative, it would be a less creative alternative for these reasons.

The account of creativity in terms of remote associations has been nicely developed in connectionist terms by Martindale. He begins by explaining defocused attention as "states in which a large number of nodes are almost equally activated" (259). This is contrasted with states in which a limited number of nodes are highly activated. The latter is the state of focused attention, which is to say, the state of uncreative people when they are approaching a problem (articulating a metaphor, formulating imagery, defining a molecular structure, etc.). One could think of it this way. An uncreative poet wants to write a love poem about his/her beloved and their relation to one another. Mentally, there is some activation pattern of the following sort. (Arrows indicate a transfer of activation from input nodes to output nodes. Parenthetical numbers indicate the resulting activation of the output nodes.)

Skin + white → lilies (+1)
      → ivory (+1)
      [nothing further]

Romance + scenery → moonlight (+1)
      → roses (+1)
      → seashore (+1)
      [nothing further]

Romance + movement → walk (+1)
      [nothing further]

Similarly, the noncreative activation pattern for DNA structure might be something along the following lines.

Shape → sphere (+1)
      → oblate spheroid (+0.8)
      → prolate spheroid (+0.8)
      [nothing further]

In each case, remote—and valuable—alternatives would receive no activation or, at best, too little activation to be available for use in solving the problem (i.e., the problem of choosing the most aesthetically effective metaphors and images or the problem of defining the shape of DNA).

Note that this account addresses the feeling of being "stuck" on a problem. We feel stuck (according to this model) because we keep going over the highly activated nodes, with no evident alternatives. The activation of those nodes has left other nodes—including those nodes that would lead to a solution—with zero or, at best, subthreshold activation. Moreover, continually reviewing the highly activated nodes may serve only to activate those nodes further, which in turn only makes the problem worse, as activation cycles back to the already overactive, and useless, nodes—lilies reminding us of ivory reminding us of lilies; moonlight reminding us of seashores, reminding us of moonlight, and so on. Indeed, the Hebb rule operates to worsen the situation here, for we keep activating these nodes simultaneously, thus strengthening their connections and thereby furthering the fruitless, repetitive cycle of error.

In contrast with this, Martindale argues that creative thought involves a more diffuse set of nodal activations. Thus, when Neruda was writing "The Insect," perhaps he had a network activation more along the following lines:

Skin + white → lilies (+0.9)
　　　　　　→ ivory (+0.85)
　　　　　　→ oats (+0.8)
　　　　　　→ whitewash (+0.7)
　　　　　　[etc.]

Romance + scenery → garden (+0.9)
　　　　　　　　→ seashore (+0.9)
　　　　　　　　→ roses (+0.8)
　　　　　　　　→ moonlight (+0.8)
　　　　　　　　→ hills (+0.7)
　　　　　　　　[etc.]

Romance + movement → walk (+0.9)
　　　　　　　　　→ journey (+0.7)
　　　　　　　　　[etc.]

The highest level of activation would still yield a moonlit walk on the seashore and a beloved who has skin like lilies. However, there is not a sharp distinction between standard and strange associations here. Unlike the uncreative writer, Neruda has a wide array of unusual images and metaphorical sources that are above the threshold of activation. At the same time, the commonplace images are not so fully and unequivocally activated themselves. Moreover, even a single innovative choice in this context may realign the entire set. For example, depending upon idiosyncracies of Neruda's lexical structure, the journey node could be linked with the hills node. Thus the partial activation of the journey node could spread activation to the hills node, and vice versa. Moreover, the oats node could be linked with the insect node such that, once "oats" is chosen for the poem—and thus repeatedly reactivated as Neruda continues writing and revising—the insect node comes to receive a high degree of activation. This node may then receive still further activation via the idea of unworthiness. This broadly spreading activation provides a striking contrast with the case of the uncreative poet, whose associations repeatedly cycle through the same, limited range of alternatives. As a result, instead of an unworthy lover walking on a moonlit seashore with his beloved, whose skin is like lilies, we have Neruda's highly creative poem.

Needless to say, this too is not all there is to it. For one thing, there has to be some limit to what is activated. The set of activated nodes cannot be too large. Nor can it simply be random. In either case, it would become too difficult to find an apt solution to the artistic or scientific problem at hand (see Martindale 266). Indeed, there are two obvious, noncreative possibilities here. Most people evidently generate only a limited set of proximate nodes, all highly activated, with little else. Perhaps some other people generate too many nodes, including a large number that are not at all apt. This may be what happens when a student gives an answer on a test or in class that seems bizarre. It is a case of overactivation of cognitive nodes, the reverse of the underactivation in the student who gives only standard answers. Tests that equate the number of associations with greater creativity are not well designed to isolate this phenomenon. In any case, creativity would fall between these excesses. More exactly, it would result from a gradient of activation that is not so steep that it eliminates nonstandard possibilities, but is not so flat that it includes irrelevant options equally with potentially apt solutions.

Though I have not come upon this idea among writers on creative cognition, it does fit nicely with other aspects of this approach. Indeed, this is presumably where knowledge or mastery enters. Over-generation of possibilities seems most likely to occur when someone has begun work in a new field, but has not achieved mastery of that field. In other words, mastery allows us to limit associations in ways that make it more likely our associations will be appropriate. On the other hand, while mastery helps to prevent over-generation of associations, it may also lead to undergeneration. Someone with mastery of a field may be no more creative in his/her area than someone outside the field entirely (though for different reasons). For example, in learning chemistry, one comes to add certain sorts of knowledge—thus certain nodes—to one's neural net, nodes that were not there previously. Initially, connections with these new nodes are fairly indiscriminate. For example, a beginning chemistry student may have links between "molecule" and a wide range of shape nodes. As this student gains expertise, those links are pared away until his/her associations between "molecule" and "shape" are fairly limited. One result of this is that someone who has mastered chemistry is less likely than a novice to come up with inappropriate possible shapes for a new molecule. On the other hand, this expert might also be less likely to come up with an appropriate but highly unusual shape in circumstances where a high degree of innovation is required. The expert is likely to have a wide range of typically appropriate shapes available to him/her. If ellipsoids are usually relevant, then he/she will know much more about ellipsoids than the novice. But the very fact that he/she knows more ellipsoids makes it much easier for his/her thought to get stuck in cycling through those ellipsoids. The point holds for poetry as well. Someone with no knowledge of poetry may have no stronger connection between the beloved and lilies than oats or whitewash.

This does not mean, however, that less knowledge is a good thing. In fact, it seems clear that less knowledge is a bad thing. Most obviously, a novice will not be able to work through difficult problems in chemistry, whatever his/her wealth of associations. There is a similar, though less technical problem in poetry. To write poetry successfully, I need to have enough familiarity with various aspects of poetic form, the historical resonances of different terms, the ways in which images interact with themes, and so on. Otherwise, I will not be able to orient my poems to a readership. I cannot have these crucial sorts of familiarity unless I know a good deal about poetry.

So, to be creative, it is apparently necessary to have a hierarchy of connection strengths that does not sharply degrade remote associations, but that at least partially reflects knowledge of the relevant domain—poetry, chemistry, or whatever. It is also necessary that one be able to integrate remote associations into one's larger project, which relies on such knowledge. The latter is particularly clear in what is often isolated as the second phase of creativity, the phase where one assesses one's novel associations/solutions. Specifically, creativity involves at least a "generation" stage and an "evaluation" stage. The two have significantly different cognitive properties. Martindale points out that creativity requires "a low-arousal [or defocused] state in order to 'search' for a solution." But, after this, it equally requires the "return to a higher arousal state [or narrow focus] to see if the solution is a good one" (261). Thus, once the novel idea has been generated, it must be assessed and developed. The assessment and development require an intensive focus on that idea. This process centrally involves the determination of an appropriate fit between the new idea and the problem. The point is obvious in the sciences, where a new idea needs to be evaluated both theoretically and experimentally. But it holds equally in writing poetry, painting, or creating music. One has an idea for a metaphor or image. But then one has to give that image full attention in evaluating its place in the encompassing poem. Part of that evaluation involves having a sense of the poem's formal properties, its relation to other poems, the associations and expectations that are likely to be triggered in a reader, and so on. In other words, it involves a mastery of schematic knowledge in the field.

It seems clear, then, that domain-specific knowledge (e.g., of chemistry or poetry) is important. But it is not all that is important. Domain-specific knowledge is what gives us tools for "second stage" evaluation. But, as we have already noted, it is also what defines and highly activates proximate associations that are noncreative and that get us stuck. This suggests why creativity is so often a matter of borrowing across related but nonidentical domains. Creative, thus nonstandard or nonproximate associations in chemistry may be drawn from physics. Creative, thus nonstandard or nonproximate associations in one art form or tradition may be drawn from another art form or tradition. Consider again the case cited by Weisberg in which an engineer solved a problem regarding the structure of the kidney by applying simple principles drawn from engineering (247). Clearly what happened here is that the engineer had systematic knowledge that did bear directly on the problem, but that had been segregated from the problem due to disciplinary boundaries. Thus standardized disciplinary constraints did not inhibit his thoughts on the problem to a few, professionally proximate associations. At the same time, relevant knowledge prevented the overgeneration of inappropriate associations and facilitated the second stage evaluation of possible solutions. Perhaps a similar process was involved in Thomas Cech's Nobel Prize winning work on RNA. Cech explains that, at crucial points in his work, he "turned to genetic engineering, with which [he] had no prior experience at the time" (11); he had "to learn a whole new technology. Yet at the end of a long road, entirely new insights were gained" (14). In Cech's case, the work was more a matter of asking new questions across disciplinary boundaries, rather than providing new answers to well established questions. But that comes to much the same thing, for, as Palade points out, "In addition to *solving* problems, the creative mind *recognizes*" and, we might add, poses, "new problems" (145).

We find parallel cases in the arts when, for example, painters innovate based on principles of optics, or where artists working in one tradition draw elements from another tradition. Picasso's use of Iberian sculpture and African masks in his paintings is an obvious instance of this sort (see, for example, Leighten 79–81 and 86–9). Picasso's "remote associations" in this case were, in effect, the proximate associations of artists at other times and places. Thus they were associations with a high prima facie likelihood of bearing on and being appropriate to visual art. Goethe's use of Sanskrit drama in *Faust* is another case in point. We find the same sort of thing when an author draws from another genre (e.g., a novelist draws on lyric poetry). In effect, these cross-domain borrowings have the best of both worlds. Coming from highly structured and closely related domains (e.g., other artistic traditions, other genres), the borrowings tend to inhibit irrelevance while simultaneously broadening the author's or artist's associations and thereby facilitating innovation. In some cases, they may even contribute to systematic, second stage evaluation, especially as this has already occurred in the other domain (e.g., in the Indic tradition's judgments regarding those staging techniques Goethe borrowed for *Faust*).

Representation and "Basic Creativity"

Of course, theories of creative cognition are not necessarily connectionist. While cognitive accounts of creativity are almost certain to incorporate spreading activation, they may—and, in fact, usually do—involve reference to standard representational architecture as well. As we have already noted, Gardner addressed creativity in terms of schemas. The research we have just been discussing, however, suggests that creative variation may be more aimed at prototypes, for the most fully activated nodes in a neural network are precisely the standard, expected features that go to constitute a prototype. Thus the prototypical beloved has skin like lilies or ivory, the prototypical movement of lovers is a moonlit walk on the seashore. Finally, it is clear from our discussion that exempla play a role in creativity as well. When Goethe wrote *Faust*, he had in mind particular instances of Indic literature, such as *Abhijñānaśākuntalam* (along with other precursor works). These nonexemplary (that is, in Goethe's tradition, nonprototypical) exempla provided the remote associations that made *Faust* innovative and apt.

In this and the following section, I will consider creativity in terms of schemas, prototypes, and exempla, discussing how writers and artists vary each type of structure. However, before going on to this, we need to return briefly to the continuity of artistic or scientific creativity with ordinary creativity. Up to this point, we have been acting as if there are only two degrees of creativity—the quotidian creativity of ordinary life and the great creativity of *Les Demoiselles d'Avignon* or Watson and Crick's work on DNA. But there is a lot of creativity in between. Indeed, almost all art and science are somewhere in the buffer zone between ordinary innovation and pathbreaking creativity. In this section, I would like to consider "basic creativity," the innovation that we find in even minimally successful works of art—from popular ephemera to admired canonical works that are considered a continuation of the tradition rather than a radical change or "turning point" in the tradition. I might equally refer to it as "normal innovation," for the idea is roughly parallel to Kuhn's notion of normal science—the sort of routine science that is crucial to advancing a particular scientific research program (as distinguished from revolutionary science, which initiates a new research program).

Since the default values of schemas are so crucial to the definition of prototypes, let us set them aside for the moment (until we turn to prototypes) and consider schemas as broad, abstract structures that give general conditions for the object in question. We have schemas for genres, for characters, for imagery, for dialogue, and so on. Indeed, we have more than one schema for each. Basic creativity does not alter schemas in this sense. Nor does it add to the set of available schemes. It does not change the basic structure in which, say, a particular genre unfolds or a particular technique is implemented. Consider point of view. Schematically, narration may be first person or third person and it may be omniscient or limited. Basic creativity does not transform this set of options. What does it do, then? The very fact that schemas are abstract indicates the necessity of specifying them. Thus the first sort of basic creativity is the specification of schemas. If one writes from a limited point of view, one must set the limits. If one writes with a first person narrator, one must develop the voice—the speaking rhythms, vocabulary, attitudes—of that narrator. The point is still more obvious with respect to story structure. If one writes a romantic tragi-comedy, one must develop details about the lovers—their physical appearance, their location in time and place, the nature of and reasons for their separation, the precise means by which they are brought together again at the end.

There are several ways in which authors may specify schemas. One is through the combination of elements from other works. Thus my romantic hero may look like the hero in one earlier work, suffer conflicts selected from heroes in two or three other works, and so on. Perhaps more commonly, at least in successful and enduring works, an author may draw on his/her own autobiographical experience to complete these schemas. To do this, he/she may remain fairly close to the original experience, modeling the hero on him/herself, the lover/beloved on some real romantic interest, and so on, or he/she may draw on real experiences in a more open manner, mixing physical and personality traits from different acquaintances and putting them into the schema without concern for the ways the biographical originals may have behaved in similar circumstances.

Variations in prototypes take us beyond the bare minimum of innovation. But that hardly means that these variations are radical. A wide range of very non–avant-garde literary works alter one or another default value or average property. More exactly, there are standard cases of genres, characters, image patterns, etc., just as there are broad, definitional or semidefinitional principles. These standard cases (thus prototypes) are often altered in one or another particular in the works that are considered lasting—including those that we see as continuing a tradition, rather than defying or revolutionizing it—and even in a wide range of works that are considered to be popular ephemera. Thus, the prototypical villain in a western wears a black hat, has a hazy past, shoots people in card games, threatens the hero's life, abducts the hero's beloved, threatening her chastity or her life, and so on. But most westerns will alter one or another of those prototypical properties. Thus, in John Ford's *Stagecoach*, we find a card sharp who wears a black hat, plays cards, has a hazy past, and so on. He even threatens the life of the hero's beloved—but he does so to protect her chastity rather than to violate it. The most common variation of a prototype property is probably a simple reversal or antonymy. In *Stagecoach*, the villain's attitude toward the heroine is reversed from one attacking her chastity to one protecting it. In Shelley's "Triumph of Life," the prototypical imagery associating good with light and evil with darkness is reversed, so that light is linked with evil and darkness is linked with good. On the other hand, in some cases, the change is more complex. For example, in sonnet 130 ("My mistress' eyes are nothing like the sun"), Shakespeare, speaking of his beloved's breasts, changes the prototypically expected white of snow to "dun" (l.3). Presumably the breasts of Shakespeare's mistress were not black as coal, which would seem to be the diametric opposite of "white as snow." To find an appropriate alternative, Shakespeare had to move to the wider set of nonwhite (thus nonprototypical) images.

Alterations in prototypical properties are common in admired works for several reasons. Among other things, it is difficult to develop a specified plot while maintaining all default and average principles. The creation of a plot involves working out highly complex interactions among characters, events, scenes, themes, and so on. It happens regularly that the necessary specification of these elements results in conflicts with prototypical properties, which then must be changed if the story is not to seem incoherent. Indeed, this is so common one might even say that part of being a prototypical narrative is incorporating nonprototypical elements.

Consider again the example from *Stagecoach*. The film is a western, but as part of its specification it takes over a theme from stories about the American south—the displacement of an entrenched gentry, who follow strict codes of tradition, honor, and social hierarchy, and their replacement by enterprising young individualists who are pragmatic and egalitarian. The villain in *Stagecoach* is one of those displaced gentry. This causes a potential problem for the western prototype. This villain's traditionalist commitment to female chastity contradicts the standard tendency of the western villain to threaten the chastity of the heroine. At this point, there are two obvious options. One would be to make the character into a hypocrite and have him assault the heroine despite his principles. Another is simply to drop the entire prototypical threat from the villain. In making the threat against the heroine into a *protection* of her chastity, Ford chose a third, more interesting alternative—a more creative alternative, one might say. In this case, the thematic and narrative coherence are preserved and the prototypical property is not simply followed or discarded, but reversed. In connectionist terms, this is not surprising. Both the prototype of the western villain and the prototype of the southern gentleman would send activation to such units or complexes of units as "female chastity." Thus a continuing concern with this topic is almost predictable. Indeed, Ford is implicitly relying on just this complex of activation operating in the viewer's mind. As the "savages" surround the stagecoach, we see the villain's revolver pointing at the head of the heroine. No one ever explains why this happens. Ford is, in effect, assuming that the connectionist networks just mentioned—along with the network recording common beliefs about savage behavior toward captured women—will provide the unmentioned information, the explanation for why this man is about to shoot the heroine.

It often happens that particularly common violations of prototypes follow broad social patterns. Shelley's reversal of light and dark imagery is bound up with the Romantic reversal of social and moral values, exemplified most obviously in Romantic Satanism, which was itself bound up with the social and political agitations of the time. Similarly, many prototype variations in recent years have been based on shifts in gender roles or sexual orientation (e.g., making action heroes female or both romantic lovers male). These are two areas which have seen broad and deep social change in the same period.

Finally, after schemas and prototypes, we come to exempla. Needless to say, creativity bears on exempla no less than it does on schemas and prototypes. There are three clear ways in which this occurs. The first involves the transformation of exempla, usually through abstraction and respecification. The second results from the use of noncanonical or unfamiliar exempla. The third is produced by shifting the domain of an exemplum. (Needless to say, the three can be combined.)

The first—transformation of an exemplum—involves more or less the same processes that we discussed in connection with schemas. For example, in *Baumgartner's Bombay*, Anita Desai draws extensively on the exemplum of Conrad's *Heart of Darkness*, taking aspects of structure from Conrad's novella and specifying them through her own experience and reading. Thus she takes the general narrative of a European adventurer entering a non-European country, but shifts the latter from colonial Africa to independent India. Specifically, in *Heart of Darkness*, Kurtz travels to the heart of Africa in search of ivory. In doing this, he is drawn into the local savagery, including strange religious practices, evidently involving cannibalism. Given the basic respecification just mentioned, Desai needed some sort of parallel in modern India. Interestingly, she preserved the cannibalism. Some people who burn corpses on the Ganges are reputed to eat human flesh as part of a ritual. Desai took this up as a way of respecifying Conrad's African cannibalism. But how would this occur, and who would the European cannibal be? Here Desai considered what Europeans come to India today, as opposed to Europeans who came to Africa a century earlier. Evidently, in Desai's view, the common reason for Europeans to visit India now is to acquire drugs. They are not colonialists, but addicts. So, she created a character, Kurt, who travels to the heart of India in search of heroin. In doing this, he becomes involved with local savagery, strange religious cults, and cannibalism.

The second way of treating exempla creatively is to take up a noncanonical exemplum, especially one that is nonprototypical in some significant respect. Of course, this must involve transformation as well, including abstraction and respecification. But the abstraction may—indeed, presumably will—stress nonprototypical properties. As in the case of prototype transformation, there are often social and political patterns to this. Modern women authors have rediscovered forgotten women writers and used them as models. Writers of the Irish Renaissance took up noncanonical Irish lyric and epic poetry. Practices such as these are clearly informed by broader social trends—feminism, nationalism, and so on.

Perhaps the most cognitively interesting way of using exempla creatively is by taking an exemplum and shifting it to a new domain. Joyce took up Ibsen, an exemplary modern dramatist, but used him as a model for the short story. He took up Homer and Milton, exemplary epicists, but used them as models for a novel. The exemplum in question may be an entire work, a character, some plot element, a style, or something else. A good example of character used in this way may be found in Romantic Satanism. Blake, Shelley, Byron, and others took up Milton's Satan, surely an exemplary villain. But they shifted this character from the character category "villain" to the character category "hero." Thus when Byron modeled his hero Manfred in part on Satan, he relied on an exemplum—indeed, an exemplar (a prototypical exemplum). But this exemplar was shifted out of the "villain" category, then combined with some of Byron's own biographical experiences (through abstraction and respecification). In connectionist terms, the exemplum of Satan did not trigger such heroic traits as winning dangerous battles. Rather it activated such nodes as "seduction" and "myself am Hell" (Milton 4.75). The autobiographical impulses behind the poem activated such nodes as "sister" and "remorse," which in turn further activated and were further activated by "seduction," and "myself am Hell." All of this combined to produce a character that, though largely composed out of existing patterns, is highly innovative (a clear product of remote associations) and, though composed out of highly diverse elements, is highly consistent and "appropriate" (in part due to its use of a well-established model from another domain—not unlike the engineer's work on the kidney).

Principles of Radical Innovation: Genius and Childhood

In the preceding section, we distinguished minimal novelty, which is merely unique specification of a schema, from the nonminimal, but still "basic" creativity that involves altering prototypical and exemplary structures. As this indicates, the movement away from minimal creativity toward greater creativity is equally a movement away from prototypes. This is just what we would expect from our initial discussion of creative cognition. Proximate associations are, again, precisely the properties that make up prototypes. Remote associations are precisely properties that are related, but nonprototypical. However, this only gives us the beginning of an understanding of radical creativity. It tells us what radical creativity is not—it is not confined to prototypes, nor even to minor alterations in the localized properties of prototypes. But what is it, then? What takes creativity beyond masterful, but still basic creativity, to radical newness (such as we find in the avant-garde) and to what we sometimes call "genius"?

One of the few cognitive researchers to have touched on the creativity of the avant-garde, thus radical creativity, is Howard Gardner. Specifically, Gardner devotes a great deal of attention to the remarkable similarities between childhood art and avant-garde experimentalism. For example, he explains that children in one study were "reminiscent of certain avant-garde artists" when they "said you could consider the noise of a car going by as music 'if people like it' or 'if you want it to be.'" This is virtually identical with the view of avant-garde composer John Cage. Along the same lines, "four- and five-year-olds often liked abstract paintings more than realistic ones" (102).

Gardner argues, however, that there are crucial differences. For our purposes, two are particularly important. First, the children lack mastery. Second, and perhaps more importantly, they lack a sense of audience. They find it difficult to take up the point of view of a reader or viewer. Gardner notes that "the youngest subjects," those of "about five years old"—which is to say, those who hold some of the most apparently avant-garde views, as just noted—"proved quite oblivious to the reactions of others" (141). The child becomes "quite sensitive" (141) to others' point of view only in the period when his/her approach to art is losing its experimental quality and is undergoing cultural systematization.

Gardner is certainly correct in emphasizing these differences. But, having noted the differences, he seems to forget about the similarities. They do not become meaningless on account of the differences. Indeed, in my view, the similarities suggest that radical innovations in adulthood are bound up with childhood art. After all, it is not very plausible that the parallels between childhood art and radical creativity in adulthood are merely coincidental.

In part, Gardner drops the issue because he is considering a different question. Gardner wonders if the child is a Picasso who loses his/her talent at the age of eight, presumably due to miseducation. This is an important question, for, if this is what happens, then our educational system is to blame for massively stifling genius. (Gardner concludes that, in fact, this is not what happens.) The question raised by radical creativity, however, is different. It does not concern the relation of children's art to genius, but the relation of genius—or more exactly the relation of radically innovative works of art—to childhood modes of thought and expression. My contention is that radical innovation is innovation that has a deep structural relation to childhood. Indeed, Gardner even touches on this relation, when he writes of "mature artists" that "much in their processes of creation is reminiscent of children" (102). But the point is general and remains undeveloped.

More exactly, there appear to be two sorts of radical innovation and both are organized and oriented by reference to childhood modes of art. They might be called "classical" and "romantic" (or "avant-garde"). I will refer to them as "progressive" and "recuperative." When growing up, the average child in any culture slowly achieves a very minimal level of competence (far below mastery) in drawing, singing, story telling and so on. This achievement of competence is, first of all, a matter of dispensing with many techniques, practices, ideas, that are not standard in the adult arts of one's culture. In other words, young children spontaneously develop a wide range of techniques for drawing, telling stories, and so on, that they subsequently discard as they learn the "right" way to draw, tell stories, and so forth. At the same time, children gain greater competence in the techniques that remain. They learn to use the remaining techniques more consistently and more rigorously. Finally, they gain a sense of and develop sensitivity to audience, learning how to take into account an audience's perspective, knowledge, expectation, and so on. I will refer to this change in children's artistic diversity and competence as "cultural selection and systematization," for the culture selects certain artistic principles from the plethora generated by the child and it develops those principles systematically.

The first sort of radical innovation, the "progressive" form—probably the dominant form of radical innovation for most of human history—involves the rigorous development of cultural systematization, the extension of the basic principles of competence so that they are followed less haphazardly, understood less loosely, and so on.[1] Probably the most obvious instance of this is the attempt by European artists from the Renaissance through the Impressionists, then to Photographic Realists, to paint "what they really saw" and not "forms they had learned" (Gombrich 394), the repeated effort to minimize painting what they knew in order to paint only what they actually perceived. By my account, this effort is one form of progressive radical innovation. At each step, there is an increase in the distance between mastery of the domain (here, painting) and childhood spontaneity (which, in drawing, is primarily based on knowledge, rather than momentary sensation). A similar development may be found in the increasingly rigorous treatment of literary point of view, culminating in the interior monologue of Joyce, Woolf, and others. Children do not maintain point of view consistently, nor do they adopt other points of view. Learning the "right" way to tell stories involves cultivating consistency in this area. Nonetheless, even professional writers often violate principles of point of view. Some writers (e.g., Joyce) devoted themselves to the rigorous development of this aspect of cultural systematization. It is worth noting that this sort of radical innovation is probably closest to that of science and is probably the form most readily illuminated through their conjoined study. Indeed, Gombrich draws directly on the philosophy and history of science (e.g., the work of Karl Popper) in treating the development of artistic illusion.

The other sort of radical innovation, alongside the "progressive," is "recuperative." This sort of radical innovation is closer to such prototype cases of creativity as the early modern avant-garde and postmodern experimentalism. It includes most of the works we would consider shockingly new (e.g., *Finnegans Wake*). From the name itself, it is probably obvious that what I have in mind is the recovery of childhood techniques that were lost in cultural systematization. However, this is not merely a repetition. It is crucial to the development of a successful avant-garde that the recuperated childhood technique be systematized, and particularly that it be developed in relation to a sense of audience. This is no easy matter. The risk of progressive innovation is that it will lead to mechanical art. The risk of recuperative innovation is that it will lead to incomprehensible art. It has certainly been the case that much avant-garde art has proven "cognitively opaque" (as Lerdahl put it, regarding avant-garde composition [231]).

Consider, for example, the case of Kandinsky. Kandinsky was one of the most important avant-garde creators of modern art, and his work was produced "partly under the influence of children's drawing" (Butler 39). Butler points out that Kandinsky believed he was "working with a language of colours and shapes which evoke specifiable emotions" and, "along with many of his abstract painter successors," he believed "that the disposition of the painting ensures that we will unconsciously have the 'correct emotional response'" (44). However, "Very few spectators of this type of painting can respond to them as Kandinsky wished" (45). In part because this problem has recurred continually for avant-garde artists, it often happens that there are "two phases of innovation." As Butler explains, the first phase is "that of radical change to the language of an art." This is "followed by a more pragmatic, audience-oriented adaptation of new techniques, which often demands a highly allusive compromise with the past" (258). In other words, there is often a sort of systematizing development within avant-garde movements whereby an initial, radical innovation comes to be reformulated, reshaped in ways that are more accessible, "appropriate" to the domain, as Sternberg and Lubart would put it.

As the preceding discussion suggests, one way of dealing with the systematization problem is to borrow techniques from another tradition in which they have already been systematized. Gardner's research gives us a better idea of why and how this is the case. The childhood array of techniques is universal. It is shared by children everywhere. Gardner assimilates childhood artistry to the beginnings of language. Initially, a child engages in "a period of babbling" when he/she produces "sounds from all languages." Learning the phonology of one's own language is almost entirely a matter of losing many of those initial sounds so that "production is increasingly restricted to those . . . in the individual's own cultural milieu" (148). In artistry, too, the child begins with a universal range of practices that is gradually restricted. Moreover, the general processes of cultural selection and systematization are identical across cultures, for they all involve the rigorous development of masterable techniques along with sensitivity to audience. Because of their common origin and their shared processes of systematization, artistic practices are far more transportable across traditions than one might initially expect. On the other hand, these techniques are not identical across traditions. As with language sounds, the particular artistic practices retained by distinct cultures are different from one another in some degree.

One result of this is that prototypical art in one culture is a good source for principles of radical innovation in another culture. Both the initial body of (childhood) techniques, and the subsequent direction of development (systematization with sensitivity to audience) are, again, identical in the two cases. For the most part, what is different in another culture is simply what our culture could have been. Each culture, each artistic tradition, can easily provide artists in another culture, another artistic tradition, with techniques that those artists already had (in a preliminary form) as children, but subsequently lost. Moreover, when a foreign tradition does provide such principles, it provides a culturally systematized version of them. That is no doubt why radical innovation in the last three centuries—from Goethe through Picasso (to take two examples we have already mentioned)—has been bound up with cross-cultural influences.

But, again, the crucial point here is the revival of childhood techniques, for even cross-cultural borrowings rely on and often emphasize the precultural aspects of those borrowings. Put differently, Picasso does not end up painting in a particular African tradition. African, Iberian, and other traditions, rather, suggest to him his own forgotten practices and they offer him preliminary systematizations of those practices. He then takes up these practices and systematizations for his own purposes and shapes them for a different audience.

The link between the avant-garde and the artistry of children has of course, been recognized by authors other than Gardner–if most often as a criticism. Butler notes that "accusations of childishness" were "made against Schoenberg, for example, in Walter Dahms's description of the *Three Piano Pieces* Op. 11: 'First a child taps the piano aimlessly'" (77). In 1908, Matisse was "greeted . . . as a painter 'with whom impressionism reaches its second childhood' and whose 'motive and treatment alike are infantile" (215).

What is much more important, however, are the specific correspondences between avant-garde innovations and childhood practices. Perhaps most obviously, children draw what they know, not what they see. Progressive innovation moves further and further away from this, perfecting perspective to the point where the painter supposedly paints only what he/she sees. In recuperative innovation, however, the tendency is precisely the opposite. Andre Salmon, referring to the avant-garde, went so far as to assert that "The great law that dominates the new aesthetic is the following: conception overrides perception" (qtd. in Butler 72).

There are still more striking and particular connections as well. The geometrization of art in Cubism was a profound and transformative innovation. But it merely systematized one tendency of children, whose earliest drawings grow directly out of geometrical forms. As Gardner explains, "In the second year of life children begin to make marks on pieces of paper and to gain enjoyment from this activity," but these are "apparently unorganized." (The most direct parallels here are of course, with certain sorts of abstract painting.) "In their third year children become able to produce a variety of geometric forms. . . . A dramatic watershed occurs around the age of three or four, when children become able to combine geometrical forms into coherent and recognizable shapes and to associate them deliberately with objects in the world." As these figures gain in complexity, we arrive at what "has been deemed the 'flowering' of artistic activity by observers of the infant painting scene" (149).

This description is deeply reminiscent of the "watershed" in Picasso's work—the development of Cubism. Indeed, with a few changes, the passage could be applied almost directly to *Les Demoiselles d'Avignon*. However, there are some crucial differences. Most obviously, Picasso arrived at this stage in reverse. He did not begin with the simple geometrical forms and move to representational accuracy. Rather, he moved from greater representational accuracy to greater stylization through geometrization. This is, of course, part of the incorporation of mastery into his innovation. In addition, despite the much publicized disdain of avant-garde artists for their audience, Picasso was deeply aware of his audience and produced a painting that would allow for general accessibility. In other words, in *Les Demoiselles,* Picasso took up a discarded childhood technique as the basis for his radical innovation. However, he subjected it to the two transforming conditions that differentiate childhood art from adult art: technical mastery and audience awareness. The technical mastery is evident not only in the finished works that preceded *Les Demoiselles*. It is also evident in the series of sketches that led up to this particular painting. Picasso did not simply produce *Les Demoiselles*. The work involved a long preparatory period, with multiple sketches, and subsequent revisions (for a discussion, see Daix 65–78 and Leighten 85–6). Moreover, a large part of that reworking evidences a clear sense of audience. No matter how avant-garde an artist might be, he/she still produces work through alternately generating and evaluating. The evaluation involves his/her adoption of a receptive attitude, the attitude of a viewer.

Both productively and receptively, Picasso's work was facilitated by his study of Iberian, African, and Oceanian sculpture. Here, Picasso found art that emphasized the geometrical elements that were part of his own childhood artistry, but that had been largely set aside in the development of Western art. At the same time, he found these elements integrated into a socially shared system of art. This not only made him aware of the possibility of geometrization. It also suggested a way in which this technique could be systematized, mastered, and socialized, which is to say, geared toward an audience. But, of course, Picasso could not simply assume this audience. He was not painting for the ancient Iberians or even for Polynesians of his own day.

Here it is worth considering *Les Demoiselles* in more detail. The geometrization of the figures and the background are obvious. The disregard for perspective is clear as well (e.g., the fruit seems as if it is about to slide off the canvas). But what is striking is that we are, in a sense, eased into the geometrization, an easing that manifests Picasso's mastery and his sense of audience. The two figures in the center of the canvas are the most traditional. Their geometrization is less pronounced and more realistically plausible than the other figures. Take figure 2 (counting from the far left). She is painted as if lying down. The bluish-white background suggests bedsheets, and she pulls part of a sheet over her leg. Her right arm is crooked behind her head in a classic reclining posture. The geometrization is simple. The arm/elbow/head form a triangle—as one would expect. The upper torso is a triangle also—somewhat stylized, but plausible in, say, an athlete. Her vulva is a realistically plausible triangle as well. Finally, her nose is a sharp triangle. Triangles obviously dominate this figure, but her breasts are semicircles, and her eyes and eyebrows are exaggerated arcs. The figure is hardly standard. The geometrization is striking, but not disruptive. It is easy to get to this figure from our schemas for other reclining nudes. The same point holds for figure 3. In this case, both arms are behind her head, and both form triangles. The eyes and nose parallel those of figure 2. A sheet covers her vulva and her upper torso is narrower and more ordinary. One breast is an arc. The other is a triangle. The representation gives a sense that her left breast (the triangle) is lifted, while the right breast droops slightly. This is in keeping with realism as her left elbow is raised much above her right elbow, and her torso is twisted in such a way that one would expect this effect.

Thus these two central figures maintain fairly clear connections with earlier, more standard nudes. Again, they ease the viewer into the picture. As Solso explains, we can focus on only a tiny portion of a painting at any one time. In viewing a painting, we scan and pause repeatedly. Thus, given "the natural course of eye movements," the "center" of the painting is the "region of the visual field" that receives "the greatest amount of traffic" (150). In connection with this, "The most frequently explored part of visual art is the center" (149). In this way, the central figures of Picasso's painting are perfectly placed to provide a sense of continuity with past tradition, to allow the viewer to enter the complex innovations of the painting gradually.

The rest of the picture changes this situation considerably. First, it depicts a single space. All four figures are parallel. Yet figures 1 and 5 (the background figure on the far right) are clearly standing, and figure 4 is seated. For figure 1, the bluish white is some sort of backdrop. She seems to be pushing away a darker curtain in the front. For figure 5, the bluish white is itself a curtain that she is pushing away before a background partially of the same color as the curtain held by figure 1. Again, figures 2 and 3 appear to be reclining. The disruption of perspective is just the sort of thing one finds in work by children. But here it is systematic. We have figures who are lying, standing, and sitting. The upright figures frame the reclining figures. The use of overlapping sheets creates a sense of three planes. A foreground figure on the far left, a background figure on the far right. Moreover, the far left and far right figures are facing the center and apparently in motion toward the center. In contrast, the three central figures are stable, motionless—two reclining, one seated. Indeed, they form a large central triangle that gives stability to the composition, while the peripheral figures give a sense of motion. All this is in contrast with the fairly random childhood disregard for perspective—again, indicating both mastery and audience awareness.

The figure closest to the two central figures is the woman on the far left. She is more strangely geometric than the two central figures. In part, she repeats their characteristics (e.g., the triangular vulva and nose, the large arcs for eyes). But the triangular kneecap is odd, and so is the way her right leg fragments into a series of triangular planes. Her breasts are a strange square. Finally, her face is darkened. That, and the triangular shadow over her nose and upper lip, give her face a more masklike quality than that of the two central figures. Here Picasso is in effect preparing his audience for the figures on the far right. The central figures have relatively natural, if geometrized faces. The figure on the far left has a more masklike face. The figures on the far right have masks instead of faces. Indeed, even here there is a difference. Figure 5 (on the far right) preserves the normal form of the human face more fully than figure 4 (the seated figure). The nose is two triangles which actually produce a sense of depth lacking in figures 1–3. It is placed at the right point on her face. But she has virtually no chin (i.e., her mouth is unrealistically low on her face). Some two-thirds of her face is the nose. And, instead of flesh-color or shadow, she has streaks of green on the nose and red streaks elsewhere. Finally, figure 4 is a highly stylized mask. Her nose is a rectangle with two concave sides, one straight side, and one convex side. Her eyes are out of parallel. Her mouth is on the side of her face, and the entire face seems to rest on some sort of base. This "base" is continuous with her arm and is thus, in part, a stylized hand. But it is also like some sort of handle, as if this mask were to be held, not worn. Figures 4 and 5 are more extreme in other ways as well. Figure 5 has only one breast and it is an entirely implausible square. Figure 4 loses almost all distinguishing bodily characteristics, even to the point where the clues for her posture are contradictory. Yet, at the same time, figure 5 is represented as moving realistically through curtains that she pushes open. Her (highly stylized) mouth is slightly open, as if she has just begun to speak. Figure 4 stares back at the viewer with defiance. They are the two figures with the fullest intentionality, the most accessible inner life. Figures 2 and 3 are like manikins with their vacuous eyes and standardized postures. Figure 1 is intermediate; partially in motion, but partially frozen, she is in some respects a moving person and in some respects a statue in a posture of motion. Only the hint of anger in her lips tends, I think, to tilt the balance toward a sense of inner life. Thus Picasso parallels the increasing movement away from standard European techniques with an increasing humanization of the figures, until the most geometrized and foreign figures are ultimately the most human as well.[2] Again, the combination of mastery, systematization, audience awareness, and childhood-based radical innovation is unmistakable.

Of course, painting is not the only art to which these principles apply. Links between childhood creativity and the literary avant-garde are equally clear. The explicit use of authorial intervention, the "breaking down of the fourth wall" in theater, the foregrounding of the fictionality of fiction are all staples of the literary avant-garde. They are also staples of childhood narrative. For example, Gardner explains that "Faced by the little girl trapped by the lion, a three-year-old will simply pick the little girl up and take her away from the lion, declaring 'she's safe now'" (173–4). For young children, "the boundary between the fictional world and the real world is highly— excessively—permeable" (174). Radical disruption of plot schemas is also a common part of childhood narrative. Sometimes a child "confuses the monster frame with the fairy-tale frame (thereby having the monster live happily ever after) or embraces a physical solution when a psychological one is wanted (thereby making the prince taller rather than happier)" (175). My only question here is whether the child is genuinely confused, or if he/she is simply happy to mix up frames and solution types in this way. In any case, the link with experimental techniques is clear. It is only at around the age of eight that children "adhere faithfully to the schemas of the culture" and are "attracted to 'formula stories'" (177). Across the arts, eight is the usual age at which childhood "radicalism" is lost and social selection and systematization become definitive.

Music is no less relevant here than painting or literature. Consider, for example, two fairly standard techniques of avant-garde jazz. The first is the partial rejection of discrete pitch in the use of "wailing" sounds produced when the performer glides from one tone to another, sometimes above the usual range of the instrument. A second is the fragmentation of melodies, breaking off one segment of a melody rather than playing through the entire sequence. Gardner explains that the first musical sequences "produced by children around the age of a year or fifteen months" are "melodic fragments." These fragments have "undulating patterns, going up and down over a very brief interval" and "are more reminiscent of waves than of particular pitch attacks" (150). Moreover, when children begin to learn songs from others—which follows their own generation of "spontaneous song" (150)—they "repeat" some "characteristic bits or embryonic tune segments." At this time, "the child is ... working with the building blocks of song: exploring small segments, practicing with them, combining them in diverse ways so that they now bear a kind of family resemblance to the target song but do not yet reveal its general structure" (151). This is so obviously characteristic of avant-garde jazz that the preceding sentence could simply be repeated, substituting "experimental jazz musician" for "child": "The experimental jazz musician is working with the building blocks of song: exploring small segments, practicing with them, combining them in diverse ways so that they now bear a kind of family resemblance to the target song but do not yet reveal its general structure."

As we have seen, Coltrane's "My Favorite Things" uses all these techniques—the undulating patterns in the highest register, the reliance on brief melodic fragments, and the diverse combination of song segments into an improvisation that bears a kind of family resemblance to the target song. We could add other techniques as well. Sloboda sees infantile babbling as one of the earliest "common behaviour[s] which could possibly be musically relevant." The infant's "intonational babbling is primarily composed of microtonal pitch glides" (*Musical* 200). Coltrane is well known for just such glides—so much so that Dean remarks "Microtonal improvising which goes beyond the usage of Coltrane is rare" (65). However, like Picasso, Coltrane eases us into these innovations, and he continues to provide us with ways of structuring them throughout the entire piece, thereby reducing the risk of cognitive disorientation, as we discussed in chapter 1. Here too we find mastery, systematization, and audience awareness combined with radical innovation based on culturally discarded childhood techniques.

Along the same lines, childhood song does not maintain a strict "sense of key and tonality," but is "generally restricted to the overall contour of the song and to an approximate sense of tonal values" (152). In reproducing songs, "four-year-olds" follow "the approximate sizes of the leaps" between pitches, but without "an accurate sense of interval mapping... and a key sense that remains stable across phrases" (153). This movement of approximate tonal value and approximate intervals is just what one finds in some chromatic improvisations and wailing glides of avant-garde jazz. Again, in "My Favorite Things," Coltrane restructures these techniques by reference to the point of view of a listener by shaping his improvisation in such a way as to make the approximate pitches and intervals mappable as thematic variations, by limiting the duration of deviations from a recognizable key, and by continually returning to a stable tonality. It is as if Coltrane makes little forays into the radical innovations of childhood—stretching even to the very origins of childhood art in what Gardner calls "the period of free exploration" (155)—but brings us back to a culturally familiar place just when we might become too disoriented (usually within about thirty seconds, a timing that is perhaps related to the dissipation of cortical arousal, as suggested in chapter 1).

As we noted in the first chapter, one technique used by Coltrane to keep his avant-garde work "appropriate," to connect it with the cognitive capacities of an audience, is the organization of the music by tacit reference to (unsung) lyrics, as in the implicit rhythmic repetition of "favorite things" or the rhythmic and melodic echoing of "a love supreme." Again, the pairing of speech with melody and rhythm is also very characteristic of children. Thus it too is a recuperative innovation. For children, song is intimately bound up with speech. Gardner points out that in the "first year of life," children's "babbling includes melodic and intonational as well as phonological experimentation." From a very early age, "children prove capable of imitating the intonational patterns of... linguistic structures" (150). The child's first approach to learning song is the repetition of the lyrics (151) and for a couple of years "the lyrics and the rhythm are still carrying the day as far as song production is concerned" (152). Moreover, the lyrics and the rhythm are not distinct here. Until the child experiences a "breakthrough" to "underlying pulse," he/she relies on "surface rhythm," which is to say, the "placement of accents in the surface lyrics" (154). Indeed, the very "four-year-olds" who lack "an accurate sense of interval mapping... and a key sense that remains stable across phrases" do "readily learn the words to the song" (153). It is precisely the words that govern the musical structure for the child. Here too Coltrane takes up a culturally forgotten childhood practice and subjects it to systematization in order to produce a radically innovative work.[3] What is unusual about this particular case is that Coltrane takes up an *organizational* structure from childhood, a structure used by children to increase their sense of musical coherence. He then uses it to increase his listeners' sense of musical coherence as well. In other words, he uses a childhood technique to make his experimental work more accessible to an audience. This indicates that recuperation may contribute not only to the novelty of radical innovation, but to its appropriateness or "adaptation to task constraints" as well.

Progressive and recuperative relations to childhood techniques hardly explain everything about radical creativity. Nor do specifications of schemas, alteration of prototypes, the recruitment of remote associations, and so on, explain everything about basic creativity. Many questions remain open, and none of the preceding hypotheses is firmly established. Nonetheless, it seems clear that a cognitive approach to creativity—both basic and radical—can prove tremendously fruitful. Smith, Ward, and Finke note that the cognitive study of creativity was "once considered unrealistic" and "unresearchable" ("Preface" vii). Current results seem both plausible and illuminating. At the very least, they indicate directions for future research that should help us to gain some genuine understanding of a topic that has been of central importance to humanistic study for centuries, but up to now has remained almost entirely mysterious.

CHAPTER 4

The Text (I)

Where the Metaphors Are

A commonplace of recent critical theory is that there is no difference in kind between literary language and ordinary language (see Pratt for an early, influential argument that "the body of utterances we call 'literature'" is not "systematically distinguishable from other utterances on the basis of intrinsic grammatical or textual properties" [xi]). The general idea is entirely in keeping with cognitive scientific views. As we saw in the preceding chapter, cognitive theorists view genius as an intenser form of ordinary creativity. The same point holds in other areas as well. For example, literary plots are tighter versions of the tales we tell every day. Understanding a postmodern novel is an exercise of the same order as interpreting life itself from the fragmentary evidences of quotidian experience. More generally, for most cognitive scientists, there is no difference in kind between the practices of literature and those of ordinary thought. There is, at most, a difference in their extent or degree.[1] Metaphor is no exception. Whatever we may think metaphor is, it is not one thing in poems of high seriousness and another thing in idle talk. It is the same thing everywhere. Indeed, metaphor is widely viewed as one of the most significant features of radical creativity, even one of its primary sources. Cognitive theorists too accept that metaphor is central to innovation. They simply stress that this innovation is to be found in everyday conversation as well as sonnets.

Of course, to say that metaphor is the same thing everywhere still leaves the issue of just what sort of thing it is. The cognitive scientific approach constrains us to view metaphor as a matter of information processing, and to understand that processing in terms of standard cognitive architectures. But that does not decide the issue. Within those limits, there are different ways in which metaphor may be explained. Two accounts of metaphor have been particularly prominent in cognitive studies. Both rely on a version of representational architecture, though one is more fully and more explicitly located within that architecture than the other.[2] The first account was developed by psychologists such as Amos Tversky and Andrew Ortony. It is sometimes referred to as a "feature matching" or "feature transfer" theory. In keeping with the general principles of cognitive science discussed in chapter 2, I will refer to it as an "information transfer" theory or, by reference to its architecture, as a "lexical processing" theory. This account begins with an explicit treatment of the structure of the mental lexicon, posits two simple processes—lexical scanning and constituent transfer—and seeks to account for metaphor using only this minimal architecture. (Constituents are any elements of a lexical entry.)

The second prominent account was first set out by George Lakoff and Mark Johnson, then subsequently developed in a literary direction by Lakoff and Mark Turner. While the information transfer approach treats metaphor as a relatively local phenomenon, Lakoff, Johnson, and Turner see metaphor as pervading human thought processes. Indeed, according to these theorists, metaphor is central to our cognition. While of course some metaphors are of only local or ornamental significance, others guide the way we conceptualize the world. These are the metaphors that concern Lakoff, Johnson, and Turner. They refer to them as "conceptual metaphors." As Lakoff and Turner treat conceptual metaphor in a literary context, I will focus on their work. The Lakoff/Turner account is less fully explicit than the information transfer account with respect to cognitive architecture. However, Lakoff's and Turner's views are broadly in keeping with representationalism. At the same time, their approach is very different from the information transfer account. Indeed, they present a great deal of evidence that, in their view, contradicts more local accounts of metaphor, such as that of Tversky and Ortony.

I will first outline the information transfer account. However, I will modify it in several ways, incorporating standard elements of cognitive architecture (e.g., procedural schemas) and differentiating processes of constituent transfer in literal and metaphorical interpretation. In a second section, I will turn to the Lakoff/Turner view, setting out its theoretical principles. Following this, I will combine the two approaches to analyze Shelley's "Triumph of Life." In a concluding section, I will consider Mark Turner's more recent theory of "conceptual integration" or "blending," which in many ways advances both the information transfer or lexical processing theory and the conceptual metaphor theory.

Minimal Metaphoricity: A Lexical Process

In a lexical processing account of metaphor, metaphorical interpretation may be understood, first of all, as a form of lexical scanning. We have a topic or a "target," and some metaphorical predicate or "source." The metaphorical statement calls on us to understand the target by reference to the source. Suppose I say that "Smith was a real lion in the department meeting." *Smith* is the target; *lion* is the source. The lexical processing account explains our interpretation of this sentence in the following way. Hearing this statement, I begin to scan my lexical entry for *lion* in order to find relevant properties that might apply to someone in a department meeting (cf. Tversky 349). My entry for *lion* includes various properties—"four-legged," "eats raw meat," "fierce," "merciless," and so on. I eliminate "four-legged" and "eats raw meat," but apply "fierce" and "merciless."

Ortony distinguishes two ways in which we might identify such properties. First, we may find that we already know these things about the target. In this case, we merely match constituents of the source and target. Thus, if we already know that Smith is fierce and merciless, we scan our entry for *lion* and discover those shared predicates. In this case, no constituents are transferred. Rather, saliency is transferred. Constituents that are prominent in our entry for *lion* serve to stress constituents that were not prominent in our entry for *Smith*. In fact, this is the use of metaphor emphasized by Ortony. The other operation involves the attribution of new information— as in the case where there was nothing in our entry for *Smith* indicating ferocity or mercilessness. How exactly does one select features for transfer? Here, I would argue, one engages in standard inferential reasoning, deciding what predicates might reasonably apply to the target in the particular context. In other words, there is no strictly prescribed method of inference here, no logically necessary sequence that yields an absolutely certain conclusion. There are, rather, various pragmatic schemas that we use to draw probabilistic inferences. To a great extent, these involve PDP-type activation patterns. For example, we come up with different interpretations for "Smith was a real lion" when spoken of a department meeting and when spoken of a steak tartar festival. Algorithmically, we would account for this by reference to multiple links among constituents of the source, the target, and various other lexical items accessed or primed in context. Thus, in the case of a steak tartar festival, "raw meat" would be primed or accessed. This would prime relevant constituents of the metaphorical source ("lion: eats raw meat"). This, in turn, increases the likelihood we will select that and associated constituents ("eats ravenously," "eats directly with mouth," or whatever) for transfer.[3] Unlike Ortony, this is the aspect of metaphor that I will emphasize—hence the name "information transfer" theory. However, it is important to recall that, in many cases, metaphor is not a matter of transferring constituents per se, but of transferring salience or, more simply, bringing previously known information into greater prominence.

An information transfer account has a number of virtues. First, it is consistent with plausible views of cognitive architecture. Second, it appears to predict accurately some perhaps surprising properties of metaphor. Consider, for example, dissymmetry. As is well known, we interpret "Billboards are pimples" differently from "Pimples are billboards." This dissymmetry is predicted by the order of lexical scanning. As we noted in chapter 2, lexical entries are hierarchically structured. When we scan our entry for *pimples* in order to understand billboards, we quickly come upon *ugly*. When we scan our entry for *billboards* in order to understand pimples, it is more difficult to come upon relevant constituents. Depending upon the context, we might isolate a property such as "sign bearing some message," as in "Joey's pimples were billboards announcing his entry into adolescence." In any case, the interpretive difference between the two sentences is predicted by this account. Moreover, as the last point indicates, a lexical processing account also suggests that metaphorical interpretation will be highly context sensitive—which is correct, and thus another point in favor of the theory.

This account also indicates that literal and metaphorical interpretation are closely related processes. Both are a matter of context-sensitive scanning of the internal lexicon. For example, suppose I am told that Smith, who has just been appointed to a hiring committee, is a right-wing Republican. This is a literal claim. Nonetheless, I scan my internal lexicon in order to isolate properties that are germane to the context. So, my lexical entry for *right-wing Republican* may include such properties as "opposes affirmative action" and "opposes capital gains tax." The former is clearly relevant to a hiring committee. The latter is not. So, I select the former and not the latter for application to Smith in these particular circumstances. It is testimony to the elegance of the theory that it does not unnecessarily multiply types of processing, but instead accounts for literal and metaphorical interpretation in much the same terms.

On the other hand, this does not mean that there is no distinction to be made between literal and metaphorical interpretation. A lexical processing account does not in and of itself generate or explain such a distinction. It does, however, allow us to formulate criteria for this distinction in a way that is more plausible than other proposals.

Probably the most common *demarcation criterion*—that is, the most common criterion for distinguishing metaphorical and literal statements—involves some inference of literal falsity. Unfortunately, this sort of criterion is not successful. As Donald Davidson has stressed, while many obvious cases of metaphor are literally false (e.g., "Juliet is the sun"), other obvious cases of metaphor are literally true (e.g., "No man is an island"). Davidson's alternative—that metaphorical statements are trivially false or trivially true—does not work either. In fact, the literal truth or falsity of a statement is sometimes just irrelevant to its status as a metaphor. Imagine, for example, the following discussion: "Smith is a real Christian." "Do you mean he believes Jesus is God?" "I'm not really sure what he believes, but he is a real Christian." In this case, the literal truth value of the statement is not even known. It is certainly not trivial.

But what, then, is the difference between a literal statement and a metaphorical one? As it turns out, a cognitive approach does not give us an answer. Instead, cognitive principles indicate that this is a misguided question. In a cognitive framework, there is nothing about a sentence, divorced from human minds, that would make it literal or metaphorical, or meaningful in any way. Meaning is just a function of cognitive processing, whether that of a speaker, a listener, a writer, or a reader. Put differently, there is no such thing as a metaphorical—or, for that matter, literal—statement per se. Rather, there are only literal and metaphorical intents and literal and metaphorical interpretations or, more technically, literal and metaphorical generative processes and literal and metaphorical interpretive processes.

Of course, this only changes the question to—What, then, are these processes? Here, however, cognitive principles allow us to give a positive answer. In the case of literal interpretation, we assume that lexical properties of the source, including default properties, apply to the target, unless we are given evidence to the contrary. For example, our lexical entry for *human* includes the default property "has two arms." We assume that this applies to any given person, unless we have specific information that he/she was born with one or no arms or lost one or both arms. Moreover, in literal interpretation, we assume that, if a default does not apply, one or another specified alternative does apply. Metaphorical interpretation simply does not involve this presumption. In other words, in metaphorical interpretation, we do not transfer constituents from source to target unless we have specific reason to do so. The difference between literal and metaphorical interpretation, then, is not a matter of the terms themselves, nor of any specific part of their lexical structure or properties, nor of the relations between these structures or properties. Rather, it is a matter of our presumption regarding the transfer of source properties to the target.

This demarcation criterion has some implications that are worth noting. First, it indicates that there probably is not any decision criterion for choosing metaphorical or literal interpretation. A *decision criterion* is a criterion that tells us when to interpret something metaphorically and when to interpret something literally. Most formulations of demarcation criteria tacitly assume that a demarcation criterion will be a decision criterion. For example, in Davidson's theory, metaphor is defined by the trivial truth or falsity of a statement and metaphorical interpretation is triggered by that same trivial truth or falsity. The demarcation criterion I have just proposed cannot serve as a decision criterion, because it concerns interpretive assumptions, not objective properties of or objective relations between the source and the target. This is a virtue of that criterion, for our actual, practical decisions are not, in fact, governed by hard and fast rules (as, for example, Ted Cohen has noted). Rather, we choose a metaphorical or literal interpretation on the basis of a wide range of empirical factors—knowledge of the speaker, of the situation, of common usage, et cetera—in connection with general concerns for logical consistency and explanatory simplicity. Put differently, this demarcation criterion indicates that you can't tell a metaphor by looking at it, and that seems to be correct. Even such "obvious" cases as "The Trojans were lions" may be intended literally in a relevant context.

Another implication of this demarcation criterion is that metaphorical interpretation will be largely prototypical. That too appears to be correct. Traditionally, feature matching theorists have tended to treat lexical entries as if they are dictionary-like lists of properties. However, as we saw in chapter 2, lexical structure is much more complicated. The mental lexicon includes abstract structures, or schemas, organized into default hierarchies; more concrete prototypes, where all the defaults are in place, and weighted averages are added; and, finally, exempla or instances of the categories. Our default values for *bird* would include "relatively small," "flies," "builds nests in trees," and so on. In keeping with this, robins and blue jays are prototypical birds; ostriches and penguins are not. The demarcation criterion I have just proposed suggests that metaphorical interpretation will not violate defaults, and thus will not deviate from prototypes, except in cases where the violation is stated. Specifically, in metaphorical interpretation, we do not assume that the nonapplication of a default entails some lexically specified alternative. In fact, it seems that we do not transfer an alternative unless it is explicitly signaled—as in "Smith is a lion without teeth."

Of course, metaphors are not confined to prototypes and explicit exceptions. They may also take up other lexical complexes such as exempla ("Smith is a real Republican on that committee." "Yeah, but still he's more of a Forbes than a Gingrich"). More importantly, they take up domains. As we saw in chapter 2, domains are sets of lexical entries that share a superordinate category and a common lexical relation. For example, the scalar relation of temperature defines a domain encompassing the various grades of cold and heat. "Bodily direction" is another domain, subsuming forward, backward, left, right, and so on. Within the information transfer framework, the systems of metaphor examined by Lakoff, Johnson, Turner, and others, may be understood largely as domain-based metaphors.

However, before going on the Lakoff and Turner, it is important to discuss the metaphorical operation of one final type of lexical structure—procedural schemas. It may not be obvious at first, but procedural structures enter significantly into our experience of metaphor. Indeed, there is evidence that procedural schemas are not only possible sources of metaphor, but even primary sources of metaphor, at least developmentally. Howard Gardner explains that "The resemblance that motivated" a child's metaphors in one study "did not, at first, stem solely from the objects themselves but were constructed out of the pretend action of symbolic play." Prior to "the age of four, the predominant type of metaphor in [this child's] speech . . . fed off the gestural transformation of an object." Indeed, "At all ages sampled," this child's "metaphors were grounded either on how an object could be handled, or on its shape, or on both" (163). Once mentioned, it is obvious that we invoke procedural schemas in analogical comparisons all the time. We tell someone that a certain dance step is like kicking a soccer ball or that they should hold up some tall item by putting their weight against it as if they were pushing a heavy piece of furniture. The purpose of these metaphors is, in effect, to transfer procedural rather than representational information. Each skilled action we perform may be understood as compiled out of "subroutines." These subroutines are smaller, unselfconscious actions that we engage in automatically. The procedural schema for kicking a soccer ball involves lifting one's leg in a certain way, bending the knee, and so on. We transfer some, but not all of these constituents to the dance step.

The metaphorical use of procedural schemas is not confined to such straightforward physical activities. It bears on art as well, and not only on such bodily arts as dance. Indeed, it is important to our experience of literature. Of course, in reading literature, we do not engage in any direct transfer of procedural subroutines—or, more exactly, we do not enact such subroutines. We do not "run" metaphorical procedural schemas from a literary work. We do, however, prime them, partially activate them, make them readily accessible to working memory. Take, for example, the sensual effect of certain erotic metaphors. That effect, I would argue, is often best understood as the result of a nonconscious activation or priming of procedural schemas. Consider an image from the fifth century Sanskrit poet, Bhartrihari, who speaks of a girl with "honey in her lips" (65). One may or may not find the image erotic. But, if one does find it erotic, I cannot imagine that this is due to a representational comparison between honey and lips, a transfer of features from the former to the latter. Rather, I suspect that its effect is due to a priming of procedural schemas for tasting honey—licking off the thick coat of honey on the surface, then gently sucking out what remains in the recesses—here aimed metaphorically at a woman's lips (just as the actual, literal use of the schema might be aimed at one's finger, a spoon, or anything else dipped into a honey jar).

It is a final advantage of lexical processing theory that it readily accounts for metaphors bearing on action, metaphors that are to be found every-where in life and in art, but are almost entirely ignored by other accounts of metaphor.

The Thinking Person's Guide to Metaphorical Thinking: Lakoff and Turner on Conceptual Metaphor

Lakoff and Turner begin by, in effect, repudiating the theory we have just discussed. They do not see metaphor as a local matter. They see metaphor as pervasive. Moreover, they see it as structuring our ideas, guiding our inferences and understanding, not only in poetry, but in everyday life. As they put it, right at the outset of their work, "Far from being merely a matter of words, metaphor is a matter of thought" (xi). Of course, in one sense, all cognitive accounts agree on this. The information transfer account does not treat metaphor as mere linguistic ornamentation. It clearly involves thought. However, in an information transfer account, the cognitive consequences of metaphor, though important, are localized. For example, physicists may try to understand the atom by using the metaphor of the solar system. I might draw on musical analysis as a model for thinking through some problem in poetry. But these are special cases. In the information transfer account, I am not usually engaged in metaphor-based cognition of this sort. This is not true for the account given by Lakoff and Turner.

Lakoff and Turner agree that thinking about the atom on the metaphor-ical model of the solar system is a relatively isolated activity. However, they argue that this is only because such explicit, comparative reflection is a peripheral use of metaphor. The crucial place of metaphor is not in self-conscious reasoning, but in unconscious processing. This processing, Lakoff and Turner argue, defines the truly important variety of metaphor, concep-tual metaphor, and it is to be found almost everywhere. Indeed, one might aptly reverse Lakoff's and Turner's fundamental claim that "metaphor is a matter of thought." By their analysis, thought is (by and large) a mat-ter of metaphor. Lakoff and Turner do acknowledge that not all thought is metaphorical. It is necessarily the case that at least some of what we think and say is literal. But metaphor is widespread, and it suffuses all areas of human cognition, whatever we might believe.

More exactly, Lakoff and Turner argue that our ideas about a wide range of topics are guided by a limited number of basic metaphors. These metaphors provide more or less abstract schemas that are specified in different ways. The most abstract metaphors are "generic-level." These are rendered more concrete in "specific-level" metaphorical schemas which are, in turn, concretized in particular expressions (81). In other words, Lakoff and Turner understand any given metaphorical utterance as nested in a set of encompassing metaphorical structures. The encompassing structures are common in a given society. As Lakoff and Turner put it, "It is a prerequisite to any discussion of metaphor that we make a distinction between basic conceptual metaphors, which are cognitive in nature, and particular linguistic expressions of these conceptual metaphors" (50). The basic conceptual metaphors are precisely what give meaning—communally shared meaning—to the particular linguistic expressions. "Basic conceptual metaphors are part of the common conceptual apparatus shared by members of a culture. They are systematic in that there is a fixed correspondence between the structure of the domain to be understood (e.g., death) and the structure of the domain in terms of which we are understanding it (e.g., departure)" (51).

Consider the common idiom taken up in a statement such as "I don't feel that I am making much progress in my life; I am just spinning my wheels and not really getting anywhere." Lakoff and Turner take utterances of this sort to be the most important instances of metaphor. They are utterances that are entirely ordinary, just the sort of thing anyone might say at any time. They are not confined to poetry or highfalutin rhetoric. They are simply part of the way we speak. But they are not only matters of speech. They also guide the way we think. They do this because of their location in the encompassing metaphorical structures just mentioned. In this case, the speaker is drawing on the standard metaphorical structure, LIFE IS A JOURNEY.[4] LIFE IS A JOURNEY is a schema. Or, rather, *journey* provides a schema that we map onto *life*. In mapping *journey* onto *life*, we actually come to understand life in terms of a journey. We specify the schema in thinking about life, but we also structure our understanding of life by reference to the schema. Life itself has no particular structure. It is diffuse and disorganized. By imposing the journey schema on life, we make life (or our idea of life) into something structured.

The most obvious thing we do in thinking of life this way is that we envision life as having a goal. Lakoff and Turner say that this is part of a still more general metaphorical structure, PURPOSES ARE DESTINATIONS. Thus LIFE IS A JOURNEY specifies PURPOSES ARE DESTINATIONS and

"I'm spinning my wheels" particularizes LIFE IS A JOURNEY. More exactly, we take the schema for a journey and we map it onto our formless idea of life. In mapping the journey schema, we must define correlates for the constituents of the schema. When doing this we are guided by the encompassing PURPOSES ARE DESTINATIONS metaphor. Because journeys follow paths to destinations, lives must have paths to goals (or purposes). Because journeys involve relatively constant progress toward a destination, lives must have relatively constant progress toward a goal. Because journeys involve some vehicle that serves to transport us to the destination, lives must have some vehicle that serves to transport us to the goal (e.g., one's job). Lakoff and Turner explain that "journeys can be seen as having well-differentiated components such as travelers, a starting point, a path, impediments, and so on" (61). So we come to think of life as having these well-differentiated components as well.

Indeed, to advert to the terminology of chapter 2, metaphorical schemas do not merely select and segment. And they do not merely render salient certain structural relations. Rather, "Part of the power of such a metaphor is its ability to *create* structure in our understanding of life" (62, emphasis in the original). Thus I become dissatisfied with my rank because I am not being "advanced." I think my job is just not "moving me along" in the way it should. My adolescent son or daughter is "lost" and "has no sense of direction"; he/she can't decide "where he/she wants to go in life." My friends "welcome a new baby into the world." The baby has "come to us" and they are "beginning the adventure" of parenthood. Someone else I know, "passes away," "departs forever," "goes to his/her eternal home."

Of course, there are other ways of explaining all this. Ortony would insist that, for the most part, these idioms are "lexicalized" (see "Are Emotion"). In other words, when we hear that someone has "passed away," we do not interpret that metaphorically. Rather, we have a lexical entry for "pass away," and that entry simply explains that it means "die" and that it is used in circumstances requiring delicacy. We do not map any metaphorical schema onto life. Moreover, the broader pattern is not due to some historical mapping that led all of us to believe life has a purpose simply because a journey has a destination. Rather, human activity is always purposive—as the intentional level of mental architecture stresses. Whatever we do is organized into hierarchies of goals. What we do in the short term is guided not only by short-term goals, but by long-term goals for which the short-term goals are means. As we succeed in achieving short-term goals that are means to the achievement of long-term goals, our achievement of long-term goals becomes easier and more likely. In using such phrases as "making progress," our ancestors at some point probably were using a metaphor that assimilates life to a journey. But it is not clear that they were adding any structure to life.

It seems that the relevant structure was already there. We already had goals. We already had means of achieving goals. We already had a sense of whether the likelihood of achieving a goal was increasing or decreasing. Understood in this way, the idioms we have been discussing do not now have profound cognitive implications, and probably never did.

At the same time, it remains a striking fact, even from the information transfer point of view, that our idioms do form a limited number of patterns. As Lakoff and Turner explain, "though there is an infinitude of potential conceptual metaphors, only a very few of these have special status as basic metaphors in our conceptual systems" (51). Moreover, even if lexicalized, it is likely that the metaphorical ideas associated with the idioms are at least partially activated or primed. That activation may guide our thought, at least in certain cases. Suppose we adopt something like the information transfer theory of metaphor and assume that idioms such as "passed away" are lexicalized, which is to say, have their own lexical entries which indicate literal meanings. Nonetheless, the activation of those entries will prime related entries(e.g., entries related to journeys, in the case of "passed away"). That is just part of our general cognitive architecture. When further discussing the target (e.g., death) we are likely to draw on the ideas and images that are most readily accessible in our lexicon. These would, of course, be the primed entries. In this way, even an information transfer account indicates that there are occasions on which the metaphorical systems isolated by Lakoff and Turner appear to have consequences for our thought. Put differently, a fully developed information transfer account must incorporate the central insights of Lakoff, Johnson, and Turner.

On the other hand, it does not follow that the metaphorical structures must orient thought in any particular way. Suppose Doe has just finished one big academic project. Smith asks Doe, "Where is your new research leading you?" or "What have you set out to do now?" Smith implies that Doe should be working on a new project. Is this idea determined by a metaphor schema? Does Smith say this because he implicitly assumes that LIFE IS A JOURNEY? This is certainly the idea that many readers take away from Lakoff and Turner. However, it does not seem accurate. Most obviously, Doe can reply, "I need to take some time to smell the roses on the way. After all, life is over before you know it and at some point you get too old to enjoy the ride." Clearly, Doe is relying on the very same schema as Smith. For Doe also LIFE IS A JOURNEY. However, in Doe's case, this does not entail an immediate commitment to a new project. Rather, it entails the opposite. Moreover, even if LIFE IS A JOURNEY had implied a single conclusion, Doe still would have been free to switch to another schema. For example, Doe might have responded, "I thought I'd just let things lie fallow for a while. Some new projects will begin to sprout eventually." The schema here is, roughly THE MIND IS A GARDEN, which is clearly quite different from the LIFE IS A JOURNEY schema. Of course, it too does not determine any conclusions. Doe could just as easily have used this schema to conclude that he should get to work right away, not leaving the garden untended.

In sum, whether one adopts an information transfer view, which stresses lexicalization and priming, or the full conceptual metaphor view of Lakoff and Turner, it does seem clear that many, perhaps almost all of our ordinary idioms fall into a fairly limited number of consistent patterns. Moreover, we draw on different aspects of these patterns when we speak and these patterns often have bearing on our understanding of and response to whatever topic we are considering (e.g., our life). On the other hand, these patterns are much more malleable than we might at first imagine. While they may guide our thought, this is not because a given schema strictly entails one attitude or one type of action. In fact, Lakoff's and Turner's metaphorical schemas appear open to virtually unlimited alteration. Put differently, if these patterns guide our thought, it is not because the patterns could not accommodate other ways of thinking. LIFE IS A JOURNEY can be specified in such a way as to fit various and contradictory attitudes about work. Moreover, like all such patterns, it is always open to negation. In other words, metaphorical or primed constituents may always be preceded by "not," and thus apparent implications may be reversed. When Smith says, "Shouldn't you be pressing ahead with your research?," Doe may respond, "Life is not a footrace." In this way, when a particular instance of a metaphorical schema does guide our thought, it is only because we have not questioned its particular validity. We have not thought through its implications, determined what evidence supports it and what evidence contradicts it. This makes metaphorical determination of thought much the same as literal determination of thought. If Smith believes "One should always be pressing ahead with one's research" that may not be fundamentally different from Smith believing "One should always be at work on some research project." Of course, there may be more subtle differences between the two. For example, it may be that biases based on metaphor schemas are more difficult to analyze critically or have greater rhetorical force and are therefore more consequential for our thought and action. But that is a difference in degree, not in kind.

In any case, metaphor schemas certainly have significance for poetry. As we have already noted, Lakoff and Turner emphasize the continuity between ordinary thinking processes and artistic creativity. We commonly believe that the metaphors employed by poets are of an entirely different order from the metaphors employed by ordinary folk in ordinary speech. Lakoff and Turner demonstrate convincingly that this is not the case. Rather, the metaphors employed by poets are almost invariably instances of the same broad metaphorical schemas that govern everyday speech. Of course, this is not to say that the metaphors of great poets are simply the same as the idioms of ordinary talk. That is clearly untrue. Rather, the metaphors employed by great poets are unusual or striking variations on the standard metaphors. As Lakoff and Turner explain, "Poets must make the most of the linguistic and conceptual resources they are given. Basic metaphors are part of those conceptual resources, part of the way members of our culture make sense of the world. Poets may compose or elaborate or express them in new ways, but they still use the same basic conceptual resources available to us all. If they did not, we would not understand them" (26).

Lakoff and Turner isolate four ways in which poets vary quotidian metaphorical structures. First, poets *extend* ordinary metaphors. The source schema for a metaphor may include a wide range of possible constituents, not all of which are used in ordinary speech. Thus we speak of death as sleep. The corpse in the coffin "looks so peaceful, as if sleeping." One unused or rarely used element of the sleep schema is "dreaming." Moreover, dreaming itself is a subschema, with its own elements, such as "having a nightmare," which takes us still further away from ordinary usage. Shakespeare extended the standard metaphor schema of DEATH IS SLEEP to dreams, and implicitly to nightmares, when he had Hamlet ask "in that sleep of death what dreams may come" (III.i.65).

A second method of developing poetic metaphors is through *elaboration*, or "filling in slots in unusual ways" (67). Lakoff and Turner give "Horace's reference to death as the 'eternal exile of the raft'" (67) as an example. They explain that DEATH AS DEPARTURE leads us to think of death as a journey away from life to another place (e.g., Heaven), perhaps in some vehicle, such as a carriage. Lakoff and Turner note that a raft is an unusual vehicle to use for specifying this schema. Another example might be drawn from Shakespeare's sonnet 97. This poem begins, "How like a winter hath my absence been/From thee" (ll. 1–2). It takes up the common metaphor schema, LIFE IS A YEAR, which includes a sort of subschema, STAGES OR PERIODS OF LIFE ARE SEASONS IN A YEAR. Shakespeare uses this schema to identify a period of separation from his beloved as winter, the time of death. What is unusual is that the winter of his life is, of all things, summer: "And yet this time remov'd was summer's time" (l. 5). What could be a more unusual specification of a metaphorical winter than a literal summer?

A third way of generating novel variations on basic metaphors is through *composition* or joining different metaphorical schemas. Shakespeare is well known for this, though he has often been criticized for it, as it is not always clear that his joined metaphors fit together. (When composed metaphors do not unite successfully, we refer to them as "mixed metaphors.") Consider the common metaphorical schema that BEAUTY IS LIGHT, which is itself presumably an instance of the still more encompassing GOOD IS LIGHT.

This schema is specified by Shakespeare in the famous line from *Romeo and Juliet,* "Juliet is the sun" (II.ii.3). But this line does not simply specify the BEAUTY IS LIGHT schema. It composes that schema with the distinct schema, DESIRE IS HEAT. Wishing to communicate both the attraction of the characters and Juliet's beauty, Shakespeare takes the relevant schemas and joins the sources in such a way as to yield a specific metaphor that instantiates both, for the sun is a source of light and of heat. Indeed, the fuller metaphor involves extension as well. Once he has thought to metaphorize Juliet as the sun, Shakespeare is able to extend the metaphor in such a way as to make the time of her appearance into morning. Indeed, this brings in yet a third metaphorical structure, a variant of GOOD IS LIGHT—GOOD IS DAWN, as when we say "There is a new dawn in our country." Another extension follows. Since dawn appears in the east, the east is available as a constituent. Shakespeare takes this up in making Juliet's window into the east (II.ii.3), which is probably unusual enough to count as elaboration as well as extension. The result of all this is a complex of metaphors that are innovative, but that follow directly from standard metaphor schemas via the processes of extension, composition, and elaboration.

The fourth and final process for varying commonplace metaphors in poetry is *questioning.* This occurs when the poet sets up the common structure in order to negate it. Some obvious instances of this could also be drawn from Shakespeare's use of BEAUTY IS LIGHT. Thus sonnet 130 begins, "My mistress' eyes are nothing like the sun" (l. 1) and continues, "If snow be white, why then her breasts are dun" (l. 3). Clearly, he is questioning the standard metaphor schema in these lines.

Lakoff and Turner treat further aspects of rhetoric and further tropes, examining images, metonymy, and so on. Of these, it is important to say a few words about one process in particular—personification, in part because personification is not separate from metaphorical schemas.

As we have seen, metaphorical schemas have "slots," structural spaces that are filled in when the metaphor is specified. These often include slots for agents. Personifications derive from those agent slots. As Lakoff and Turner explain, basic metaphors "provide the roles which can serve as the sources of personifications" (17). Take, for example, the metaphorical schema, PEOPLE ARE PLANTS. We find this used in such expressions as "Billy just shot up like a weed since I saw him last" and "Sally has really blossomed in her new work." Sometimes the plants are crops, as when someone says, "We have a whole new crop of students coming in this fall." If the plants are crops, then the source schema provides agent constituents that may lead us to create or posit agents in life corresponding to the agent roles in the source schema. Thus we may see God as planting new people on the earth. Or we may see parents as gardeners, tending to their children. One standard specification maps human death onto the death of crops, metaphorizing death as a sort of harvest. This mapping provides a very salient agent role—if death is a sort of harvest, then there must be someone who does the harvesting, which is to say, causes the death. Historically, this led to a standard personification in which the cause of death became the Grim Reaper.

Personification plays a particularly important role in literature, most obviously in allegory. For example, in *Midnight's Children*, Salman Rushdie takes up the common idiom of "the birth of the nation." He allegorizes the birth of India in the birth of Saleem Sinai, who comes to personify the nation, sharing its historical tribulations, even its physical features (e.g., Saleem's teacher allegorizes Saleem's face, explaining, "Thees birthmark on the right ear is the East Wing; and thees horrible stained left cheek, the West.... Pakistan ees a stain on the face of India" [277]). As usual, this involves a nested hierarchy of metaphor schemas, including NATIONS ARE PEOPLE and, above that, GROUPS ARE INDIVIDUALS. These schemas lend themselves particularly well to personification. But personification is common—in and outside literature—even for metaphor schemas that do not obviously focus on agents.

Living the Bad Life: Shelley's "Triumph of Life"

Needless to say, no single approach will provide "the key" to a poem as complex and rich as Shelley's "Triumph of Life."[5] Nonetheless, an examination of metaphor, particularly an examination that combines both the conceptual metaphor approach and the information transfer approach, seems particularly promising, given the obvious metaphorical density of this work.

The title of Shelley's poem already draws on two life schemas. As Perkins explains, the word "triumph" here "refers to the processions through ancient Rome by which the senate and people honored a victorious general. At the head of the procession came the senators and magistrates, followed by trumpeters, trophies of war, and prisoners. The general was carried in a chariot drawn by four horses" (1061). Thus, the title implicitly takes up LIFE IS A JOURNEY and LIFE IS A BATTLE/DYING IS LOSING A BATTLE AGAINST AN ADVERSARY. Specifically, it refers to a triumphal march—a sort of minijourney—which itself announces that the battle of life has been won (i.e., that dying/the loss of the battle has not occurred) and thus that the journey of life will continue. Shelley extends, elaborates, and composes these schemas. But he also questions them. Though we cannot yet know this from the title, it soon becomes clear that perhaps the main purpose of the poem is to challenge—indeed, to reverse—many of the standard schemas regarding life. The triumph of life is, in fact, a terrible thing.

The first two lines are: "Swift as a spirit hastening to his task/Of glory and of good, the Sun sprang forth." These already indicate that the attitude of the poet is one of questioning—more exactly, of negation and reversal. Moreover, it is negation and reversal that are, so to speak, doubled (without thereby producing a positive). First, Shelley reverses the usual operation of metaphor here. Metaphor typically uses a concrete or perceptual source, which is well specified and well comprehended, to understand an abstract target, especially one that is vague and ill comprehended. Here we have an unnamed and unspecified spirit used as the source by which we might understand the sun and we have the spirit's "task" operating to explain the dawn. As if this were not strange enough, Shelley specifies one constituent that we are supposed to transfer from the source to the target, "swift." He also names two other constituents of the source, which we are presumably intended to transfer also—"glory" and "good." Yet a reader cannot help but notice that the sun does not move "swiftly" in the sky. It does not "hasten" in the way an incorporeal spirit would hasten. Thus it seems we have no choice but to read the explicit constituent transfer as ironic.

Here as elsewhere irony is easily treated in the information transfer account. The interpretive process is the usual one, except that now we take up the antonym of the source, or we scan the original source and apply antonyms of any relevant constituents. Again, lexical items are not linked simply through similarity of meaning, but through other relations as well, such as antonymy. It is easier to access the lexical entry for *short* from *tall* than from any irrelevant term (e.g., *desk*). Suppose Jones says "Smith is on a diet? Well, I understand. He's a real whale." Now suppose that Smith is almost emaciated. We then understand the metaphor as ironic because the constituents relevant to *diet* (e.g., "having much blubber") are not only false of Smith, but the opposite of what truly characterizes Smith. Note that the irony of the second assertion reacts back on the first assertion, so we infer that Smith's being on a diet is *not* understandable.

Along the same lines, given that we infer irony with respect to the "swift" and "hastening" constituents in Shelley's poem, we need to do the same thing with the other named constituents as well. Thus we assume that the not swift and not hastening sun is also not "good" and not "glorious." Put differently, the association of the sun with goodness and glory is an instance of the metaphorical schema, GOOD IS LIGHT. But the implication of irony in these lines indicates that Shelley is questioning this basic conceptual metaphor, perhaps even to the point of reversing it and suggesting that BAD IS LIGHT and GOOD IS DARK.

In the following lines, night is referred to as "the mask/Of darkness" worn by the earth. This suggests the standard view that night is concealment and deceit, perhaps contradicting our interpretation of the opening lines. Yet, due to the sun, "altars of the mountain snow/Flamed" (ll. 3–6). If darkness is genuinely deceiving, then the light should be revealing. Indeed, one of our basic metaphorical schemas is KNOWING IS SEEING, as when we say, "I see what that means." Here the mountains are altars, thus we transfer to them the property, "place of sacrifice." "Flamed" indicates that we are dealing with a sacrificial holocaust. But, in fact, there is no sacrificial fire here. There is only the deceptive crimson of the light reflected from the unmelted snow. What is really there on the mountain—snow—is in effect the opposite of the apparent flame. Thus, rather than KNOWING IS SEEING, we have DECEIT IS SEEING and, instead of TRUTH IS LIGHT, we have FALSITY IS LIGHT.

These lines also begin to introduce religious themes, which are deeply bound up with the metaphorical structure of the poem as well. Thus "altar" might be seen as transferring such constituents as "holy" or "religious" to the mountains. The point is extended in the following lines when we find that the ocean prays, the birds sing hymns, and the flowers swing censers filled with incense. The collection of images leads us to transfer the constituent "holy" to nature as a whole. But the target is not nature only. It is nature at a certain time–nature as it emerges into light. The point is emphasized by the fact that the birds are singing matins. Indeed, the whole of nature not only receives the general constituent "holy," it receives more specific constituents from the source "Christian service."

There is nothing that directly contradicts or ironizes this metaphorization of nature at dawn as a holy, Christian ceremony. But the reader is prepared for irony at this point. Thus we expect problems. The question is, where will the problems arise? Is the problem one of the imagery alone? Or is the problem one of religion itself? In other words, at this point, there are two possibilities. The connection of Christian ritual with light may be a false connection, such that organized Christian religion is actually associated with darkness, thus good (in the terms of the poem). Alternatively, the connection of Christian worship with light may be apt, in which case organized Christian religion—perhaps Anglicanism and Catholicism in particular—is being damned to the same reversal of position. In other words, it is unholy.

In fact, the rest of the poem makes clear that the Christian church is generally a force of evil. The idea is not uncommon in Romanticism. It is most obvious in the typically Romantic reversal of Satan's status as the personification of evil. As we have already noted, the very title of the poem suggests the metaphorical schema LIFE IS A BATTLE. One common religious variant of this is LIFE IS A BATTLE BETWEEN GOOD AND EVIL, which readily generates personifications for both good and evil. This is itself often composed with DYING IS LOSING A BATTLE AGAINST AN ADVERSARY such that the adversary in the second schema is identified with evil in the first schema. Satan is, of course, this personification of evil and adversary of life. However, for a number of Romantics, Satan—at least the Satan of *Paradise Lost*—was a hero. Thus the usual personifications were reversed. Shelley took up this idea elsewhere, writing famously that "Milton's Devil as a moral being is . . . far superior to his God" ("Defense" 1081). The point bears not only on religious institutions, but on political institutions and other oppressive structures that characterize anyone who defies them as Satanic.

With this in mind, we may begin to suspect that the poem deals broadly with the socially accepted world as the inverse of what is true and good. What is elevated in ordinary life is what should be denigrated. The suspicion is confirmed when Shelley turns to the great world leaders, the people who are revered in history. They are clearly people who should not be revered, but reviled.

On the other hand, this way of putting it implies that Shelley may have in mind some group of people who deserve praise—perhaps an underclass who should be elevated (as in those Romantic writings that celebrate the peasantry), or "primitive peoples" who have preserved their relation to the nature, or some foreign, "mystical" culture from the East. But, if this is the case, Shelley does not emphasize it. Rather, he characterizes "all things that in them wear/The form and character of mortal mould" (ll. 16–17) as partaking in this pseudo-sanctity.

The introduction of Christian ceremony does, however, raise the issue of one particular individual—Jesus. Does this problem extend all the way back to the founder of Christianity? The relation of all this to Jesus and to the story of Jesus becomes clear in the next stanza. The central ritual of Christian worship commemorates the self-sacrifice of Jesus, the Son of God. He took on the burden of all human sin and suffered for the freedom of humanity. He died and then rose from the dead to redeem all of us. But the worship depicted in Shelley's poem recounts somewhat different events. First we find that all the worshipers "Rise as the Sun their father rose." In terms of priming, "sun" might activate both *sun* and the homophone, *son*, recalling Jesus. (Priming commonly extends to homophones [see Garman 293–4].) Given only the word "sun," this sequence is possible, but fairly improbable. However, the reference to "father" certainly primes *son*, thus making it likely that the lexical item *son* will be activated, at least briefly. Moreover, the references to rising prime the various meanings of *rise*. When, in the context of reference to a father, we read that the Sun has arisen, and when we read "Sun" with its capitalized first letter (suggesting personification), the entry for *Jesus*, primed by both, is likely to be activated.

Thus we have a potential for either allegory or irony. Given the development thus far, we might reasonably expect irony, which is what we get. The irony is already suggested by the fact that the Sun is the "father," thus not the Son. More significantly, when all the worshipers rise, they do so, not to gain new life, but "to bear/Their portion of the toil" (ll. 18–9). The term "bear" in this context may lead to a partial activation of Jesus's bearing of the cross. But here we find that the worshipers bear something. Moreover, what they bear is "toil," reminiscent more of the Fall of humankind and the expulsion of Adam and Eve from Eden. Indeed, we arguably have a sort of implicit metaphor in which the sin and punishment of Adam and Eve are the (unstated) source for understanding these worshipers (as target of the metaphor). In connection with this, we might transfer such constituents as "false pride," "greed," "desire for excessive greatness," "believing Satan rather than God," "suffering enduring exile and death."

The point is extended when we read further about the punishment, the "toil" suffered by the worshipers. This toil was what the Sun formerly "Took as his own and then imposed on them" (l. 20). The irony here implicitly relies on our having activated the entry for Jesus. Jesus took as his own the burden that God had earlier imposed on humankind. But, here, the Sun/father reverses the sequence, imposing on the worshipers a suffering that had initially been his. Thus the worshipers are not being relieved of their burden of hereditary sin, the continuing legacy of their expulsion from Eden. Nor are they worshiping a savior. Rather, they are receiving a burden that is not their own, and they are worshiping someone who does not liberate, but enslave them. Once again, Shelley engages in systematic metaphorical reversal.

At this point, the speaker of the poem is introduced. Unsurprisingly, he is contrasted with all that went before, and with all normalcy. For example, he is "wakeful" at night (l. 22). This suggests that he has not succumbed to the error of the worshipers (who are, again, associated with light), nor is he subjected to their punishments. One of the more peculiar statements about the speaker is that his waking "thoughts . . . must remain untold" (l. 21). Especially in Romantic poetry, the whole point of bringing in a speaker is to allow him/her to engage in self-expression. As soon as we read a poem by a Romantic poet, expectations of this sort are triggered. More technically, we bring into effect certain schemas regarding Romantic poetry. It is odd, and disconcerting, that Shelley tells us the speaker had thoughts that we are not going to hear. It is even stranger that these thoughts not only will remain untold but *must* remain untold. This creates a degree of mystery about the speaker—a mystery that is, in fact, not entirely uncommon in characters that have elements of the Romantic Satan.

The mystery is increased by the fact that "before me fled/The night" (ll. 26–7). Literally, this refers to the fact that the speaker is facing west. But the phrasing is strange. Night is personified as someone in flight. Our lexical entry for *flee* tells us that a person flees danger and does so in fright. We transfer the latter constituent (*fright*) onto night and the former (*danger*) onto that which causes the fleeing of night–"the day" which "rose" "behind me" (l. 27).

But night here is not merely night. The movement of night clearly represents the movement of time. As Lakoff and Turner explain, TIME MOVES is a common metaphorical schema for time. There are "two versions: in both, we are located at the present and are facing toward the future with the past at our back. The views differ on whether it is the future that is moving toward us, or whether we, at the present moment, are moving toward it" (44). When the speaker is facing west, he sees night, thus the past. He is not moving toward the future, nor watching the future move toward him. He is watching the past flee. Of course, the future (i.e., day) is coming toward him, in keeping with one version of the standard schema. But it is coming toward him from the wrong place (behind, not in front). Thus, the speaker is located at a metaphorically contradictory point in time, an inverted place where the future is behind and the past is ahead, though the future is coming and the past is going.

The temporal contradiction fits with what went before, but also with what follows, for the speaker soon sees the entire history of humankind all as one present moment—though a present moment that moves in time. That present moment of all time that also moves is precisely the "triumph of Life," the procession of Life that marks its victory over so many people, people who are, in fact, not alive, but dead.

The speaker is also at a contradictory point in space: "the Deep/Was at my feet, and Heaven above my head" (27–8). "Deep" here refers in part to the darkness. But that is strange, for the darkness should be far away from him by now, moving swiftly on its own (personified) feet. Indeed, placing it at the speaker's feet perhaps links him with the fleeing night. Moreover, he in effect remains in the darkness, despite its motion and his immobility. "Heaven" is, in part, the day from which night flees. But "Heaven" is also the place of God, "above my head." Again, light, day, dawn, the Sun, are identified as divine, spiritual, the objects of worship, in keeping with the (ironized) schema GOOD IS LIGHT. In this context, "Deep" suggests not only the night, but a particular place, comparable to Heaven—especially as they are both capitalized. That deep place is, of course, Hell. Our lexical entry for *Hell* is primed by the term *Heaven*. *Deep*, operating as a probe among primed entries, activates *Hell*, the deepest deep. Thus the speaker is located just at the conjunction of Heaven and Hell.

The speaker is, then, a sort of cosmic person, centering space and time in himself, a sort of alternate God. But he is not God in being powerful or omniscient. In fact, he is neither of these. He does not act on anyone, unlike the Sun who brings light and toil to worshipers. Moreover, his spiritual knowledge comes almost despite himself. It arrives as a "trance" which brings not light but a "shade" (ll. 29, 30), a darkness that is yet so "transparent" (l. 31) as to provide a "Vision" (l. 40)—precisely what should require light. Here too, then, he reverses the standard schema that KNOWLEDGE IS LIGHT, making knowledge into darkness.

These forty lines form the first section of the poem, the first narrative sequence. We cannot go through the entire 547 lines. However, this gives a good sense of what follows. The rest of the poem continues the same general project, extending, elaborating, composing such schemas as LIFE IS A JOURNEY, DYING IS LOSING A BATTLE AGAINST AN ADVERSARY, GOOD IS LIGHT, and systematically questioning them, in part through the manipulation of such lexical processes as constituent transfer and priming. Clearly this is a poem that both manifests and demands a great deal of cognitive work. It is also a poem that is difficult to understand without analyzing that cognitive work, especially the cognitive work of metaphor.[6]

Mixing It Up: Conceptual Blending and Working Memory

Mark Turner has gone on from his work with George Lakoff to develop a broader and more flexible theory of metaphor. Indeed, he has articulated a theory of human thought processes generally, processes that include, but extend well beyond metaphor. In a series of writings on his own and in collaboration with Gilles Fauconnier, he has argued that metaphorical thought is an instance of what he calls "conceptual integration" or "blending."

Turner came to recognize that standard accounts of metaphor, including the Lakoff/Turner account, were limited in ways that do not fit the data of metaphor. Specifically, in treating sources and targets, theories of metaphor have assumed that the generation and understanding of metaphors are "direct, one-way, and positive" (*Literary* 60). Against this view, Turner argues that concepts may blend so that metaphors operate indirectly, in more than one direction, and negatively. Thus, in contrast with theorists who employ source/target models, Turner argues that metaphor—and, indeed, all thought—involves two or more inputs or *input spaces,* as he calls them. These input spaces *project* some properties to a *blended space*—thus the projection does not go directly from a source to a target. The resulting blend may then project back to a particular input. That input may then be considered the target. In other cases, there is no backward projection, thus no target. In still other cases, the blend may project back to more than one input. In those cases, the blend is not unidirectional, for it may involve indirect projection from input A to input B and vice versa. Moreover, the blend is not confined to the mere combination of the projected (or, equivalently, transferred) properties. There is, in addition, an *emergent structure* that results from the combination itself. Finally, Turner emphasizes that blending is recursive and thus a blend may itself operate as an input to another blend.

Turner illustrates his points with complex literary metaphors as well as idioms of the sort treated by Lakoff. However, the general idea works perfectly well for the most banal, literal statements. Take the following sentence, spoken by a doctor: "The patient weighs 180 pounds." We may analyze this as involving input from several spaces. One is the concept "patient." Properties such as "human," "having some illness," "seeing a doctor," and so on, are "projected" into the "blended space." One property of being a person is having some weight. In this case, the weight is specified. It is specified by projection from another input space. This would be the space defined by "180 pounds," which is itself a blend of a number and the concept "pound." (This illustrates the recursiveness of blends.) The result is a blend in which there is an individual sick person, with a weight of 180 pounds, who is seeing a doctor. Now consider a second sentence, spoken by the doctor immediately after the first sentence: "He is 5′2″ tall." This second sentence forms a blend. The blends for the two sentences are projected into a third blended space. The resulting blend not only tells us that the person has a certain height, etc., it also tells us that he is overweight. "Overweight" is an emergent structure. It is not to be found in any of the input spaces—"patient," "180 pounds," and so on. This blend clearly projects back to the input "the patient" (not, say, the input "180 pounds"), for it indicates that this particular patient is overweight (not that 180 pounds is overweight or that 5′2″ tall is overweight). Thus it has a specific, single target. (For a schematic representation of this analysis, see figure 5.)

An example of a blend that projects back to more than one input may be found in the cynical (and usually sexist) aphorism, "Translations are like spouses. If they are beautiful, they are not faithful; if they are faithful, they are not beautiful." This creates a blend that comments on (i.e., projects back to) both translations and spouses. Thus it does not have a particular target. On the other hand, Turner notes that, in cases such as this, if one or the other input is the focus of attention in a given conversation, then that input is the *topic* of the blend (though it is not the target in the technical sense). Suppose two people are talking about the problems with a particular translation and one of them quotes this aphorism. In that specific case, "translations" is the topic, but it is not the target (and "spouses" is not the source).

Turner views conceptual blending as a development of Lakoffian cognitive metaphor theories. However, in its basic principles, conceptual blending theory is neutral between cognitive metaphor and information transfer accounts. Indeed, a fully algorithmically specified information transfer account would have to come to a version of conceptual blending (though, as far

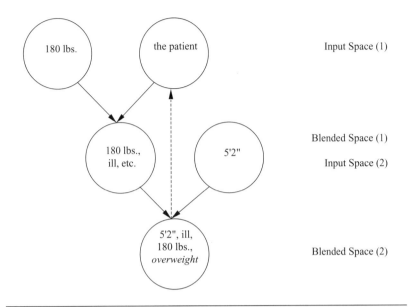

Fig. 5. A simplified version of conceptual integration for the sentences, "The patient weighs 180 pounds. He is 5′2″ tall." Italics indicate emergent structure. Projection back from the blended space to an input space is indicated by a dashed line.

as I know, no one has developed such an account). In this way, information transfer accounts can benefit greatly from Turner's ideas. At the same time, I believe that Turner's account can benefit from the standard representational architecture in which information transfer accounts are usually formulated. Turner develops his ideas in a way that is, so to speak, neutral with respect to architecture. But I believe his points would be clarified, extended, and rendered more algorithmically rigorous by reference to standard principles of memory structure.

Specifically, the "blended space" is clearly located in working memory. Blending is itself a process of integrating information from long-term memory through working memory. Note that Turner's main points follow directly from this. Clearly, there is no information transfer directly from one lexical entry (a source) to a second lexical entry (a target). Rather, there is always a recruitment of information from different lexical entries into working memory. Moreover, the synthesis that occurs in working memory may be transferred back to one lexical entry, changing that entry, or not. Indeed, it might be transferred back to more than one entry, or it may not change any entry. Thus there may or may not be a "target" in the usual sense. In addition, working memory allows for attentional focus on one or another item. This attentional focus defines precisely Turner's "topic." The idea of emergent structure fits here as well. Working memory operates not only to join bits of information, but to draw inferences, make predictions, and so forth. In other words, one of its main functions is to produce emergent structure. Indeed, connecting emergent structure with working memory is important in that it emphasizes the active cognition required to produce emergent structure. My mind has to do something to get from height and poundage to a normative judgment regarding weight. The emergent structure does not just appear on its own.

This is not all. Several details of Turner's analysis are directly entailed by standard architecture. For example, the recursive nature of blends is only to be expected, given the cyclical nature of working memory. The use of multiple inputs is also in the very nature of working memory, which operates to synthesize information from sensory processors, specialized (e.g., linguistic) processors, buffers, and long-term memory. In connection with this, Turner also stresses that blends often involve associated images (*Literary* 76). There is no obvious reason why this would be the case given Turner's account alone. However, it makes sense in the context of standard architecture for two reasons. First, lexical entries presumably include a range of visual images along with semantic properties. If these are not directly accessed, they would at least be primed, and thus very likely to enter working memory, given even fleeting attention to the visual properties of any input. Second, a prominent part of working memory is the visuo-spatial sketchpad, which our working memory tends to use even in cases where the current concerns are not strictly visual.

The mention of priming brings up two other issues in Turner. Turner notes that blends often involve "metonymy." For example, our image of the Grim Reaper as a skeleton is a blend of death with a "metonymy" of death (the skeleton). But there is no reason for Turner to use this rhetorical concept (metonymy) when the standard cognitive process of priming is much more obviously relevant. The links isolated by Turner under the rubric of "metonymy" are precisely the links one would expect from standard processes of priming. Thus, when considering an image for a personified death, the human mind would select some image that is readily accessible in lexical scanning. The idea of death would prime a set of images. The idea of a person (necessary for personification) would further prime a subset of those images—perhaps only "skeleton" and "corpse." Insofar as the personification involves a sense of timelessness or eternity, *skeleton* would receive still further priming. (In contrast, a personification that stressed decay might be more likely to prime corpses.) Thus a priming account yields just what Turner says a theory should yield on this score. It is not clear that metonymy could explain this as successfully. Related to this, Turner discusses the importance of emotion in blends (*Literary* 79–80). It is well known that priming is congruent with emotion. As Bower puts it, when an "emotion is aroused . . . activation will spread out along its connections, thus priming and bringing into readiness . . . associated ideas and memories" (389). Thus the link with emotion is entailed by standard architecture as well.

Turner also emphasizes that input spaces tend to operate via prototypes (*Literary* 82). For example, when we hear "The patient weighed 180 pounds," we automatically assume a prototypical patient—for example, we assume that he/she is human. In other words, we project "human" into the blended space. But, if we were operating only by necessary and sufficient conditions, we would not do this. Thus, if we projected only "living organism that may become ill and be treated medically," we would not be surprised if the next sentence were "The farmer said that she was not the only one of his sows that had fallen ill." This operation of prototypes is predicted directly by an account of the mental lexicon which identifies prototypes as our basic lexical constituents, thus just what would be brought into working memory as a default.

I should stress that none of this diminishes the value of Turner's analyses in any way. In fact, quite the contrary, the convergence of Turner's work with standard architecture gives further support to both. Thus Turner's account simultaneously enriches and is enriched by synthesis with standard representational architecture.

But this is not all there is to Turner's account—and not all that may be "blended" with standard architecture. An algorithmic account of blending (or synthesis of information inputs to working memory) should further specify just how the synthesis occurs. In connection with this, Turner introduces the notion of counterparts. Unfortunately, in my view, the idea of counterparts is too imprecise to serve as a technical concept. Turner seems to introduce it as an identity term, which is to say, a term that refers to distinct items in the inputs that are to form a single item in the blend. However, he goes on to indicate that counterparts need not be fused in the blend. Turner then explains that "It is not possible to blend two stories without some counterpart connections between them to guide the blending" (*Literary* 86). But this hardly tells us anything. I would rather say that we need to know what input items are counterparts in the initial sense (i.e., which input items are fused to form which blended items) and how all the resulting, blended items are related. In short, we need a structure for the blended space—which is ultimately Turner's point anyway. As Turner puts it, "Blends can be constructed if two stories can be construed as sharing abstract structure" (87). This is where Turner returns to his work with Lakoff, for in many cases this abstract structure is provided by metaphor schemas. However, even here Turner differs from Lakoff and Turner, for he emphasizes the "partial and flexible use" of these structures (81), their "partial, selective, and transforming" operation (83), et cetera.

Here too I believe that an integration of blending theory with representational architecture is beneficial to both. In a standard representational account, what Turner describes might work its way out along roughly the following lines. Some experience (e.g., a perception) serves as a probe to activate particular procedural schemas, involving attention, lexical scanning, etc. It also activates certain representational structures—schemas, prototypes, and exempla—not as objects of lexical scanning, but as organizational principles for the contents of working memory. These schemas, prototypes, and exempla provide the structure for the blend. They set out a sort of grid in the general workspace of working memory. The case here is comparable to my entry into HBL 127, described in chapter 2. When entering HBL 127, I open a schema in working memory—say, the schema for a room. This schema provides a broad structure through which I can organize and direct my perceptions of HBL 127. It is, in effect, the organizational structure for a blended space.

As to flexibility, procedural schemas have default values and alternatives. Moreover, while representational schemas and prototypes have standardized properties, they are also linked with schematic alternatives, nonprototypical exempla, and so on. The order of lexical entries and of lexical features within entries are continually shifting through the vagaries of spreading activation. The interaction of the procedural and representational structures with one another and with new information, all in the context of the ever-changing orders of lexical activation, cannot even allow for the sort of mechanical and univocal processing to which Turner rightly objects. Thus, in its actual operation, standard representationalist architecture leads necessarily to the partial, flexible, selective, and transforming operation posited by Turner.

Since this has been all very abstract, we should consider an example. One of Turner's main emphases is that even the most banal thoughts involve tremendously complex blending. I will therefore confine myself to a small illustration, Cordelia's plea, "I cannot heave/My heart into my mouth" (I.i.96–7). The most basic blending analysis gives us an explicit physiological input, concerning the heart and the mouth, and an implicit mentalistic input, concerning, among other things, speech. The implicit input is carried over from Lear's initial question, "what can you say" (I.i.90) and his subsequent admonition, "Speak again" (I.i.95). The organizing structure in the blended space is not overt, but it is clearly the human body, specifically Cordelia's body. This is constructed in the visuo-spatial sketchpad, based on activated lexical items, perception of the actress, etc. It is then passed on to the general workspace. The counterparts (i.e., the input items that should be fused in the blend) are mapped onto the same parts of the body. Most obviously, the mouth in the (explicit) "heave" input is identified with the mouth in the (implicit) speech input as both are mapped onto the mouth of the organizing body schema in the blended space of the general workspace. What about the heart? Here, Turner's account again benefits from the representational architecture. *Heart* is lexically ambiguous and its utterance will at least prime (if not actually activate) all meanings (again, see Garman 293–4). While the "heave" input most obviously activates the physical organ meaning of "heart," the "true inner feelings" meaning is also activated in the implicit input space. This second activation is facilitated by the fact that Lear's question concerns feelings. Thus the entire discussion has primed items related to emotion. Both meanings, then, map onto the heart of the organizing body schema. As a result, we have a blended space in which Cordelia's mouth as a physical space that can contain something solid is identified with her mouth as an organ of speech and her physical heart is identified with her feelings, all through the organizing structure of Cordelia's body.

But thus far the blend leaves open the counterpart for "heave." What happens here? Heaving is what moves Cordelia's heart into her mouth as a physical space. Its counterpart must be something that moves Cordelia's feelings into her mouth as an organ of speech. Here we engage, once again, in lexical scanning. Such items as "speak," "feelings," "mouth," and so on, serve as probes that activate "express" or some related item, making it the obvious choice. But further processes of evaluation in working memory should reject "express," for "express" does not actually bring one's feelings out of one's body into one's mouth. Rather, expressing one's feelings involves reporting those feelings. The feelings remain "inside." After much scanning, we may come to the conclusion that there is no counterpart for "heave"— which is right, for that is precisely what "cannot" suggests. Just as there is no physical process for "coughing up" one's heart, there is no mental process for bringing one's inner feelings into the outer, sharable world. Cordelia can surely express (i.e., report) her feelings. She says "Nothing" because she cannot bring her feelings themselves out of her mouth. The point bears on the broader, contrastive blend that relates Cordelia to her sisters—who illustrate quite clearly that an expression of emotion is not a matter of bringing true inner feeling out into the common world.

Indeed, even that is not all that is going on here. A fuller analysis of Cordelia's statement may indicate that the (partial) blend involves more detailed and specific elements from the lexical entry for *heave*, including its implications of sickness, along with images of choking or suffocation. It may also generate an emergent structure, that of death—for anyone who literally heaved up his/her heart would die. This has further implications for the failure of the blend with respect to emotion and speech, and for other aspects of the play as well. It may even have implications for the most encompassing blends bearing on the imagistic coherence of the play as a whole, for Cordelia does ultimately die by choking and suffocation (from hanging). In these ways, conceptual blending theory may help us understand, not only particular metaphors, but many levels of complexity in literary works—and in our response to those works. Indeed, with regard to the latter, one of the most remarkable things about blending theory and other cognitive approaches is that they reveal to us the subtlety of our ordinary reactions to literature and the arts. In the case just discussed, we have already performed almost all these difficult, elaborate blends spontaneously when reading the play, even if we were not self-consciously aware of their implications. If we did not do this, we could not possibly experience the play as we do. For, in the end, our experience of the play is necessarily the experience of a complex, blended space that we have made, cognitively.

CHAPTER **5**
The Text (II)
Narrative, or Getting the Story Straight

A central distinction in narratology is that between story and discourse, what happens and the presentation of what happens. Imagine a murder. There are facts about who committed the murder and why. There is a sequence of events—psychological, physical, social—that lead up to the murder. Roughly, that real sequence of events is the story. Smith fired Jones from his job. Jones's life fell apart. He blamed everything on Smith. He began to think about killing Smith. He went to buy the gun. He began target practice. He hung out at Smith's apartment building, to learn when Smith enters and leaves, and so on. Now suppose you are a juror at Jones's trial. You first learn that Smith has been murdered, and that Jones is accused of the crime. The first witness discusses seeing Jones at Smith's building on the day of the crime. The next witness testifies that Jones bought a pistol two weeks earlier. The third witness testifies that the caliber of the bullet that killed Smith is the same as that in the gun bought by Jones, though the gun itself has not been recovered. In the trial, you pick up bits and pieces of what happened. You hear about parts of events from different times and places. The order of the testimonies is not the same as the order of the events in real life (e.g., one witness talks about the day of the murder, then a later witness speaks about a time two weeks earlier). Indeed, some of what you hear may be untrustworthy. Perhaps someone testifies to seeing Jones across town at the time of the murder. Other things you hear may be irrelevant. Thus someone else testifies that Doe had shouted at Smith, "I'm gonna kill you for this!" after Smith backed into Doe's new car. This jumble of mixed and partial retellings is the discourse.

In a sense, the task of the jury is to reconstruct the story from the discourse. This is also the task of the reader of a novel or the viewer of a film. In each case, we are presented with an array of materials—partial, fragmentary, disordered, perhaps contradictory, untrustworthy, or irrelevant. From this, it is up to us to figure out "what happened." Of course, there is an obvious difference between fiction and nonfiction. In the case of nonfiction, there are facts about what actually happened (i.e., about the story). That is not the case in fiction. On the other hand, even in reality, the story is never directly accessible to us. In life as in art we only have the discontinuous, partially disordered fragments of experience. We are in much the same cognitive situation in the two cases. Unsurprisingly, then, we follow the same cognitive procedures. Specifically, given an array of fragments, we construct agents, objects, actions, events, and causal sequences, hoping that we "get the story straight." Here, as elsewhere, the human mind proceeds in the same way, whether it is dealing with nature or with art.

Some of the most significant work in literature, film, and cognition has been devoted to isolating the cognitive procedures we use in making stories out of discourses. Indeed, the importance of cognitive study in film could probably be dated from David Bordwell's *Narration in the Fiction Film* which sets itself just this task.[1] In this chapter, I will take up the work of Bordwell, along with some related empirical and theoretical studies (such as those discussed by Gerrig in his influential *Experiencing Narrative Worlds*), in order to consider just what cognitive processes are involved here, how they operate, and how isolating them can reveal things about film and about our response to film. After considering this in some detail, I will turn from discourse inference to story structure per se. Specifically, I will discuss, much more briefly, some story universals and the cognitive reasons for these universals.

Figuring Out What Happened

A film begins. First there is a shot of Jones. He looks left, off camera. There is frantic music playing in the background. Then there is a shot of a man in a trench coat, walking toward the camera. Then another shot of Jones, still looking left. Jones reaches into his pocket and begins to pull something out. Then there is a close-up of a pistol. The hand holding the pistol fires twice. After this, a shot of the man in the trench coat holding his gut, grimacing, and collapsing to the ground. Following that, a shot of Jones turning quickly into an alley, then running away from the camera. A series of shots such as this is entirely disjointed—and yet very easy to put together. We immediately interpret the man in the trench coat as the object of Jones's gaze. We immediately connect the pistol firing with the man collapsing. We infer that he has been shot by the pistol. We do not assume that he is suffering from gas pains and that the pistol signaled the start of a footrace, perhaps in another city and even at another time—though this is a logical possibility. In short, we constitute the story from the discourse easily. This constitution is an ordinary cognitive process. But just what is that process?

Bordwell sees a film as a series of "cues" that signal to the spectator that he/she should "execute a definable variety of *operations*" (29).[2] These operations involve the running of procedural schemas. As we discussed in chapter 2, procedural schemas are cognitive structures of action. They allow us to do everything from walk to play music. In the case of narrative, they allow us to construct the story from the discourse. That construction involves, first of all, the application of a vast wealth of information—prominently including an array of representational schemas—from our experience in the real world. Speaking of literary narrative, Gerrig points out that "readers . . . must construct . . . situation models, which integrate information from the text with broader real-world knowledge" (6). Indeed, we evidently follow "a *principle of minimal departure*" (13), according to which we assume maximum continuity between the real world and the world of the fiction. In other words, we basically assume that the world of the story is identical with the world of our lived experience except in those specific cases where there is a direct contradiction from the narrative. As Branigan explains, "a perceiver uses a schema to automatically fill in any data that is deemed to be 'missing' in the text" (16). Indeed, Branigan understates the case when he uses the word "deemed." We fill in a great deal of real-world information without ever becoming aware that anything is missing from the text (e.g., that we do not see actually a bullet leave the gun and hit the man in the trench coat; needless to say, these data are also missing in parallel real life experiences).

Of course, not all the schemas relevant to understanding narrative are drawn from general life. There is also a set of schemas that are specific to narrative and to the particular sort of narrative at issue (cinematic, literary, or whatever). In the case of film, these would involve particular ways of understanding relations between shots (e.g., "eyeline match" where we see someone looking off screen, then we see some object in a separate shot, and we infer that the person was looking at the object), how to relate the optical point of view of the camera to the optical point of view of a character (a much more complex process than one might expect), and so on.

In short, when watching a film, our construction of the story from the discourse involves the application of procedural schemas to representational schemas and other information from ordinary life; representational schemas and other information from reading or hearing narratives, watching other films, and so on; and, of course, perceptually encoded sequences from the particular film under consideration. The schemas from life and those from narrative allow us to put together the perceptually encoded sequences from the discourse of the film into the story of the film—synthesizing them, drawing inferences, generating emergent structures, and so forth, all in the general workspace of working memory. In some ways, this is obvious—perhaps so obvious as to be banal. What is interesting and valuable comes when we begin to consider precisely what tasks are involved in constructing the story and just what schemas contribute to this.

Establishing Identity and Correlation

As Gerrig points out, when watching a film, we must continually form and revise situation models of the story, detailed structures with characters, events, motives, and so on. Perhaps the most basic part of this is the construction of identity.[3] Consider, for example, *Titanic*.[4] In the course of this movie, as in any movie, we continually see momentary apparitions of persons and we must construct our story world in such a way that these apparitions coalesce into particular individuals. Such-and-such figures in these various scenes are all Jack. These others are all Rose, and so on. Of course, characters are not all that we need to identify. We need to identify the ship as the same, parts of the ship as the same, rooms as the same. More generally, we must continually group figures from different shots together, locating them in the situation model as the same or different—or both, as when we must identify the old Rose with the young Rose, while still differentiating them by age.

In order to accomplish this, we probably rely on a schema for identity. The schema in all likelihood involves material continuity or persistence through time in the case of objects and mental continuity or persistence through time in the case of persons. Thus, we subsume Jack getting on the boat and Jack clinging to the raft under the schema for identity as there is both material continuity (of his body) and mental continuity (i.e., a set of ideas, desires, experiences, memories carried over from the time he enters the ship until the moment he dies). We do the same for young and old Rose. Indeed, the film is in many ways about identity, and difference within identity. The theme is suggested at many points, as when old Rose holds her mirror, dredged up from the floor of the Atlantic, and says that it is the same mirror, but the reflection has changed. In most of these cases, memory is directly implicated. This makes sense, for one major component of our sense of personal identity is memory. Drawing on work with amnesic patients, Schacter writes that "our sense of ourselves depends crucially on the subjective experience of remembering our pasts" (34). LeDoux goes so far as to say that "we are our memories, and without them, we are nothing" (*Synaptic* 97). The main story of *Titanic* is a memory that develops the theme of identity precisely by foregrounding difference. In keeping with this, through the encompassing frame, we are continually faced with dissolves between 1912 and 1996, the image of the wasted ship at the bottom of the sea transformed into the grandest ship ever made in 1912, then dissolved back to the wreck on the ocean floor. In each case, we must subsume the images under the schema "identity." The dissolves facilitate this—but at the same time they make the differences within identity salient. Note that this is not in any way cognitively paradoxical, for the application of the identity schema presupposes difference, at least difference in time or location. Identity means a certain sort of continuity, and, to have continuity, one needs distinction.

We must apply the identity schema not only to objects or narrative "contents," but also to more specifically cinematic elements—for example, entire scenes. These applications too have thematic significance, and significance for audience response. The film opens with a sepia-tinted view of the Titanic departing on its voyage, the sepia tint suggesting silent films from this period, though the gauge of the film, the resolution, the camera movement all indicate its modern provenance. The camera passes behind someone making a movie of just this moment—in this case, cranking the film by hand to produce the sort of motion picture that could have been made in 1912. Indeed, the film we are watching has slight blurs in motion that are clearly intended to recall early films when the shooting speed was slower, and more irregular. The scene is resonant with themes of identity, and we are clearly supposed to link the film we are watching with the film this camera-cranking fellow would have made in 1912. Though contemporary, the scene gives the opening a documentary feel. This shot—including the 1912 film maker with his hand-cranked camera—is repeated a few minutes into the film, only this time without the sepia tint and without the noticeable blur. Evidently, we must subsume the two instances of this entire scene under our identity schema. What is the effect of this? That is an empirical question, but two effects seem likely. Insofar as the subsumption is unself-conscious, it probably contributes to a sense of reality. Having already viewed this scene as if in a documentary, its repetition without the foregrounding of the film itself (through the tint and the blurring) may serve to make the current film (*Titanic*) appear more like a direct experience, or at least something close to what a 1912 documentary would have recorded. On the other hand, insofar as our identification of these scenes occurs self-consciously, the connection may operate in precisely the opposite way. A great deal of the film is concerned with issues of narration and film, including the ways in which cinematic narration can be false and insincere—as when Lovett films part of his work, then turns off the camera, saying, "Enough of that bullshit." In this context, the identity of these two shots could serve to emphasize the fictionality of the film. Put differently, in the first (unself-conscious) case, we might implicitly apply the identity schema, not only to the two stretches of film, but to a directly parallel historical reality. In the second (self-conscious) case, we might explicitly recognize nonidentity between the shots of the film, on the one hand, and the reality a camera would actually have recorded in 1912, on the other; we might see the application of the identity schema as illusory.

In keeping with this, the film repeatedly thematizes the relation of identity or nonidentity between art and history. The entire story is triggered by Jack's drawing of Rose. Lovett sees the drawing and focuses immediately on the necklace. He wants to identify it as the diamond he is seeking. To do so, he cannot compare it with the original, so he compares it with a photograph. The sequence is something like this: artistic representation is identical with documentary representation that is, in turn, identical with reality (as we learn when we see the diamond around young Rose's neck, then later in old Rose's hand). Of course, the schema of identity is slightly different in this case. The default value of our schema for identity is material and/or psychological continuity, as already noted. However, there are alternatives to the default, depending on context. In the case of art, a figure may be identified with a real object if it adequately resembles that real object and if the resemblance is caused by that real object (as in a photo) or results from the artist's knowledge of the real object (i.e., it is not simply coincidence). This specified alternative identity schema applies implicitly to the film itself. By a simple cognitive process of homology, the internal representation of the work of art (the drawing), the documentation (the photograph), and the reality (the actual diamond) transfers onto the movie *Titanic* itself and its relation to documentation and to history. Insofar as the film is successful in getting us to recognize the tragic experience of the Titanic, it relies on our identifying the story (i.e., the work of art)—including the objects and characters it depicts—with the history, in part by way of the photographic documentary suggested at the outset (with the hand-cranked camera, etc.).

For the most part, identity construal must operate automatically and unproblematically, in *Titanic* or any other film. We simply could not make sense out of a movie in which our identifications were continually disrupted and we were repeatedly asking, "Is that the same man? Is that the same ship? Is that the same room? Is that the same necklace?," and so on. However, against this background of easy identification, films often problematize certain specific identifications. *Titanic* does this briefly at several points, usually with a quick resolution—as when Rose's granddaughter openly doubts that Jack's drawing represents her grandmother. However, as we have already seen, there are also points when the issue is raised more significantly, and is not fully resolved—at least not for some viewers.

The last point is worth considering in slightly more detail. Richard Maltby has argued that classic Hollywood movies often included scenes with contradictory information, such that different audience members could interpret the scene in contradictory ways. Maltby's concern is with sexual innuendo. When the Production Code[5] was in effect, the studios could not produce movies with extramarital sex (unless the illicit relationship led to punishment). Thus they would sometimes construct scenes which a "naive" viewer could take as involving no sex, but a "sophisticated" viewer could take as involving elliptical implications of sex. The practice, however, is not confined to the period of the Production Code, nor to sexual topics. In *Titanic*, there are scenes with just this sort of ambiguity that concern identity and history, not sex. (Perhaps in keeping with postmodern trends, the eroticism in the movie is straightforward; it is the epistemology that is ambiguous.)

One very interesting scene of this sort concerns, again, art. Rose has purchased a series of paintings. She says that she wants the paintings put up in order to give the room some "color." The paintings are readily identifiable. One is a Monet; another is a Degas; a third is a Picasso. Cal refers to these as "finger paintings." Rose disagrees and says that she has taste in art, while Cal does not. She refers to Picasso, forgetting his first name. Cal pompously says that this Picasso fellow will come to nothing. As this is going on, Rose is holding up a painting that is recognizably in the style of Picasso. I take it that the basic reading of this scene would be one in which the viewer takes everything at face value—Rose has taste; Cal is a pompous idiot; the events of the story are closely and appropriately linked with the real history they represent, as indicated by the reference to an historically real artist. Something more interesting happens, however, with a viewer who has basic familiarity with Picasso. Such a viewer will identify the painting in Rose's hands with one of the most famous of Picasso's works, *Les Demoiselles d'Avignon*. In other words, such a viewer will identify the painting in the story with a painting in history. This may seem to reinforce the identification of story and history. However, a viewer who recognizes the painting is almost certain to know that it did not sink to the floor of the ocean with the Titanic. In this case, then, the identification of the painting in the story with the painting in history would seem to work against the identification of the story with its precedent history.

But that is not all. There is yet a third viewer here. This viewer is familiar enough with *Les Demoiselles* to see that the painting in Rose's hands is *not* the pathbreaking work of 1907. The differences are multiple and overt. There is no attempt at forgery here. This recognition is almost certain to be self-conscious and to suggest neither the simple truth (i.e., identity with history) nor the simple falsity of the film, but rather an ironic distance between the film and the history it apparently purports to capture (but, perhaps, does not really purport to capture). This is a particularly interesting case cognitively because the viewer must do several things. First, he/she must not subsume the story painting and the historical painting under the identity schema.

Second, he/she must recognize that many viewers will do just this. Finally, he/she must understand that most viewers will schematize the film more generally as reflecting history or as falsifying history, whereas in fact the film's relation to history is not definable by identity schemas.

Marking Time

Another crucial cognitive task for a viewer is sorting out temporal relations. Even when identifying two instances of Rose (e.g., old and young Rose) or of the Titanic (e.g., in 1912 and 1996), we must rely on differentiation in time, for it is differences in time that allow us to see the instances of Rose as two figures that may be subsumed under the identity schema. Moreover, it is time that allows us to structure the relations among these figures, who are necessarily in part different while being identified. Indeed, one of the most basic elements of inferring the story from the discourse is getting the temporal order straight. As Bordwell explains, "While watching a narrative film, the spectator takes as one goal the arranging of events in temporal sequence.... If the narrative presents events out of chronological order, we must fall back on our ability to rearrange them according to schemata" (33).

When we are watching a film, our minds set up a sort of template (specifically, an organizational schema in the general workspace of working memory) into which events are slotted. First, there may be a gross division into broad time periods. Second, there may be a more fully specified rearrangement into specific temporal sequences within a given time period. This more fine-grained organization often involves particular narrative schemas—or prototypes—such as those for particular genres. It almost always involves at least some causal schematization. Temporal schematization is not simply a matter of assigning particular dates and times to particular events. Rather, it is a matter of assigning *significant* temporal relations. The significance of temporal relations is not simply a matter of temporal location, but of temporal location as this affects causal/narrative developments. Take a murder mystery. It begins with Columbo on the crime scene. Smith has been murdered. This activates a schema or a prototype for murder. Our murder prototype involves several components—one or more murderers, a murder weapon, a motive, a sequence of events leading to the murder. Without conscious reflection, we set up this template to organize further information. As Columbo gathers information, we assign it to the appropriate categories. Smith had a violent argument with Jones that morning. We put this event in a temporal sequence with the murder, slotting it under "morning before the murder." In doing this, we mark it as a possible motive. Indeed, categorizing it in relation to the murder ("the morning before the murder") already indicates this. We do not locate the argument in some neutral temporal grid. We locate it in relation to causal/narrative concerns.

In some cases, temporal reconstruction can be a very difficult and uncertain process. However, this is rarely the case in Hollywood movies. Indeed, murder mysteries are among the rare cases where there is any temporal complexity at all. They begin near the end and work explicitly to stitch together the series of events that preceded the murder. In watching a murder mystery, much of our cognitive effort is a matter of placing events in their proper order. In most Hollywood films, however, the bulk of the story is presented in its actual temporal sequence. In other words, discourse order is, for the most part, the same as story order.

There are two common exceptions to the direct parallelism of discourse sequence and story sequence in Hollywood cinema. One is the establishment of simultaneity. Filmmakers could in principle show simultaneous events all at once on a split screen. However, they rarely do this. Rather, they use a relatively simple technique for establishing simultaneity, a technique that makes minimal demands on a viewer's cognitive resources—they intercut simultaneous scenes. In one scene, the stagecoach is being attacked. We cut to the cavalry charging. We cut back to the stagecoach, still being attacked. We cut back to the cavalry, still charging. This sequence of cuts makes limited demands on cognition, first of all, because our minds are set up in such a way that they assume object and motion continuity across short breaks in observation unless they are given reason not to. When we see a ball roll under one end of the sofa and then emerge from the other end, we assume that it is the same ball and that it continued to roll under the sofa when we could not see it. Suppose I am looking at a dancer, then I turn to look behind me at someone who is talking loudly, then I look back at the dancer. I assume that the dancer has continued to dance the whole time. Similarly, when we see an attack on a stagecoach, then something else, then the attack on the stagecoach, our minds assume continuity unless they are given reason not to.[6] We find an example of this sort in *Titanic* when Rose and Jack are at the party in steerage. We cut to Cal and the other men smoking cigars, then back to the party. We automatically assume that the party is going on the whole time—that is, we automatically schematize the party as continuous.

But how does this lead to the schematization of simultaneity (as opposed to continuity)? Our default schema for temporal ordering is that order of experience equals order of occurrence. In other words when we see A, then B, then C, we assume that A actually happened first, then B, then C, unless we have reason to believe otherwise. The continuity schema gives us a reason to believe otherwise in the cases just cited. We do not assume that the stagecoach was attacked, then the cavalry charged, then the stagecoach was attacked, then the cavalry charged, and so on. Rather, we assume that both the attack and the charge were continuous. However, here as elsewhere, we also assume minimal deviation from the default. Thus we automatically preserve the narrative order in the reconstructed story order insofar as this is possible given the schematization of continuity. The result of this is schematization of simultaneity. Simultaneity allows us to assume that at least some of what happens in the first attack sequence preceded what was shown in the first cavalry sequence, that at least some of what was shown in the second attack sequence followed what was shown in the first cavalry sequence, and so on. In this way, simultaneity allows us to preserve as much of our default temporal ordering as is consistent with the schematization of continuity.

The other common Hollywood exception to standard story/discourse temporal parallelism is the use of a frame narrative or some other division into a past and a present. This is found in a range of films, including *Titanic*. Viewers of such films have to set up two broad cognitive categories, past and present—more specifically, 1912 and 1996, in the case of *Titanic*. Any given event in the film must be entered into one or the other category before we can place it in any further temporal sequence. The opening of *Titanic*, in sepia tint, establishes 1912 as one temporal category. The first scene, however, shifts to the present. Thereafter, we must locate each scene in one category or the other, though once we have done so, the internal sequencing is easy, since story order is maintained in each case. How do we divide events into the two categories? First, we quickly come to identify most people and things in the film with one category or the other, since most of them appear in only one time period. Moreover, the one character who does show up in both, Rose, is sharply distinct in visual appearance. In addition to Rose, a few objects overlap as well—such as the Titanic itself. However, these too are sharply distinct in appearance. Thus, the temporal disjunction is very easy to follow through. There are multiple cues as to whether we are dealing with the present or the past. The cues serve as probes to activate the relevant schema and temporal organization proceeds swiftly and automatically.

Clearly, even in this case, the temporal division is a function of causal/narrative significance. The division into 1912 and 1996 is consequential for our understanding of the causal sequences defining the narrative. That is why the temporal division is important. But there is more to temporal cognition than establishing the order of events in relation to bare, objective causality. Part of temporal schematization involves our sense that a story sequence is or is not "appropriate." The sequence and duration of the story events should not only be comprehensible and plausible (interms of causality). They should also be apt. Specifically, a filmmaker tries to communicate a feeling that the story time fits the story's action. Clearly, for this to happen, events need to occur in the right order (e.g., we cannot have the event that motivates the murder occur after the murder). But events also need to take the "right" amount of time (e.g., a crime of passion must occur quickly after the initiating event; a cold-blooded murder, in contrast, must involve time for fiery anger to cool into calm hatred). The "right" amount of time is in part a function of the particular experiential quality of the events. Thus it is not simply a matter of sequence and objective causality. It involves other sorts of temporal structuration as well. Specifically, it involves the activation of narrative schemas—or, more often, narrative prototypes—that have their own temporal norms.

Consider, for example, our narrative prototype for romance. Most of us may have the sense that romance involves a particular amount of time that is appropriate for the heightening of intimacy. Sometimes people may seem to have known each other too long to experience fiery passion; the time seems right only for warmth and companionship. Sometimes people may seem to have known each other too little for real intimacy to develop, so that the relationship is simply one of physical desire. In the case of *Titanic*, Cameron is faced with the task of making the relationship between Jack and Rose appear to be of just the right duration. The right duration, in this case, would give Jack and Rose both passion and an intensity of love so great that each is willing to sacrifice his/her own safety for the well being of the other. Indeed, in this case, the film has an even narrower task—to make the temporal organization right for adolescents, perhaps especially adolescent women. In effect, the film adopts a contemporary dating prototype to produce this sense of temporal aptness. This dating prototype might involve a sequence along roughly the following lines: an initial meeting; a period of learning about one another in an informal setting (i.e., a sort of informal date); a couple of formal dates, often involving food and dancing; some interaction of the boy with the girl's parents (perhaps only when he goes to pick her up for the date); some point at which the potential lovers tell each other everything that is important to them; then, after say three dates or so, sexual intimacy, often in a car, since adolescents usually do not have any other place where they can be alone without adult supervision. There may also be a period of conflict and uncertainty, as the lovers decide precisely what they want from the relationship. (Note that this prototype need not represent actual adolescent behavior. It roughly represents one common conception of such behavior—or did when I was in high school and college—whether true to life or not.) We typically envision this sequence of events as stretching out over several weeks, or perhaps months. However, *Titanic* collapses this sequence into a few days. The result is a sort of disjunction between our knowledge of the real time sequence and the feeling (at least the feeling of many viewers) that the time of the romance is apt.

Specifically, there is an initial meeting of the lovers—a rather dramatic one that immediately establishes trust. The following afternoon, there is an informal interaction between them, where they share not only their histories, but their feelings. Jack even broaches the topic of love, though Rose refuses to talk about it. (Here, as elsewhere, the film reverses the standard gender roles of the romance prototype.) They nearly part, but then come together again in what almost counts as a third meeting. (Jack actually shows Rose his etchings in a literalization of a sexual cliché.) That night, Jack has the unpleasant task of meeting the parents, or parent, in this case. He makes it through a formal dinner before taking Rose out to dance. The next day, a bit of conflict follows in which Rose cannot make up her mind about the future of the relationship. She relents, they share more talk and time together in an increasingly erotic evening—a third, fourth, or even fifth date, depending on how one counts. This culminates in sex, in the back seat of a car. Though the time involved is only about forty-eight hours, it seems apt (at least to many viewers) in part because the temporal duration of the dating prototype has been activated and we have tacitly assimilated the events of the story to that prototype.

Making Room

In good Kantian fashion, another crucial aspect of our cognitive construction of a film involves the organization of space. Broadly speaking, spatial organization operates in the same way as temporal organization. We distinguish a limited number of general categories and subsume individual scenes under those categories, all in the context of ongoing causal/narrative schematization. But in some ways the cognition of space is more elaborate. First, we typically need to keep track of more places. Second, the relations among these places are more complex. Finally, the spatial relations within these places are more complex.

We may think of spatial cognition as beginning with a broad schema of "place." Whenever we view a scene, we subsume the scene under some place schema. First, place is a mere marker of difference. This thing happens in one place (place A); that other thing happens somewhere else (place B). But "place" is not wholly contentless. We structure space around agency, most often human agency. Thus, given any scene, we organize it in human terms, as a space in which someone could live, walk, swim, fly, sleep, whatever. In connection with this, place schemas differ by type, forming a limited list that we draw on in locating scenes. These types may be organized first into indoor and outdoor, then into private room, public room, urban outdoor (city), rural outdoor (country), and so on. Each place schema begins to define a set of relations to the larger world. Again, we assume identity between the real world and the fictional story unless given reason not to do so. Thus a private room implies a larger building, with other rooms. An urban scene implies connecting streets, people, shops, and so on.

Once we have subsumed a particular scene under a place schema, we must determine whether or not other scenes should be subsumed under the same schema or under different schemas. In general, identity of place is marked by continuity of action (e.g., a character walking from one part of a room to another), continuity of perception (e.g., characters in one shot hear characters in another shot), and continuity of scene, as marked by stationary objects—trees, houses, furniture, mountains, whatever. In other words, we judge two shots as referring to the same story space if people move without apparent delay between the spaces shown in the shots, if persons or objects in one shot can be seen or heard by persons in the other shot, or if the two shots contain the same nonmoving objects. In the absence of these cues, we tend to define spaces as different, though in some cases we may find their relation uncertain. After we have established two or more shots as defining one story place, we must form a situation model of that place. For example, we must establish a sense of where the various characters are relative to one another. This can be a difficult task. One main purpose of the continuity editing system (the standard system of editing in Hollywood) is to facilitate this. By setting up an imaginary line between focal characters, and keeping the camera on one side of that line, the viewer is never faced with disorienting shifts and is less likely to lose sight of place-defining, stationary objects. Establishing shots (which give us a broad view of the larger space in which the scene occurs) provide considerable aid in building situation models for space as well. They help us keep track of where everything is even when subsequent shots are a series of close ups which otherwise provide no cues as to spatial relations.

Parallel to this, once we have subsumed two shots under different places we must cognize the encompassing spatial relations between those two places. Think again of the stagecoach under attack intercut with the charging cavalry. We must first define these as two distinct places, with distinct situation models. However, it is very likely that the two will share a place type. For example, both might be a desert area. This already places them in some sort of relation. Though they are clearly separate—we do not yet hear the bugle of the cavalry in the stagecoach scene—there is nonetheless some object continuity. Perhaps there are distant mountains, visible from both places, or perhaps the cavalry is passing a ranch that we saw earlier from the stagecoach. Thus we subsume both places under an encompassing model of a larger, less local space. In the context of this larger space, we subsume motion under one or another schema of spatial direction. The primary schemas for motion in this context are "toward" and "away." This is true especially in those cases where one of the two places draws our emotional interest. Thus, when we are concerned with the stagecoach, we make that the focal point of our spatial construction. All other places, and all other motions, take their spatial orientation from this center. Thus the cavalry is either coming nearer to the stagecoach or moving farther away. The cavalry finally reaches the same local place when we and the characters in the stagecoach hear the bugle, sound continuity signaling local unity of place.

Titanic makes particularly interesting use of spatial cognition. In viewing this film, we need to construct several sets of spatial relations. The most obvious is the great ship itself. This involves cognizing various private rooms (e.g., the quarters of the main characters, as well as those of such ancillary characters as the Irish woman with her two children, and the old couple that die in their bed). It involves the larger separation between steerage and first class, and the organization of steerage into a series of spaces below deck that can be gated, effectively imprisoning the steerage passengers. A few specific places are particularly prominent—the grand staircase, with the clock where Rose and Jack have their rendezvous; the first-class dining area; Rose's rooms, with the safe. We also must construct models of the promenade areas of the ship, of the stem where Jack announces that he is King of the World and later sings the flying machine song, and the stern, where he saves Rose from suicide and where they hang on when the ship sinks. In viewing the movie, we have to keep all these places distinct and we have to subsume particular scenes under each of them as necessary. In fact, this is not much of a problem. Our minds are pretty good at storing and recognizing local places, especially local places associated with significant human actions. What is a problem, however, is determining the relations among these places. Of course, the basic spatial relations must be fairly comprehensible. We should not become so disoriented that we cannot follow what is going on. In other words, story space must for the most part be automatically reconstructable from the discourse. But there are points where this reconstruction becomes problematic. Specifically, a casual viewer—and even a very self-conscious viewer, working with a videotape and watching scenes over and over—is unlikely to be able to make detailed sense out of many relations among local places.

The interior of the ship, with its series of corridors, is particularly baffling. At both the beginning and the end there is a shot of a Middle Eastern man trying to figure out his precise location by looking at signs on the walls and consulting a book, presumably a dictionary. His bafflement is roughly parallel to that of the viewer. Jack and Rose wander from first class down into the furnaces, then up onto the deck through a series of labyrinthine passages that I suspect no viewer could not easily plot out. In this case, the sequence may be unobtrusive. But Cameron draws our attention to this sort of thing later when Rose asks Andrews where a prisoner would be kept. Andrews gives her a series of complicated directions. Rose is undaunted. But the viewer is probably lost—I certainly am. When Rose actually does try to follow the directions, she too falters, and neither she nor the viewer has any sense of the spatial relation between Jack's prison and the corridors where she is wandering. Finally, we learn that Rose, Jack, the corridors, and Jack's prison room are part of one local space when Jack hears Rose's voice and shouts for help—the continuity of sound providing the signal for singularity of place.[7] Nonetheless, the complexity is only exacerbated when Rose goes looking for help and moves through a series of identical corridors, then when she and Jack eventually escape and move through a baffling array of places. They eventually break through into steerage, where they are locked in with all the other steerage passengers. It is all like a dream in which one passageway leads to another then to another but with no clear logic. This no doubt has different consequences for different viewers. Some viewers are likely to become exasperated and dismiss the sequence as incoherent. Others, however, are likely to find that their inability to define spatial relations gives them a sense of the enormity of the ship (even more than the sweeping, computer-generated shots of the entire exterior) and of the incomprehensible, nightmarish quality of the disaster.

This nightmarish quality is enhanced further by our relative inability to organize spatial relations when Jack and Rose fall with the ship into the water. There is the ordered space of the lifeboats. But separate from that is the entirely disorganized space of the drowning individuals. We can hardly locate Jack and Rose in any spatial schema. There are no fixed or clear relations. When Rose climbs onto the door, we cannot situate her anywhere. The point is emphasized by the door itself, for a door usually serves as one signal of a well-defined interior space. Some sense of spatial order returns only when the lifeboat comes and enters into Rose's local space with the sound of Officer Lowe's call and her response—recapitulating her own earlier discovery of Jack.

Construing Character

Perhaps the most obvious use of cognitive structures is in the development and understanding of character. Authors form characters based on types and we recognize types, or, rather, given certain cues, we subsume characters under types. Many of the character structures activated in watching a film are the same ones that are activated in watching the world. Others are particular to narrative, to film, and so on. In each case, our view of a person's/character's ideas, motives, likely behaviors, our evaluation of him/her, our feelings about him/her, are a function of both direct information and schemas—or, more likely, prototypes—cued by that information. This may seem very constraining, and in some ways it is. But these schemas and prototypes are in fact quite numerous and diverse, perhaps more so than we commonly assume. For example, as is well known, there are plenty of patriarchal character types—the gold digger, the unfaithful wife, and so on. There are also feminist character types (e.g., different sorts of patriarchal oppressor). And there are character types that bear directly on gender, but do not fall into either category. Moreover, the number of schemas and prototypes available, their precise organization and properties, and their degree of relative accessibility will vary from viewer to viewer, yielding greater diversity within and across audiences. A film will limit the range of structures we are likely activate for a given character. At the same time, a particular viewer may be inclined generally to apply one sort of structure more than another. Thus one viewer will be more likely to apply patriarchal schemas, while another will be more likely to apply feminist schemas. Given the very same character presentation, two readers may have radically different understandings or responses, if the structures they apply are different. In addition, schemas and prototypes are not inflexible. They structure our experience of a character. But they are also responsive to odd properties of characters, at least to some degree. In keeping with this, character structures are not a straightjacket for authors any more then they are for viewers. Authors may try to avoid particular schemas or prototypes entirely, or they may try to use unusual permutations. Again, a schema involves a set of default properties and relations. One obvious way of altering a schema is to shift one of those properties or relations into some alternative of the same general kind. If a character of a particular sort is schematically male, make the character female; if a character of this sort is schematically a parent, make him/her a child or a sibling. The same kinds of variation may be used equally with prototypes, as we saw in chapter 3.

Titanic relies on a number of standard character prototypes—including the physical aspects of these prototypes whereby the villain has dark hair and the hero has fair hair. On the other hand, Cameron introduces some significant variations, largely of a political nature. Specifically, there seem to be two crucial parameters in Cameron's use of character structures, especially general or "real world" character structures: class and gender. Rather than developing characters in a corporate or patriarchal manner, *Titanic* cues anticapitalist and feminist prototypes, at least superficially. In addition, the film takes up common cinematic structures—especially from the western— and alters their gender characteristics.

Consider the final point. Jack is a character drawn directly from westerns. He even characterizes himself as a "tumbleweed blowing in the wind." He should be a strapping cowboy. But he is the smooth-faced, lean-limbed Leonardo DiCaprio, described by one of my female graduate students as "disturbingly androgynous." Indeed, he seems particularly flimsy next to the robust figure of Kate Winslet. The character of Jack should be the rough farmhand that kindles the fiery passion of the genteel lady, who in turn spurns the foppish girly-men of her own class. But he is not. The film constantly stresses the class difference between the two. When Rose meets Jack again in a dream at the end of the film, he is wearing his working-class clothes. Just before they have sex, he pretends to be her chauffeur. But, far from the studly worker and cowboy, he is really the girl in the relationship. He is sensitive. He is artistic. When she thinks of suicide, he saves her— through comforting talk. The next day, he is the one who wants to discuss feelings and she is the one who finds the idea distressing. Perhaps most strikingly, he takes the role of Little Nell, tied to the railroad tracks, and Rose has to do the manly work of cutting him free with a hatchet. Indeed, when someone tries to inhibit her rescue of helpless Jack, she bundles up her fist and bloodies his nose like a good cowboy in a saloon brawl. In this way, Cameron takes up character structures from the western, but mixes up the gender characteristics.

Cameron pays close attention to other aspects of gender in the film as well, cuing different gender schemas and prototypes for different purposes. For example, while the character of Cal owes something to the villain in westerns, he also derives from more contemporary prototypes. Specifically, Cal is designed to trigger a "domineering and oppressive male" prototype for many viewers. He physically prevents Rose from smoking, though he smokes himself; he orders her food, and admits that he does not know if she likes what he has ordered; he says that he will have to control what she reads; he behaves violently, breaking dishes and shouting at her; he insists that she "honor" him "the way a wife is required to honor her husband." It may seem initially that these are just bad traits, and that a dislike of Cal is based directly on his actions. Perhaps this is the case for some viewers, but probably not for most. Cal triggers a prototype that most viewers would not have had fifty years ago. He is a brutish, patriarchal husband with superficial cultivation in polite company, a common enough figure in feminist influenced writing of the past several decades. It is this prototype that initially makes us dislike Cal. By the end, our worst suspicions are confirmed. But most of us loathe Cal well before we have any good reason to do so. Our loathing is prototype-driven. The point may be seen more clearly if we switch the characterization of Cal and Rose. Suppose Cal is marrying Rose because Rose is rich and he is poor. Cal is openly insulting to Rose—for example, announcing that she has no taste in art. When Cal pulls out a cigar and his mother complains, Rose, deferring to Mrs. Hockley, pulls the cigar out of his mouth and rubs it out. She then orders food for both of them, asking Cal afterward if he likes the choice. Cal insults everyone present with a crude Freudian joke about how women are obsessed with size, then stomps off. Rose says that she had better watch what he is reading. Cal has a rendezvous with a young woman from steerage and spends the evening dancing and drinking with her. The next morning, Rose has a fit. She shouts that she is effectively his wife and that he will honor her and not do anything like that again. In the course of this, she pushes the dishes off the table to the ground. For me, at least, the two sequences do not produce the same sense of character—though the actions are the same. For example, in a feminist prototype, the man marrying the woman for money is a parasite and a con man whereas the woman marrying the man for money is a victim of social circumstances. There is, of course, some truth to this. In 1912, the man presumably had employment opportunities that were not open to the woman. Nonetheless, the extreme difference in judgment and evaluation is not explained by the simple statement of the facts. Rather, our early understanding of Cal as almost unspeakably evil is largely the result of assimilation to a prototype. The particular actions of Cal trigger this prototype, which in turn organizes those actions into a pattern, fills them out, assigns significance to them, and explains them in terms of (prototypical) character traits.

On the other hand, depending on the viewer, there are possibilities for a dual perspective here, at least initially. The fact that Rose is marrying Cal for his money and is clearly disdainful of him—while he does evidence some affection for her—might very well trigger a gold digger prototype. Indeed, it might even trigger a "whore" prototype. In keeping with this, Rose refers to herself as Jack's whore, and his sketch of her clearly parallels the other prominent portraits in the film—those of the Parisian prostitute and *Les Demoiselles d'Avignon* (also prostitutes). In addition, we learn that she is sleeping with Cal (hence Cal's insistence that she is his "wife in practice, if not yet by law"), but she still initiates sex with Jack. The feminist "independent woman" may be the prototype viewers are most likely to find activated by the events of the film. Nonetheless, the sexist "whore" and "gold digger" prototypes may be activated as well. Thus, even in this case, the same elements in the narrative may fit into quite different cognitive structures, yielding contradictory assessments and feelings, depending on the propensities of the particular viewer.

Needless to say, these are not the only ways in which schematization and prototype assimilation operate in the cognition of a film. One fascinating topic is the schematization of a narrator. It seems clear that sometimes we schematize a narrator as such (i.e., as a narrator) while at other times we do not—even in a work that has an explicit narrator. Moreover, we can schematize a narrator in different ways (e.g., as reliable or unreliable), with different degrees of attentional focus, different relations to other aspects of narrative schematization, and so forth. Cameron manipulates these narrator schematizations quite self-consciously in the course of *Titanic*. Moreover, he does this in connection with our similarly fluctuating schematization of optical point of view. Unfortunately, it is not possible to discuss all aspects of such schematization and prototype assimilation in a short book.[8] Nonetheless, the preceding discussion should give some sense of the extent and complexity of cognitive operations involved in the seemingly simple process of constructing the story from the discourse.

Stories: Universal Prototypes, Cultural Stereotypes, Idiosyncratic Exempla

Up to now, we have been considering the ways in which a reader or viewer takes a discourse and puts it through various cognitive processes until he/she comes to an understanding of the story. We could imagine some sort of reverse process by which the author produces the discourse from the story initially. In both cases, we would be assuming the prior existence of the story. But how does the story come about? Are there patterns to story structure? How might we explain stories themselves cognitively?

There are many issues one might take up in connection with cognition and stories.[9] In this section, I will briefly consider one—universals of prototype narrative.[10] In order to discuss this, I need to begin by explaining universals, for the concept is widely misunderstood in the humanities.[11]

Universals are, first of all, patterns that recur across genetically and areally distinct traditions. Two traditions are genetically distinct if they do not derive from some common tradition. In linguistics, for example, two languages are genetically distinct if they do not derive from some common ancestral language. If we find that a particular linguistic property is shared by Spanish and French, that does not count as evidence for the universality of the property because Spanish and French descend from a common ancestor, Latin. Areal distinctness means that two traditions have not influenced one another through contact. Suppose we find that Basque and Spanish share some property. Basque and Spanish are not genetically related. However, they have had extensive areal contact for a long period. Thus the property in question may be the result of that contact.

To say that universals occur across traditions is not to say that they occur in all traditions. The technical definition of a universal is a property or relation that occurs across more traditions than would be predicted by chance. The definition does not require that a universal occur in 100 percent of traditions. When we wish to distinguish universals that occur in all traditions, we refer to "absolute" universals. When we wish to discuss universals that occur in almost 100 percent of cases, then we speak of "near absolute" universals. When considering universals that occur in fewer than 100 percent of cases, we say "statistical" universals. This usage may seem strange, but, first of all, it is the way the term is used in linguistics, the area in which universals have been studied most extensively, most rigorously, and most successfully. Moreover, it is not some peculiarity of linguistics. It reflects the usual approach in the natural sciences. Thus in most physical and biological sciences, there are plenty of statistical laws; statistical universals are directly parallel. There is no reason to hold literary study up to higher standards than the physical and biological sciences. Finally, this use of the term "universals" has the advantage of stressing the continuity of statistical with absolute universals. As such, it reminds us of one important task in a research program on universals—refining statistical universals in the hope of eventually articulating a formulation that is absolute.

The idea of moving from statistical to absolute universals brings us to another common misunderstanding that we need to address before going on. It may seem that the best way to make our formulations more encompassing (thus, in a loose sense, more universal) is to make them more abstract. In a way, this is true. If, say, 50 percent of traditions use images of birds to suggest romantic love then, as a matter of logic, at least 50 percent of traditions (and probably much more than 50 percent) use images of some sort to suggest romantic love. In cases such as this, abstraction may be valuable. However, in these cases, there is a strict, logical relation between the initial universal and the reformulation. There is, however, a looser use of "more abstract" where there is no such logical relation. For example, necessary and sufficient conditions are not more likely to be absolute than what we consider standard cases, though the former are in some sense more abstract than the latter. Indeed, quite to the contrary, standard cases are much more likely to be universal than necessary and sufficient conditions. The point becomes more intuitively plausible if we phrase it slightly differently. Border conditions (given by necessary and sufficient conditions) tend to be different from tradition to tradition. In contrast, central tendencies—thus, prototypes—tend to remain fairly stable. The best known example of this is color. When we ask people in different cultures to note the precise point where, say, red becomes orange or orange becomes yellow, then we seem to find no correlation across languages. But if we ask them to point out the best case of red or the best case of yellow, they largely agree. As Comrie puts it, "even where colour term boundaries are very different across languages, there is agreement as to foci" (34). I emphasize this point because it applies equally to stories. Narrative universals, like universals of color, are based on prototypes, not on necessary and sufficient conditions.

For years, I had been reading extensively in the literatures of genetically and areally distinct traditions. These were primarily written traditions, but included work from the more numerous but necessarily less well preserved oral traditions. In reading this work, I was struck by the nearly constant repetition of three structures. I came to the conclusion that these are the dominant and prototypical narrative structures across all or nearly all traditions of literature and orature. In *The Mind and Its Stories,* I have defended this view and further argued that these structures derive from specifiable cognitive processes. Specifically, they are the product of the way humans think about emotions—the way we think about happiness, to be exact. These universal narrative structures derive from prototypes for happiness that are themselves universal. More precisely, happiness prototypes vary with context, just as other prototypes do. (As Kahneman and Miller point out, our prototypical dog in the context "a farm in Maine" is different from our prototypical dog in the context "Manhattan apartment" [140].) But the contexts and the resultant prototypes recur everywhere. Specifically, the happiness prototype in a personal context is romantic union. The happiness prototype in a social context is individual domination within the in-group combined with in-group domination over out-groups. Finally, the happiness prototype in a physical context is plenty of food.[12] One prominent narrative structure is generated by each happiness prototype.[13]

All three dominant narrative structures are tragicomedies. In their fullest form, they involve the achievement of a prototypical goal of happiness. But, prior to that achievement, they pass through the its opposite, the correlated prototype for sorrow (the death of the beloved, the complete loss of social power, and famine, respectively) or some approximation to this. Again, these are prototypical structures. They do not provide necessary and sufficient conditions for story construction. Rather, they provide standard cases. Thus they are very flexible and open to considerable variation. Nonetheless, they are remarkably consistent across cultures and they serve to guide the production and reception of stories even in many cases of radical narrative innovation.

The most prominent structure, not only in the West, but globally, is romantic. The fullest form of the romantic tragicomedy begins with two people in love. Their union is opposed by society, often by their parents, usually due to some difference in social category (e.g., class or ethnic origin). There is most often a rival whom the parents prefer. The conflict leads to the separation of the lovers. In tragic versions, the separation leads to death. In the complete comic version, there is often a near death or imagery of death. In both tragic and comic cases, the separation often involves some sort of exile (usually for the man) and/or some sort of imprisonment or confinement (usually for the woman). There may be progress toward marriage with the rival as well. However, in the full, comic version, the lover manages to return from exile, defeat the rival, and marry the beloved. This may be due to a change in status of one or the other lover, either through some sort of discovery or through some accomplishment. For example, the lover may be rejected by the beloved's family due to his social status. It might then be discovered that he really is has right social status, or he might accomplish something that changes his status (for example, in Chinese works, he may pass the imperial exams, thus securing a position in the bureaucracy). The final union often involves spiritual overtones and even in tragic versions there is often an implication of spiritual union after death.

It is not surprising that *Titanic*, the largest grossing film in history, follows this structure very closely. Of course, most works will not follow the structure precisely. They must vary it somewhat. Otherwise they will seem merely repetitive. As I noted in chapter 3, a prototypical work almost necessarily involves some nonprototypical properties. Thus *Titanic* involves some fairly simple variations. It begins with Rose, the heroine, engaged to Cal. Cal has been chosen by Rose's mother due to his wealth. Rose has agreed to the marriage, but obviously loathes Cal. Thus we have the standard rival figure, with the slight (and fairly common) variation that he is introduced before the romantic hero or lover. Cal and Rose fall in love, despite their class difference. Rose's mother vehemently opposes this connection. There is no real possibility for exile, since they are on a ship. But Jack is imprisoned. Here we find two small variations. First, there is the gender switch, as the heroine is somewhat more likely to be confined (though confining the hero is hardly unknown). Second, the confinement is often the act of a parent. In this case, however, the rival takes on that parental role. This too is hardly unknown. But what makes the variation more interesting in this case is that, throughout the film, Cal is ambiguously father and husband. For example, he escorts Rose's mother far more frequently than he escorts Rose, and his general attitude toward Rose is the attitude of a father to a child. In part, this may be due to a sort of cognitive pressure exerted by the prototype. In any case, Jack manages to escape and rejoin his beloved, but he dies and they are permanently separated—until the end of the film when we see the young Rose and the young Jack reunited before the camera swirls up into the light, suggesting either a dream or a heavenly reunion after death.

The second universal prototype structure is heroic. Heroic tragicomedy begins with a stable society. The rightful leader of the society is either deposed or prevented from assuming his position, often by a close relative (e.g., a sibling or parent). This leads to his exile, an exile usually accompanied by imagery of death. In the full version, when the leader is in exile, a threat arises against the home society, most often some foreign invasion. The hero (i.e., the deposed leader) returns to defeat the threat. Having defeated the threat, he resumes leadership of the society, often reconciling with the relative who deposed him initially. In a peculiar development, this seemingly perfect ending is often followed by a sort of epilogue in which the ruler laments all that has happened, perhaps giving up leadership again for a period of time during which he wanders and, in some cases, undergoes punishment for the devastations of war. (The reasons for this epilogue are complex. I discuss them in chapter 4 of *The Mind*.)

King Lear provides a fascinating case of this structure, more complexly varied and more innovative than *Titanic*'s version of the romantic plot. The story begins with a sort of convoluted usurpation where Lear himself surrenders the throne to his deceitful daughters. A more classical case of dispossession occurs shortly thereafter when these daughters deny him the vestigial powers he had retained. Though Lear initiates the usurpation, it is the daughters who carry it through. Another variation here is the shift in sex from male to female, for it is rarely a female character who usurps power. When Lear is fully deposed by Goneril and Regan, he is exiled as well, which is to say, he is sent away from home to live a wandering, homeless existence. There is ample imagery of death as well.

It is just at this point that the threat to the kingdom arises in the form of a foreign invasion. Here the strangest and most engaging variation occurs: Lear is on the side of the invaders. This variation is not unheard of. But it is certainly unusual as it places the deposed hero on the wrong side. The variation is further complicated by the presence of Cordelia, whose story is a second heroic tragedy involving dispossession by a relative and exile. Indeed, there is even an element of this in Albany who is also denied his rightful position. (Recall that Albany was in line to inherit the entire kingdom.) In keeping with this last point, Albany now arises as the rightful heir who defeats the invasion and, in so doing, overcomes the usurpers (both Lear's and his own). This leads to further complexities at the end, since Lear, Cordelia, and Albany all seem entitled to the throne—for Shakespeare has in effect given us three heroic plots, one for each of these characters. Shakespeare solves this problem by having Lear and Cordelia die. This is fitting in that Albany's character most closely follows the prototype. Though he is not exiled, he defeats the invaders, rather than joining with them. At this point, a very short epilogue begins where Albany expresses deep distress over the events and indicates that he cannot be king. In addition to all this, the heroic structure is manifest yet again in the Gloucester subplot. Part of Shakespeare's genius was his ability to generate these multiple and innovative variations on a standard structure and weave them together into a tightly unified drama.

The final prototypical narrative structure is what I call "sacrificial." It begins with some communal violation of nature or divine will. This is routinely an act of pride, greed, or both. It is usually a violation involving food, but this varies considerably. The sin leads to communal devastation, either famine or something close to famine, and death. The only way to stop the communal devastation is through sacrifice, most often a human sacrifice. The sacrifice serves as recompense for the initial violation. On its completion, the society is restored, usually through great plenty. This sort of story is different from the heroic and romantic structures in that, outside agricultural societies where famine is a constant worry, it is not frequently retold in multiple versions. However, it does appear in all or almost all societies, and it often appears with singular importance. For example, in the West, the number of canonical sacrificial narratives is far smaller than the number of romantic or heroic narratives. However, the single most important narrative in the Western world (sometimes referred to as "the greatest story ever told") is the story of the fall and redemption of humankind. The fall was caused by a hubristic violation of divine law and nature, a violation involving food, that led to communal devastation in our exile from the Eden, a garden of plenty. Our triple curse in this exile was to have to labor to produce food, to have to labor in childbirth, and to die. The only way we could return to the garden and its plenty was through sacrifice, specifically human sacrifice. This was performed by Jesus.

In *The Mind and Its Stories,* I have argued that, cross-culturally, the majority of lyric poems are implicitly narrative and that the narratives they imply are, most often, just these three as well. I will conclude with a brief discussion of "The Triumph of Life" as an implicit sacrificial narrative. Though Shelley's poem does not present a complete story, it suggests a narrative context—specifically, the context of sacrificial tragicomedy. Certainly, Shelley has put the prototype through some significant variations. Nonetheless, the poem preserves prominent features of the genre. First, we are clearly dealing with communal devastation. In keeping with the reversals in the poem, this devastation is "Life" rather than death. But the poem makes clear that life is genuinely death. This is hardly unique to Shelley. It is after all one main point of the Christian sacrificial narrative which makes life the period of exile from the garden. Indeed, in Shelley's poem, the devastation of the society is contrasted directly with the Edenic surroundings (e.g., "the fountains whose melodious dew//Out of their mossy cells forever burst" [ll. 67–8], as opposed to the path of society "Thick strewn with summer dust" [l. 45], "that path where flowers never grew" [l. 65]). Moreover, this devastation has resulted from the greed of the frenzied masses who follow the chariot and from the pride of the leaders condemned in the course of the poem. It is a communal sin which has produced communal devastation, more or less directly on the model of Eden.

But sacrifice itself—the crucial element—is apparently missing from Shelley's poem. Of course, poems are not complete plots. They are portions, moments of such plots. Moreover, this is a fragment, an unfinished work. Thus one need not expect sacrifice to appear in the poem. However, there is in fact a strong suggestion of sacrifice. Specifically, the poem gives us two heroes, two figures who have escaped communal devastation—Socrates and Jesus. In the Christian world, Jesus is the sacrificial victim par excellence, the paradigmatic hero of the sacrificial plot. Socrates, in contrast, is not widely viewed in this way. But he too was an innocent man killed by society. I believe it is important that Shelley lists Socrates here and that Socrates' execution has not been viewed as a salvationary sacrifice. Had Shelley named only Jesus, we might take him to be making a religious point. We might imagine him to be saying that Jesus did perform the sacrifice that allows our restoration, even if, individually, we repeatedly recommit the sins that keep us exiled from the garden. In other words, we might take Shelley to be advocating the truth of the Christian sacrificial narrative. But by including Socrates, he seems to suggest that such sacrifices are simply a manifestation of the pernicious "triumph of life." They are not salvationary. They cannot be.

I'm sure Shelley had never formulated to himself anything like the structure of sacrificial tragicomedy. Nonetheless, in this poem, he is both implying and in effect disputing that structure, along with the principles that underlie it. Communal devastation is not the mystical result of ancestral transgression and it cannot be reversed by sacrifice. Apparent sacrifice is simply the murder of innocents by the state. The point is related to Shelley's political views and connects with the military imagery of the "triumph." In this way, Shelley's poem is a particularly apt example for a discussion of literary universals. It manifests a universal structure. But at the same time it shows that such universality is not determinative. We can reject the social and political implications of our common prototypes even as we are, in part, repeating them. Shelley's poem is also an excellent example for it shows the interpretive value of seeing individual works in relation to universal structures. Placing "The Triumph of Life" in the context of sacrificial tragicomedy reveals things about the poem—including political implications—that we would not otherwise be likely to see.

CHAPTER **6**

The Reader
How Literature Makes Us Feel

For many years, affective psychology—the psychology of emotion—was widely seen as an entirely separate field from cognitive psychology. Feeling was viewed as something noncognitive. However, in the past decade or so, emotion has become an increasingly important topic in cognitive science. Far from being the opposite of thought, emotion is now viewed as intimately bound up with thought, to such an extent that one cannot fully understand cognition without understanding emotion, and one cannot fully understand emotion without understanding cognition.

Standard cognitive accounts treat emotion as a form of "appraisal." In other words, emotion results from a type of evaluation in which one judges the implications of a certain situation for oneself. One implicitly weighs the possible consequences of the situation in terms of their likelihood and their degree of positive or negative consequence. (The word "implicitly" is important here. As Smith and Kirby note, "most appraisal theorists have . . . maintained that appraisal can occur automatically and outside of focal awareness" [84].) The higher the probability and degree of consequence, the stronger the subsequent emotion. The stronger the subsequent emotion, the more likely it is that emotive responses will displace reasoning processes and result in involuntary actions (such as flight in fear). The knowledge that there are snakes in this part of the world may give rise to a little concern and particular attention to one's feet, but will probably not displace ordinary, meandering cognition. The presence of an unpleasant looking dog in the distance may give rise to greater fear, with proportionately greater likelihood of flight, and so on. The appearance of a wolf nearby will almost certainly give rise to flight (or freezing, another involuntary fear response) and the suppression of all unrelated cognition.

Crucial foundational work on emotion and cognition was done by Nico Frijda in the mid-1980s. Ortony, Clore, and Collins did important early work on the topic as well. All this has bearing on literary study. However, the cognitive theorist who is perhaps most directly relevant for understanding art and emotion is Keith Oatley. Oatley too was one of the early writers on this topic. Indeed, he coauthored two classic essays on emotion with Philip Johnson-Laird, one of the fathers of cognitive science. His work is no less mainstream and no less foundational than that of Frijda, Ortony, and others. Nonetheless, there are some significant differences between Oatley's work and that of other cognitive scientists. In part, these stem from Oatley's unusual background. He is not only a cognitive scientist, who has worked in neuroscience (see his *Brain Mechanisms* and *Perceptions*). He is also an award winning novelist. His *Case of Emily V* received a Commonwealth Writers Prize in 1994. Moreover, Oatley's two careers are not unrelated. Oatley has a deep *psychological* interest in literature and one of his central contentions is that cognitive science needs to address literature—to study literature, to rethink its hypotheses and analyses in light of literature. For Oatley, experimental research is very important. However, it is incomplete. Judging response times to isolated words flashed on a screen tells us something, but it does not tell us everything. It does not tell us the sorts of things literature tells us. Perhaps most importantly, it does not tell us about the complexity of human relations. And these relations are central to understanding emotion.

In the following pages, I will make occasional reference to other theorists, such as Ed Tan, one of the most influential writers on emotion and film. However, I will focus on Oatley's work—recounting, but also extending it at points—as it is not only influential and highly plausible, but also uniquely suited to the study of art.

Just What Are Emotions?

Oatley begins his major work on emotion and literature, *Best Laid Schemes,* with a general, *functional* account of emotion that draws on and extends the standard appraisal theory outlined above. A functional account sees emotion as having a purpose within some system—here, cognition. As Oatley puts it, "emotions are part of a solution to problems of organizing knowledge and action in a world that is imperfectly known and in which we have limited resources" (*Best* 3). Suppose I am out on the savannah. I have limited knowledge. Specifically, I do not know that a lion is moving in my direction, but is currently out of visual range. If I knew this, then I would not have gone out to the savannah. Suddenly, I see the lion. If I had unlimited cognitive resources and unlimited knowledge, I could think through the problem of what to do. However, I have limited cognitive resources and limited knowledge. Reasoning will take a long time, and perhaps lead to the wrong conclusion anyway. An emotion—here, the emotion of fear—solves that problem. It halts my inferential reasoning, which might otherwise get bogged down in trying to weigh uncertain outcomes, and supplies an actional response (flight).

But how exactly does this work, algorithmically? Oatley (developing the earlier work of Oatley and Johnson-Laird) maintains that the specific function of emotion is "communication." This communication is twofold. First, there is internal communication. The human mind is *modular*. In other words, it is organized into numerous systems. The relative autonomy of cognitive systems is important because it allows us to do many things (e.g., walk and talk) at the same time, and to do many things even when a particular system or module is damaged. On the other hand, modularity gives rise to problems. Different systems may issue contradictory directives. One system may be saying, "Keep walking" (i.e., it may be executing the procedural schemas and subschemas for walking), while another is saying, "Stay here, a car is coming." We need cognitive means of hierarchizing these directives.[1]

Extending Oatley somewhat, we may say that there are two sorts of process that can (and do) solve the problem of competing directives from different modules. One is purely mechanical—some principle that, automatically hierarchizes systems in a fixed way. In Oatley's account, that is the function of emotion. The other process is rational decision. That is part of the function of the central executive. Of course, given these two, our problem recurs. What if a mechanical principle conflicts with a central executive decision? Suppose that I am in the field. I am thinking about gathering food. I hear something. This is processed by some system and identified as the roar of a lion. Fear, in this model, is not first of all a feeling but the communication of one system's information to all other systems. What is there to prevent the central executive from overriding the message about the lion, including the system-prescribed action of flight? If I can override the mechanical rule, doesn't that just put me back in the original situation where my thought processes may lead me to faulty conclusions—in short, where I try to decide what to do while the lion comes and eats me? Though Oatley does not discuss it this way, preventing this situation is clearly the function of the dysphoric *feeling* of fear. It is very easy to have a default mechanical directive without any associated feeling. This happens, for example, in grammar. I have no feeling associated with using either "went" or "goed." I can easily override the mechanical rule that ordinarily leads me to use "went." The feeling of an emotion (e.g., the feeling of fear) helps prevent this in emotion-eliciting circumstances. Considered from the other side, if emotion is generally functional, the feeling that accompanies an emotion should have some function also. It seems most likely that this function is to discourage any overriding of the mechanical rule (e.g., "Run away!") by the central executive. Fear is unpleasant. I want to put an end to it. I do put an end to it by engaging in the relevant action, which is to say, by running away. If I do not run away, the feeling of fear remains. The motivation becomes more intense as the fear becomes more intense, eventually reaching the point where the central executive can no longer override its imperatives. While the point is obvious for fear, it works equally for anger and aggression, disgust and avoidance, and so forth.

But, again, Oatley's focus is not on the experiential feeling. Rather, it is on the mechanical principle, which communicates crucial information to other cognitive systems. In connection with this, Oatley and Johnson-Laird distinguish two different types of message that can be communicated from an emotional system to other systems. The first is a *control message*. This is what serves directly to hierarchize systems. Suppose that some food-gathering system is currently dominant. I hear something which some aural monitoring system identifies as a lion. That system then sends out a control message, rehierarchizing modules so that the system dealing with escape predominates rather than the system dealing with food-gathering. The second type of message is a *semantic message*. This gives the reason for the control message. In the preceding example, the other systems and the central executive would receive the message "lions are about" (or something along those lines). It sometimes happens that the control message appears without an accompanying semantic message. In that case, one becomes fearful (angry, happy, or whatever), but without understanding why. As Oatley explains, "the connection between the control and semantic parts is not necessary. The potential for dissociation enables long-lasting moods to occur, as well as emotions happening for no apparent reason" (*Best* 63).

I mentioned above that Oatley and Johnson-Laird distinguish two communicative functions for emotions. We have been discussing internal communication among systems. The other communicative function is external and social; it involves communication among people. Developing Oatley's point, we may say that this also has two varieties. The first is, so to speak, "parallel"; the second is complementary. For a parallel case, we may modify the preceding example only slightly. Jones and Smith are out gathering food. Jones sees something dangerous. Part of the emotion of fear is a spontaneous expression—a facial gesture, a cry. Jones lets out his cry or contorts his face in dread. Smith hears the cry or sees Jones's face and she immediately feels fear as well. She is implicitly fearful of whatever caused Jones to cry out. For a complementary instance, imagine Jones's response when Smith expresses anger at Jones. Certainly, Jones won't be angry with himself. Rather, he may be fearful of Smith (cf. Brothers 123 on the "complementary" nature of "anger" and "submissive fear"). In both cases, the communication of emotion is not only intrapersonal, but interpersonal as well.

As already noted, Oatley's account of emotion triggering is a version of appraisal theory. Oatley particularly emphasizes agency and aims. As he puts it, "emotions depend on evaluations of what has happened in relation to the person's goals and beliefs" (*Best* 19); "Perhaps the most fundamental postulate of Oatley and Johnson-Laird's theory is that emotions are elicited not by events as such but by evaluations of events relevant to goals" (*Best* 98). Specifically, we all have numerous goals. For example, I want to have enough food. In order to have enough food, I construct subgoals. Oatley refers to any series of subgoals leading to a goal as a "plan," though such a plan need not be devised self-consciously, nor need it be complete. One of the subgoals in my implicit plan is gathering food regularly. This entails further subgoals, down to the goal of getting this particular piece of fruit right now. Another big goal is not being harmed or killed by wild beasts. That goal is the one relevant to the presence of the lion. As Oatley explains, "Monitoring mechanisms evaluate both ongoing and dormant plans and goals. They communicate these evaluations to other modules" (*Best* 51). So, my various cognitive systems are organized around goals. These systems are continually open to appraise the current situation in their own terms. My "personal safety" module is continually open to assessing conditions in terms of personal safety even while "dormant," which is to say, even when it is not the predominant system, even when my "adequate food" module is active and I am running the procedural schemas for gathering food. Specifically, Oatley argues that these modules are sensitive to significant changes in the likelihood of achieving their dominant goals. He refers to "changes of evaluation of the likely outcome of plans" as "junctures" (*Best* 51) and maintains that "Emotions emerge at . . . significant junctures in plans" (*Best* 25). I am plucking fruit from the tree when I hear a lion. The presence of a lion radically changes the likelihood of achieving my goal of not being harmed or killed by wild beasts. In turn, this change triggers my "personal safety" module, producing the emotion of fear, with its particular control signal and resultant hierarchization of systems.

Here, we might ask just how many control signals there are, which is to say, how many emotions or *basic emotion signals* there are. Oatley and Johnson-Laird follow the lead of writers such as Ekman in positing a small number of *basic emotions* from which other emotions may be understood to derive. The Oatley/Johnson-Laird list comprises happiness, sadness, fear, anger and disgust. Oatley and Johnson-Laird do not claim the list is complete.

They accept that there may be additions to this list. For example, Ekman adds contempt, surprise, and interest. However, Oatley and Johnson-Laird do emphasize that the complete list will be quite limited.[2] In any case, for Oatley and Johnson-Laird, our various goal-directed systems monitor situations and, when there is a significant change in the likelihood of goal achievement, the relevant system sends out one of five (or perhaps six or seven) control signals. The happiness signal occurs when a goal is much more likely to be achieved or is being achieved. Fear occurs when a particular type of goal—a self-preservation goal—is threatened. Sadness occurs with the complete loss of a major goal. The anger signal results from the frustration of a plan that is currently active. Disgust is aroused by the violation of a "gustatory goal" (55).

There is clearly something odd about this account. Fear and disgust respond to particular types of goal. But they are not even types of the same general sort. A self-preservation goal might be of the same type as, say, a pleasure goal (if we posit that self-preservation and pleasure are two overarching aims of humans). In contrast, a gustatory goal would seem to be parallel to some other sensory goal (e.g., an auditory or visual goal). Anger rests on a distinction between goals that are active and goals that are dormant. But none of the other emotions bears on this distinction. Sadness stresses the complete loss of a major goal, but no emotion refers to the partial loss of a goal, or the complete loss of a minor goal. In short, the defining criteria for these basic emotions do not seem to be of the same logical type. Perhaps it turns out that emotions are not distributed logically and that only some combinations of disparate factors produce emotions. For example, it may be that gustatory goals bear on emotion while other sensory goals do not. Things like that do happen in biological evolution. Nonetheless, it would be valuable to address that issue, to consider the other possibilities and why they do not occur.

In any case, this is the list of emotions that Oatley and Johnson-Laird see as basic. To say they are basic, however, is not to say that they are unanalyzable. They are, of course, not analyzable into component emotions (that is what makes them basic). However, they do share the common structure of emotions and therefore have the following structural components:

> *Eliciting conditions.* These are the circumstances that give rise to an emotion (e.g., an attacking lion is an eliciting condition for fear).
> *Action readiness.* Action readiness is one's orientation to engage in the particular sorts of action that fit a given emotion. For example, the action for anger is aggression or attack. Thus, when the control signal for anger goes out, the procedural schemas for attack are

brought up; one's body is set for attack (facing the source of the goal frustration, leaning forward), and so on.

Conscious preoccupation. When we feel an emotion, we think about it and about things relevant to it. When angry, we think angry thoughts, focusing in particular on the eliciting conditions for our anger. Put differently, an emotion includes a particular attentional focus. When I am walking in the dark and become fearful, I begin to pay attention to potentially dangerous items.

Expression. Expression is one's spontaneous manifestation of the emotion externally in sounds, gestures, et cetera.

Bodily Disturbance. This is the spontaneous manifestation of the emotion internally in physiological changes, such as respiratory rate.

Phenomenological Tone. This is the experiential feeling associated with the emotion.

These different components bear on different aspects of Oatley's model. Eliciting conditions are the conditions that indicate a significant change in the likelihood of one's achieving a particular goal. Action readiness and conscious preoccupation are the result of the rehierarchization of cognitive systems by the control signal. Bodily disturbance may be the manifestation of physiological changes that are part of the control signal or they may be necessary conditions for action readiness. Though Oatley does not focus on phenomenological tone, I have suggested its function in dissuading the central executive from overriding emotional control signals. Finally, expressive outcomes are what allow the external or social communication of emotion.

This still leaves the issue of the precise nature of the goals. In many ways, the goals that define our cognitive systems are unremarkable. Some concern self-preservation (getting food, not being mauled). Others concern reproduction (having sex). However, there is one important pattern to emotion-defining goals that is emphasized by Oatley. These goals—or at least the plans that lead to these goals—are often deeply social. Specifically, our most important goals and sub-goals are bound up with what Oatley calls "joint plans," plans that we share with other people, plans that we enact cooperatively with others. Indeed, Oatley goes so far as to maintain that "human beings are cognitively specialized for interacting with other cognitive beings in joint plans" (*Best* 13). According to Oatley, the most intense and consequential instances of most emotions bear not on individual plans, but on joint plans. Thus, "anger . . . is primarily an emotion of joint plans, in which the other person has not done his or her part as he or she should" (*Best* 211). Similarly, "Sadness occurs with the loss of a role relationship. In its largest and most obvious social form, it is the grief of bereavement or separation in which the loss involves that part of the self that was engaged in joint plans with another" (*Best* 213). Hatred—which Oatley and Johnson-Laird consider a form of disgust—involves "Discontinuation of joint plan or disengagement" (*Best* 213). Perhaps most importantly, both for ordinary life and for literary study, love too is centrally a matter of joint plans: "To declare that one loves someone is not just to say one likes that person. It is to commit oneself to that person in a long-term role. It anticipates a future of joint activity, asserts that one will engage in it willingly and wholeheartedly" (*Best* 213).

Here, too, we might extend Oatley's analysis slightly. Oatley often treats joint plans as if they were simply a matter of a division of labor. Thus, Smith (who installs appliances) gets angry with Jones (who sells appliances) because Jones has failed to deliver the washing machine that Smith has been hired to install. They share a joint plan—one delivers the machine; the other installs it. Anger results when one partner fails to fulfill the obligations of the joint plans. However, it is important to distinguish joint plans that are based on a division of labor from joint plans that are based on an actual sharing of what might be called "defining" goals—and, even beyond that, an incorporation of another person's goals into one's own plans. Consider Smith and Jones. In a sense, they share a goal. They both wish to install the washing machine. However, this "shared" goal is itself defined by distinct goals for each of them. Smith wants the washing machine installed so that she will receive her payment and so that she will continue to have a good reputation for installing such machines and will have steady work. Jones wants the machine installed so that he will receive his payment (e.g., the machine won't be returned or the payment won't be delayed) and so that he will continue to sell such machines. Smith's goals have no intrinsic value for Jones, and Jones's goals have no intrinsic value for Smith. In each case, the success of one person's goals is purely instrumental for the other. In reality, marriage is probably the same. However, our idea of romantic love—the idea that is addressed in literature—is one where each person's goals become intrinsically valuable for the other person. In other words, the defining goals of one lover become incorporated into the life plans of the other lover, not as mere means to egocentric goals, but as defining goals themselves. Indeed, in the ideal case of this, the lover hierarchizes the beloved's goals above his/her own. Moreover, the lover's own goals become bound up inseparably with the presence, activity, experience of the beloved (e.g., he/she does not just want a nice home; he/she wants a nice home with the beloved). Thus, in literature, the most intense form of sadness is typically the death of one's beloved, because it necessarily devastates one's goals. Conversely, the most intense form of happiness in literature is most often union with one's beloved—not momentary joining, but the continuous sharing of life—because this is a necessary condition for one's most important goals. In order to distinguish this from the more common division of labor (which is also part of literature and romantic love), I will refer to the mutual incorporation of goals as shared or joint *projects,* rather than shared or joint plans.

Literature, Emotion, and Indirect Appraisal

This account of emotion is, in my view, quite plausible. We care about our goals and plans, and we feel things when our plans are successful, when they fail, and when they seem to be succeeding or failing. But this account apparently runs into difficulties when it comes to literature. After all, we do not have goals or plans with respect to literature—or, rather, the goals and plans that bear on emotions are not ours. When Juliet dies, that bears on the plans and emotions of Romeo. Why do we feel emotion here? In *Best Laid Schemes,* Oatley has a fairly straightforward account of this: "people can mentally simulate the plans of others and understand their emotions, just as they can run simulations of their own plans and test their own emotional reactions in advance. In understanding narrative a subject may identify with the protagonist of a plan, and the simulation can have many of the properties of real plans, including the property of eliciting emotions appropriately to the junctures that the plan reaches" (*Best* 107–8).[3] Of course, for this to work, "we need to postulate that a person can identify with a protagonist taking on goals and plans as if they were his or her own as a narrative unfolds" (*Best* 108).

But there are two theoretical problems here. Both are suggested by Oatley's reference to identification. The first, and most obvious, is that a literary narrative most often presents us with a fiction, so there are no real goals and plans at stake in the story itself. The second is that none of our own goals bears on the story either. Even when I witness some real situation, I may not share the emotion of those involved if I have no goals implicated in that situation. Why, then, is it that in literature we do commonly identify with the protagonist, despite his/her fictionality and the noninvolvement of any of our own prior goals?

We will return to these questions in the final section of this chapter and, again, in the next chapter. For now, I will simply assume that identification occurs (as it clearly does).[4] Given this, we can understand the response of a reader largely in terms of the experiences of the main characters in the narrative. In this way, an understanding of character emotion should go a long way toward explaining audience emotion. As Oatley puts it, "In cognitive terms a plot is typically a plan of one or more characters. A plan meets some vicissitude, perhaps a reversal of the fortunes of the protagonist. Communication of emotions to a spectator or reader occurs at such a juncture, because a plot allows a spectator or reader to identify with a character. But then it is our involvement in the plans of the plot that causes our own emotions" (*Best* 400).

Before going on, however, we need to develop this point a little further and make it slightly more complex. Ed Tan's *Emotion and the Structure of Narrative Film* sets out to present an account of audience emotion with a particular emphasis on problem solving and interest. Tan is concerned with what keeps viewers watching a movie, what keeps them engaged in the narrative. This is a different issue from what makes them cry or laugh. However, Tan's answer to this question has consequences for Oatley's concerns. Tan argues that a viewer remains interested in a film to the extent that he/she is able (1) to envision "a number of possible structures" resulting from the current narrative situation, (2) to "continually test [the] probability" that any one of those structures will be realized, and (3), in the course of this testing, to feel that there is "progress made in the direction of closure, or more precisely, the *preferred final situation*" (98). Thus, for Tan, the viewer does have goals and he/she continually evaluates progress toward these goals in the course of the film. Specifically, the viewer sees part of the film—boy meets girl, say. He/she begins to construct possible outcomes for the narrative, possible scenarios of what might occur in the future. Most importantly for our purposes, these possible outcomes include a preferred final outcome for the entire narrative—the two marry and live happily ever after, the woman realizes that the man is too patriarchal to make a suitable husband and leaves him to become a filmmaker, or whatever. Our interest is sustained to the degree that we feel we are advancing toward the final outcome, but without a full conviction of what that outcome will be and of precisely what will lead to it.[5]

Oatley's account assumes, somewhat too simply, that we all identify with the protagonist and desire the fulfillment of his/her goals. Tan's account assumes, somewhat too simply, that interest relies on something like suspense. However, each one does indicate something important about our emotional response to narrative. If we add Tan's account to Oatley's, we see that the audience member's response to a narrative may appear to be a direct function of the protagonist's goals. But in fact it is a result of the reader's formulation of a goal (the preferred final outcome), even though that is a goal for the characters rather than for the reader him/herself. Thus our emotional experience of a literary work is a function of junctural evaluation of narrative events in relation to our own goals—specifically our preferred final outcome, a goal that need not be the same as that of the protagonist (e.g., we may feel that the hero is pursuing the wrong woman and should really end up with someone else).[6] Of course, Oatley is right that the reader's goals are most often the direct result of identification with the protagonist.

Indeed, whether we fully identify or not, the junctural points in appraising the likelihood of our own preferred final outcome will usually coincide with the junctural points in the protagonist's appraisal of his/her situation. The crucial difference is that our appraisal (thus our emotion) need not be the same as that of the protagonist. Indeed, it need not be the same even when we share the protagonist's goals (which is usually the case).

This final point too is clarified by Tan. Specifically, drawing on Frijda, Tan takes appraisal to bear on the "situational meaning" of some event or condition. The situational meaning is the significance of some situation to a person. In Oatley's terms, we could say that the situational meaning is the relevance of a given situation to the achievement of one's goals. As Tan notes, it is quite possible for there to be "differences between the situational meaning structure for the viewer and the situational meaning for the character. For instance, characters may be aware of only a part of the total situation seen by the viewer" (184). When Romeo finds Juliet in the tomb, the situational meaning for him is completely different from the situational meaning for us—and it is that discrepancy that makes Romeo's suicide so tragic. Had Juliet actually died, we would no longer be sustaining the hope that the two would be united (i.e., the hope that our goal of their union would be achieved). Romeo's suicide would only complete and in a sense resolve the destruction of that hope, a destruction already accomplished by Juliet's death. However, we know that Romeo is just on the edge of being able to live with Juliet. Thus we lose our preferred outcome, our goal is destroyed, just at the moment when it could finally be fulfilled.

Causing Junctures: Plans and Projects in Titanic

Here, we might ask a seemingly simple question: Why do junctures in plans occur as they do? How does it come about that our assessments change so much and so frequently with respect to the likelihood of achieving our goals? It is obvious to everyone that this happens. And, in particular cases, it is obvious why it happens. But what conditions allow for the ubiquity of such changes, changes that leave us almost constantly in some emotional state?

Oatley says that junctures result from three sources: "first, that human action has many goals not just one; second, that such action takes place in a world in which we have limited resources and imperfect knowledge; and, third, that much of human action is undertaken jointly with others" (*Best* 12). We may consider these one by one.

Knowledge. If our knowledge were perfect, then we would judge the likelihood of achieving a particular goal correctly from the outset. But, in fact, we continually learn new things while pursuing our goals. This learning leads to a change in our perceptions. It is well known that dramatic tension in literature and film often results from the manipulation of knowledge. From the beginning, *Titanic* relies on the audience knowing that the ship will sink and that most of the passengers will die. We have this information when Rose learns that there are too few lifeboats; when Ismay (managing director of the White Star Line, which owns Titanic) convinces the captain to forge ahead with full engines, despite possible dangers; when the captain receives an iceberg warning; when a member of the crew remarks that the stillness of the water will make icebergs more difficult to spot; when we learn that the lookouts' binoculars have been lost. Each of these points becomes a sort of juncture for us, though they are almost insignificant for the characters. In fact, this discrepancy gives rise to interesting complications, in some ways like the moment when Romeo enters the tomb to find Juliet apparently dead.

Perhaps the most interesting aspect of this discrepancy is that, given our knowledge of the historical outcome, our junctures operate differently than they would have operated for the crew of the Titanic, had they realized that these were junctures. Consider, for example, the moment when the captain receives the iceberg warning. This becomes a juncture for us in the opposite direction from what it should have been for the captain at the time. The captain should have experienced the warning as a point where the likelihood of hitting an iceberg suddenly increased. However, looked at from the perspective of the ultimate sinking of the ship, we see it as a moment when the seeming inevitability of the collision is significantly reduced. It is reduced because the captain had information that could have led him to avoid the iceberg. Indeed, every junctural moment bearing on the accident is of this sort. In relation to our own ordinary lives, these are akin to junctures of retrospectively recognized opportunities that we have missed. By way of contrast, imagine a version of the movie in which the captain of the Titanic had taken all possible precautions. There were enough lifeboats. They traveled at a reasonable speed. They avoided the area where there was an iceberg warning. Yet, somehow, they hit an iceberg anyway and, for uncontrollable and unforeseeable reasons, the lifeboats were rendered useless.

The oddity here is that the captain and the crew certainly did have staying alive as one important goal. Moreover, they were certainly aware that the sinking of the ship would prevent the satisfaction of that goal. Nonetheless, they did not experience these very significant changes in the likelihood of hitting an iceberg as junctures. They did not reorder their cognitive hierarchies, reevaluate their practices, and so on. Why not? Part of the answer is simple, and a matter of knowledge. Our assessment of junctures is just as fallible as our assessment of initial likelihoods.

Multiple goals. But, of course, that is not the whole answer. The movie points to other explanations as well. It is clear that Ismay does not want to let concerns about safety get in the way of increased profits. The captain suppresses worry about icebergs so that it will not interfere with the glory of his final voyage. This brings us to another of Oatley's explanations for why junctures occur. Junctures occur because we have multiple goals. What difference does that make? Sometimes our goals conflict. Sometimes we have to make decisions favoring one goal rather than another. Sometimes a change in the likelihood of goal achievement has nothing to do with external circumstances, but with our own actions, as necessitated by another goal. Ismay certainly had a goal of the ship not sinking. But aspects of the plan leading to that goal (e.g., the exercise of caution in speed of travel) contradicted another goal—that of breaking records in speed of travel and thus gaining greater publicity. The captain too suffered from goal conflict, whereby the plan guaranteeing the ship's safety tacitly contradicted the plan to achieve celebrity on his last voyage. Of course, this is just the sort of dilemma emotion was supposed to resolve. The problem is that, in this case, all the goals were involved with emotion. Indeed, emotion probably was the decisive factor here too. Unfortunately, as it turned out, the wrong emotion won.

Oatley does not fully discuss the mechanics of this process. However, it would seem to be something along the following lines. Contradictory junctural messages in effect inhibit one another. If one is stronger, then the system is hierarchized according to the stronger message. If neither is stronger, then perhaps the decision is thrown over to the central executive, or perhaps the entire system gets locked up, like a computer trying to execute some problematic command. One could understand this in connectionist terms. One set of experiences activates fear inputs. Another activates desire inputs. The level of activation and the connection strengths determine the degree to which fear or desire is activated. If one or the other is activated much more strongly, then its control message—and presumably its semantic message—will predominate. Imagine the following situation. Bob and Jane are strongly attracted to one another. Each has a series of sensations and thoughts that give high activation to inputs that have high connection strengths with sexual desire. At the same time, they experience relatively weak activation of inputs rather weakly connected with fear (of, say, pregnancy). This may give rise to a situation in which the fear signal is entirely inhibited. It may give rise to a situation in which both signals are sent, but the desire signal predominates strongly. In this case, Bob and Jane may adopt precautions against pregnancy if it is easy for them to incorporate this into the actions guided by desire (e.g., if a contraceptive device is ready to hand), but not otherwise. In other words, the desire-based action readiness, conscious preoccupation, and so on, would be the ones they follow, with the contradictory fear signal having little or no impact.

Here we can consider the case of the captain. Evidently, the prospect of honor at the end of a swift passage gave a high degree of activation to input units that were themselves strongly connected to goals involving social esteem. In other words, the mere discussion of a highly celebrated early arrival was enough to give strong activation to some units that were very strongly linked to motivationally effective goals (i.e., goals with strong behavioral links). In contrast, the iceberg warning, the stillness of the water, and so on, evidently gave only low activation to inputs that were themselves only weakly connected with the goal of keeping the ship afloat. Moreover, this goal was itself only weakly linked with behaviors. All this has come about for the usual Hebbian reasons—the captain had not been on a sinking ship before, so the connections of warning signals to saving behaviors had become very weak. The weakness of these connections is actually addressed in the film when Lovett explains that the captain was relying on twenty years of experience. This experience was codified in connection strengths. Over two decades, each time the captain received a warning, but encountered no iceberg, the connection strength between warnings and icebergs decreased. Since encountering an iceberg is one eliciting condition for fear in this context, the decrease in that connection was simultaneously a decrease in the fear—thus a decrease in the action readiness, attentional focus, and so on—produced by such a warning. In consequence, each new warning item produced only a slight activation that dissipated quickly in the captain's neural network. In ordinary circumstances, that still might have sufficed. Even one item (e.g., the iceberg warning) may have been enough to result in a mild fear that would have led to caution, and thus perhaps to the prevention of disaster. But any such mild feeling, and consequent behavior, were overridden by the much more strongly activated feeling of ambition.

What is interesting here—and also true to life—is that the various danger signals appear much more real and significant to an observer. The captain's ambitions are excited by talk and conjecture only. The fear should have been a response to real, palpable conditions. This illuminates the importance of imagination. The captain's imagination of his own honor was so vivid and salient that it was more real—more consequential for his cognitive systems—than aspects of the real world. (In chapter 7, we will see how this is possible cognitively.) The point bears not only on the literal progress of the plot. It implicates art itself, including *Titanic,* for art has this same vividness and salience and can easily become more real for us than reality.

Joint action. The plot sequence we have been discussing—the part of the story that leads to the sinking of the ship—is implicitly bound up with joint plans. For example, the captain's internal goal conflicts would have been tragic enough had they affected only him. But they did not. They were part of joint plans with the crew and with the passengers. The magnitude of the tragedy results, in part, from the disastrous failure of the captain in following through on his part in those joint plans.

The romantic plot of the film also treats joint plans—or rather joint projects. Indeed, it does so more explicitly and in many ways more intensely. This is just what one would expect. Joint projects are most often closely bound up with family relations. The ideal marriage is one in which the partners incorporate one another's goals into their own plans. The ideal parent is one who incorporates his/her child's goals—or at least those that are in the child's best interests—into his/her own plans. Thus the ideal husband makes his wife's professional success part of his own plans, and the ideal wife does the same for her husband. The ideal parent incorporates the child's goals of success into his/her own goals, working to give the child education, and so forth.

One problem with joint plans is that they often conflict with individually held plans. Emotionally, such conflict is worst in those cases where two people are supposed to have a shared project. The most extreme form of this occurs when one person not only fails to incorporate the other person's goals, but actually sets out to impose his/her own egocentric goals on that other person—when, for example, a husband tries to impose his self-serving preferences on his wife, or a mother tries to impose her egocentric preferences on her child.

These are, of course, the central conflicts in the romantic plot line of *Titanic.* One might expect Rose's mother to be concerned with Rose's happiness and fulfillment. However, far from incorporating Rose's goals into her plans, she instead imposes her own goals on Rose. Thus she makes Rose part of a joint plan—marriage to Cal—in which Rose has no interest whatsoever. The dissymmetry is repeated with Cal himself, who makes it perfectly clear that he is going to decide everything that Rose does, or even thinks. Oatley points out that anger is the result of goal frustration. This is precisely Rose's response at the beginning of the film, where she explains that, though outwardly calm, "inside, I was screaming."

In addition to the anger, we find suicidal depression when Rose runs to jump off the back of the boat. The gesture is symbolic in a psychoanalytic sense. Rose feels that she is being left behind as Cal and, more importantly, her mother forge ahead with their own plans. The attempt at suicide is, in a sense, a communication of that despairing emotion. Oatley explains that depression results in part from a sense that important goals, especially goals important to self-definition, have been lost (300–3). Certainly, that is Rose's sense. She sees no possibility for ever following out her own goals, for defining herself through choosing and engaging in concrete pursuits, including pursuits that would involve others in mutually fulfilling joint projects. Looking ahead, she can only see a future in which she must surrender her goals to others—to Cal and her mother.

Cases such as this—cases where one loses one's own goals in joint plans imposed by others—may make it seem that the social nature of goal pursuit is simply a curse. But these negatives are balanced by positive factors in those cases where another person genuinely incorporates one's goals into his/her plans, thus facilitating one's happiness, rather than inhibiting it. The presence of such a genuine joint project in *Titanic* is almost too obvious to mention. Jack first meets Rose when she is threatening to commit suicide. He insists that he is involved in her life simply by being present at that moment and that he has no choice but to join her in her action. "You let go and I'm gonna have to jump in there after you," he tells her, introducing an important motif that recurs later in the movie. Though they are not, strictly speaking, sharing a project here, Jack has incorporated into his own plans the very possibility of Rose having any goals, or any future at all. The next day, Jack shows the same sort of concern with Rose's goals when he asks if she loves Cal. Rose repulses Jack after this question, just as she had repulsed him when he first came to prevent her suicide. The parallel is obvious and the audience can see that here too Jack is intervening to prevent a suicidal destruction of Rose's future. Thus, once again, he is concerned with the preservation of her future goals. The point develops through a detailed sharing of small goals as Jack promises that he will teach Rose how to do a number of things, such as ride a horse. The instance is specific, but the point is general. Cal operates to stifle all Rose's future goals, to subordinate them to his goals. Jack, in contrast, functions to facilitate and expand Rose's future goals. This talk of horseback riding is merely an instance of the larger freedom and independence that Rose discovers through this relationship with Jack. The point is developed to its logical conclusion when Jack leads Rose to a raft where she can survive. He does not look for a way to save himself, but stays with her, encouraging her, in effect setting aside his own goals for survival and substituting hers. His success in fostering her goals is shown at the very end of the movie. Rose sleeps beside a long row of photographs. The camera passes each one. The last is a photograph of her riding a horse.

Remembering the Way You Feel and Feeling the Way You Remember: Emotive Response to Art

But we are still left with our initial questions about the nature of literary emotion—why we feel it for events that are fictional and with which we have no egocentric involvement.

The sources of literary emotion have been examined by a number of European thinkers, beginning with Plato. But the accounts most closely related to cognitive science are probably those that derive from the ancient and Medieval Sanskrit theorists. It is worth considering the ideas of these writers before going on to a full-fledged cognitive account—in part because some recent cognitive treatments of literary emotion (including those by Oatley) have drawn heavily on the Sanskrit tradition.

A central principle of classical Indian aesthetics is that artistic works communicate emotion through their *"dhvani"* or suggestiveness. Dhvani includes all the associations that cluster around anything that a reader encounters in a work of literature or a viewer encounters in a performance. It derives from individual words, patterns of imagery, scenes, characters, narrative sequences, and so on. The suggestions themselves comprise not only other words, but a wide range of nonverbal associations (e.g., images) as well. Dhvani is in effect a PDP network. It is the set of all activated nodes connected to the work of art in any given reader's or viewer's mind. As a concept in literary and aesthetic theory, dhvani is actually quite radical in this way. *Dhvani* is not a metaphorical meaning, nor even a connotation. It is much broader—and much more clearly (one might say, algorithmically) psychological.

A millennium ago, the great Sanskrit philosopher, Abhinavagupta, asked just how this cloud of associations (in our terms, the spread of activation across a neural network) produces emotion in a reader or viewer of art. According to him, all our experiences leave traces in our memory. These traces bear with them the emotions we felt at the time. The mind accumulates these traces and they contextualize each new experience. We respond to the present in terms of the collective effect of the traces left in our memories by the past. For Abhinavagupta, this point applies both to real life and to the experience of literature. More exactly, any current experience has certain features that link it with our experiences in the past. These features are not narrowly defined, but include the entire range of *dhvani* or suggestion— verbal, imagistic, and so on. Particular suggestions may be understood as matching up with particular memory traces. In some cases, that match will lead us to recall the memory explicitly. For example, walking into a hospital, I may be reminded of the last time I was in a hospital, when my mother was having surgery. However, Abhinavagupta explains, the chain of suggestions might connect to a memory without actually leading us to recall that memory. In both cases, we, in some degree, reexperience the emotion of that memory. In other words, we feel fear, anger, sorrow, or joy as we felt it in the memory, not (necessarily) as it is relevant to the current situation. Of course, in real life, memories are not the only source of emotions. Real, current situations involve direct, new emotions, emotions that are bound up with the consequences of real events. There may be something similar in literature, resulting from simulation and identification. But, again, there are problems here. We are dealing with events that are fictional and that do not involve any of our own egocentric goals. Thus it still remains unclear why we feel emotions at junctural moments in literature. Abhinavagupta provides a possible explanation. He argues that literary emotions are the result of emotion-laden memories that have been triggered by literary events, characters, and so on, but are not self-consciously recalled.

About ten years ago, when I first read Abhinavagupta's theories, I was struck almost immediately by their coherence with basic principles of human cognition as understood in cognitive science. Centuries before the development of modern psychology, Abhinavagupta had articulated an account of literary emotion that was highly plausible and had great explanatory potential. It only lacked an adequate cognitive architecture to be developed fully and compellingly. In "Toward a Cognitive Science of Poetics," I explored this idea, relating Abhinavagupta's account to recent developments in cognitive science. (For a more fully developed version of this discussion, see chapter 2 of my *The Mind and Its Stories*.) Later, the argument of this essay was taken up by Oatley, extended, and integrated into a more encompassing account of literary cognition.

My basic argument was the following. The notion of *dhvani* may be specified in terms of the mental lexicon. *Dhvani* is all the entries that receive activation at any given point in one's experience of a work. Thus the triggers for *dhvani* include all aspects of the work that communicate activation to lexical entries. Moreover, the suggestions themselves (i.e., the items receiving activation) include not only words, but images, prototypes, exempla—and, crucially, experiential memories. I see now that this requires some refinement. Most importantly, I should have said that *dhvani* is all the elements of any memory system (lexical, episodic, or other) that receive activation as a result of the experience of the literary work. In any case, I went on from here to argue that episodic memories often bear with them the emotions that one experienced at the time of the memory. In other words, they do not merely record the fact of the emotion. Rather, they include elements that can give rise to the original emotion a second time. I left aside the issue of just how this could occur. We will discuss some possibilities in the next chapter, possibilities derived from brain research. In any case, these emotions are latent as long as the memories are latent. However, as the memories become activated, the associated feelings become activated also. This is, of course, just Abhinavagupta's view, reworked in terms of current theories.

But what about Abhinavagupta's idea that, in experiencing literature, we do not explicitly recall the memories that inspire our feelings? For Abhinavagupta, this nonrecollection is not merely incidental. It is crucial to the experience of literature. If I am watching a sad love story and begin to think self-consciously about some sad romance of my own, I will stop concentrating on the play. At best, my attention will be divided. I will no longer be thinking through and responding to the play. At least in part, I will be thinking through and responding to the biographical situation I am remembering. Thus the relevant memories, though not entirely latent, must not be fully activated either.

As it turns out, it is not at all difficult to give a cognitive account of this intermediate state of semi-activation. The state of semi-activation posited by Abhinavagupta has a direct parallel in the well-established phenomenon of priming. As we discussed in chapter 2, an item in memory is primed when it is activated to a high degree, but just below access. My contention, then, was that relevant memories are continually primed in our experience of literature. Moreover, if full activation leads us to reexperience at least some emotions, it seems likely that the partial activation that occurs in priming would have a similar, if perhaps reduced effect. Thus one might expect priming to produce just the sorts of consequence that Abhinavagupta attributed to unconscious memory traces.

On the other hand, a question arises here. If priming effects can produce the sort of intense emotions we experience in literature, then how is it that they seem to produce only relatively peripheral effects in ordinary life? One difference between literature and the world of daily experience is that in literature the memory triggers are fairly consistent and continuous for particular primed items. Thus a love story will continually prime memories of romance. This is important because priming effects decay rapidly. In daily life (e.g., in ordinary conversation), a memory will be primed once, but then it will fade, replaced by other primed memories in rapid succession. When this occurs, the primed memories are likely to have few and limited emotional consequences. In contrast, the suggestions of literary works keep the emotion-laden memories primed for long stretches of time. Thus their cumulative effect may be very strong.

In making this particular use of cognitive architecture, I was not simply appealing to Abhinavagupta's authority or common intuition. There is a great deal of empirical research on literary response that fits this account. I have pointed out elsewhere that there are many problems with this research (see, for example, *Philosophical Approaches* 308–12). However, one thing the research seems to indicate overwhelmingly is that personal memories are crucial to our emotional response to literature. Work by Seilman and Larsen indicates that literary texts elicit more "remindings" of personal memories than nonliterary texts (see also Larsen, László, and Seilman; and Halász "Emotional" and "Effect"). Research by Oatley, Angela Baison, and Seema Nundy suggests a close relation between literary emotion, empathy, and personal memory (see the accounts of this research, especially that on gender, memory, and association, in "Why" 113–4 and "Emotions and the Story

Worlds"). In short, experimental studies clearly support Aghinavagupta's ideas and the cognitive reformulation of those ideas as just outlined. At the same time, as with any other hypothesis, more research is certainly in order.

In addition to its intuitive plausibility and close relation to the empirical data, there are other advantages of the view set out in "Toward a Cognitive Science of Poetics." Perhaps the most significant is that it accounts readily for differences in response and for certain patterns across differences. It is a commonplace that our responses to literature change in the course of life, that we like different works in youth than in middle age. Intuitively, it would seem that these changes are the result of changes in experience. A memory-based account of response indicates how this could occur. The emotive nature and quality of our experiences change as we age. These changing experiences become new memories. Moreover, earlier memories fade. As a result, the collection of our memories is continually altered, and it is altered systematically. In middle age, a person is more likely to have more easily accessible memories of raising children than of having no date on a Saturday night. Similarly, male and female responses to literature differ. There are no doubt several reasons for this, but one is very likely to be systematically different memories.

The obvious objection to this theory is that it relies on a disjunction between the source of an emotion and the target of an emotion. When reading a romantic tragedy in which one of the lovers dies (e.g., *Romeo and Juliet*), the source of my sorrow (by this account) is some set of personal memories. However, the target of my sorrow—the object to which I connect the sorrow—is the death of the lover. This may seem odd. It may seem that if I feel sorrow because a romantic loss or separation hurt me, then the target of my sorrow has to be me; it can't be the fictional lover. Moreover, in responding to the work, in feeling the emotion, I clearly think that the death of the lover is the source of my sorrow. After all, if I thought otherwise, I would not be sorry for the lover, but for myself.

Initially, this seems to be a problem. However, the misattribution of causality in emotional experience is widely documented. In fact, such misattribution is pervasive in real life. We standardly attribute emotion to some salient event or agent in our environment, and we are quite sure that it has caused our emotion, even when that is totally false. For example, one study found that, when people's moods were affected by the weather, they misattributed their positive or negative feelings (caused by sunny and rainy days, respectively) to events or conditions in their lives (see Clore, Gasper, and Garvin 125–6; see also Ortony, Clore, and Collins 162 and citations). The point holds across a range of conditions and feelings. Jones is stimulated by the swift speed at which he is driving, but thinks that his enthusiastic attitude is due to his traveling companion. I feel happy because my indigestion has lessened, but I attribute it to the session I am attending at a conference. Note that these misattributions are consequential. For instance, I may praise the session widely after misattributing my mood to the papers. The consequences of misattributed anger even have an idiom associated with them—"I don't know what's bothering you, but *don't take it out on me.*" "Taking it out" on someone is acting toward them on the basis of misattributed anger.

In short, a split between the source of an emotion and its target is well-established empirically. Moreover, it makes a good deal of sense that there would be such a split in literary response in particular, given the fictionality of the target (i.e., the literary work) and its irrelevance to the reader's egocentric goals.

In some recent essays, Keith Oatley has taken up this account of literary emotion and incorporated it into a broader theory of literary cognition. Specifically, Oatley argues that there are four cognitive structures in any literary work. Following standard narratology, he refers to two of these as "story" and "discourse." He adds to these what he calls the "Suggestion Structure." This is, precisely, *dhvani.* Oatley understands it as a "structure" because it is systematically patterned in a literary work. Again, *dhvani* or suggestion is relatively unpatterned in much ordinary conversation, nonliterary reading, and so on. But, in literature, authors organize their works in such a way as to cultivate particular patterns of suggestiveness (whether they self-consciously recognize they are doing this or not). Finally, Oatley adds the "Realization Structure." The realization structure is what phenomenologists such as Ingarden would call the "concretized" version of the story. It is the story as we imagine it, including the precise ways we fill the "gaps" in the text (as Iser would say), infer unmentioned causal connections, complete the personalities of the characters, visualize particular scenes, and so on. This bears on our present concerns, for the "realization" (or concretization) of the literary work is entirely personal to the reader and it is to a great extent the result of recruiting personal memories. In other words, the "realization structure" results from *dhvani* priming personal memories. Those personal memories not only contribute to the reader's emotion. They also provide the materials for the reader's full imagination of the work.

Oatley presents strong empirical evidence that realization results from such an incorporation of primed memories. Though Oatley does not indicate precisely how this occurs, the basic algorithmic sequence is clear enough. Events and characters in the literary work are defined by some properties. These properties prime particular memories in a reader. The memories are the source of the reader's emotive reaction to the work. But they are also primed items with representational content. Like the story itself, the memories too involve persons, settings, and events. When the reader begins to fill in any indeterminate aspect of the story—from hidden causes to scenery—he/she necessarily scans his/her lexicon or memory systems for relevant material. He/she comes upon the primed material first. As a result, this primed material has a particularly important place in completing the work.

Note that this process has a cyclical effect on the emotions. As our emotional response to a work develops out of a particular set of primed personal memories, those memories begin to guide our realization or concretization of that work. As a result of this concretization, the memories themselves are reprimed and thus our emotional response is reinforced or enhanced. If a particular character primes the memory of someone I dislike, I will probably imagine details of that character's motivation or appearance by implicitly drawing on that aversive memory. One result of this is that I come to dislike the character all the more thoroughly. Put simply, I begin to distrust a character due to a memory. The priming of the memory leads me to imagine the character with an untrustworthy face or a hidden motive. My imagination of the untrustworthy face or the hidden motive further primes the memory that led me to distrust the character initially and thus reinforces the distrust.

We may develop the point still further by drawing on recent memory research, which considerably alters the commonsense conception of memory storage. In the commonsense view, memories are like little videotapes and accessing a memory is like running the tape. We have more or less complete and more or less coherent memories of episodes in our past life—ranging from our first day at school to our wedding to whatever we did yesterday. But neurobiological research indicates that this is not the case. As Daniel Schacter explains, it seems that our memory storage is in fact very fragmentary and discontinuous. We have partial and isolated memories of past events; "only bits and pieces of incoming data are represented in memory . . . fragments of experience" (Schacter 40)—snippets of conversation, glimpses of faces, an occasional scent or taste. Not only are memories fragmentary, they decay, and they decay, so to speak, from the bottom up. In other words, the specific details decay, leaving more general structures (see Schacter 91). Clearly, then memory retrieval is not simply a matter of running a videotape. In fact, "retrieving" a memory is a highly elaborate and constructive process. We access fragments from the relevant time period and link them together, often using broad schemas. In other words, we do not really remember the past, we reconstruct it—often in a way that reflects our present concerns as much as our past experience, sometimes in a way that does not reflect our past experience at all. As Schacter explains, "even the seemingly simple act of calling to mind a memory of a particular past experience—what you did last Saturday night or where you went on your first date—is constructed from influences operating in the present as well as from information you have stored about the past" (8). Sometimes the present conditions virtually create the memory (104–13).

Now we may return to aesthetic experience. Our response to a novel, a play, a movie, would begin with a series of fragmentary observations and imaginations. In reading, we cluster together traits for scenes, characters, events. We engage in an ongoing synthesis of these in working memory. As we do this, we envision the scenes, and so on, in partial and fragmentary ways. When watching a play or film, our attention shifts from one part of the visual array to another, from one sound to another. We cluster these together as in reading. We synthesize these in working memory. As this is going on, the various fragments of perception, meaning, imagination, and so on, spread activation throughout our lexicons and episodic memory systems. Earlier, I argued that this leads to the priming of personal memories. Here we may go so far as to say that it leads to the actual activation of personal memories, not merely their priming. But these memories are in their fragmentary state. And they are not the object of attentional focus. Ordinarily, when thinking about a past event, we would activate not only a few isolated fragments, but whole sets of related fragments. We would bring them into working memory as the central objects of attentional focus, in order to synthesize them and to reconstruct the past event, often via some organizing schema. However, in reading, we are already engaged in an ongoing synthesis or reconstruction that is structurally parallel to the reconstruction of memory. Thus the reconstruction of memory does not go forward. Rather, the activated memory fragments are brought into the task at hand, the ongoing synthesis of the literary work. These memory fragments, then, become part of that literary synthesis, contributing to our understanding of characters, our concretization of scenes, our inference to the unstated causes of events.

In sum, Oatley's suggestion structure and realization structure each appears to be a function of our episodic memories. Fragmentary memories complete or fill in our imagination of a work and simultaneously give rise to our emotional response. In keeping with our general tendency to explain emotions by reference to salient experiences, we attribute that emotional response to the events of the work, which are the objects of our attentional focus. This is in part a misattribution. But it is not entirely a misattribution, for our imagination of these literary events incorporates elements from the actual, biographical source of our emotions.

I will conclude this section by returning briefly to *Les Demoiselles d'Avignon*. Much research on personal memory and aesthetic response has focused on relatively full, articulated recollections. I am somewhat skeptical of this research. In an experimental situation, test subjects strain to produce coherent memories. They then develop those memories reflectively. In other words, the readers in these studies often explain their responses by reference to developed and precisely verbalized personal reminiscences. I believe that these elaborate and detailed memories are most often an artifact of the testing situation. At the very least, it is clear that we do not engage in such extensive narrativizing of our own pasts while reading or while watching a film. This is true for the Abhinavagupta reason that, if we do engage in such detailed (and reconstructive) reminiscence, we have stopped reading or watching the film. Again, the preceding arguments indicate that a work of art triggers memory fragments that are not integrated with one another in a post facto reconstruction of a past autobiographical event. Rather, they are integrated into our developing comprehension of the work. These memories are not well-developed, memoirlike ruminations. In discussing my response to Picasso's painting, I will of course mention some aspects of particular, personal memories. However, I will refer primarily to more general connections, broader categories of memory. The sorts of specific, fragmentary memories that fall under these broad categories should be easy enough for readers to fill in.

My strongest emotions in viewing Picasso's painting are inspired by figures one and five (counting from the far left). I find the face of figure one very sad (though there is anger in her expression, especially in the set of her lips). Objectively, I suppose, there is nothing about the painting that demands this.[7] My interpretation here already incorporates the memories that give it a particular emotional tone. In any case, when I look at the sharp distinction between the color of the woman's face and the color of her skin elsewhere, I see this as a signal of age. Her face seems to me shriveled and sunken. It fills me with a sense of shock at a sort of unexpected decline. It recalls for me seeing a woman without make-up when I have seen her for years only with make-up. Suddenly, I see the accumulated effects of time, effects that had been hidden. There are, of course, specific instances that come to mind. One is particularly striking—a neighbor who died from cancer when I was young. I don't know if it is accurate, but I remember her face as darkened and shriveled too. Perhaps this memory entered into my imagination, even my encoding of this figure, and my emotional response to her.

I have a similar response to figure five. Indeed, if anything, it is stronger. I feel a great deal of tenderness for her. In some ways, my initial or most accessible associations are light, almost trivial. Her arms are like the arms of someone opening a shower curtain. The squares that mark her skin remind me of skin seen through the translucent pane of a shower door. I realize that, in my imagination, her hair is wet. Indeed, the blue around her is also like water, which probably contributes to the association. Here I have memories of my swimming team when I was young (I will spare the reader the particulars). These contribute to the affection. But there is something more sinister about the blackness around her. Indeed, there is more shadow around her face than around the faces of any other figure. Her arms are by far the thinnest, suggesting the greatest frailty. In general, she does not seem well. The absence of her left breast almost suggests a mastectomy (an association linked with particular memories, of course), and it is presumably no accident that the missing breast is the one closest to her heart. The blackness of her left eye goes along with this. On the whole, I feel that she is the woman who has suffered most.

But what I find most moving here is not the suffering per se. Rather, I associate her act of entering the room and speaking with consolation. That is what most draws me to figure five. Depending on where I stand before the painting, she seems to be addressing figure one, who now appears lost in thought. There is no real evidence in the painting that figure five is being supportive or generous. But the vague memories that fill out the frozen narrative for me—memories of which I was unaware before I began considering my emotional response—are memories of two people sharing a sense of sorrow in a larger and indifferent group. I see figure one as both sorrowful and angry. Though derived from my memories, this sense of ambivalent or contradictory emotion does fit the painting as well. Indeed, imagining emotional contradiction in her attitude and motivation helps to explain some conflicts in her representation, such as the evident motion of her left leg and her complete frigidity in the right leg, for the anger would compel her to act, while the sorrow would constrain and immobilize her. In any case, in connection with this, I see figure five as addressing that sorrow empathically (from her own experience). Again, this is not because the painting requires such an interpretation, but because it has triggered certain memories which link figure one with the sorrow and anger of recent bad news (e.g., that she is ill) and figure five with generosity of spirit and empathy despite her own pain. Indeed, this is enhanced by the fact that figure five has barely opened her lips. I have an almost kinesthetic sense of my own attempts at saying something consoling, but finding that nothing comes (after an initial, awkward "uh"). Indeed, I can think of very recent instances of just this sort, as with a friend whose spouse had died a few months ago. At the same time, all this is connected with the fact that the delicate pink curve of figure five's hip is almost the only thing in the picture that I find erotic. This relates to the swimming memories and the sense of change and loss with age that I have felt only in the last few years, a sense that is obviously inseparable from particular memories.

My emotive response to the rest of the painting is fainter. I feel a certain level of distress at the torso of figure two, for it reminds me of a young male athlete. This connects with the swimming memories already mentioned, for the sheet on her thigh recalls the towel grabbed by a swimmer after a race, and the triangle below her waist is like the male swimsuit. But this may be an artifact of the present analysis. Having mentioned swimming memories earlier, I am now more inclined to think of them in connection with other aspects of the painting. Figure three, in contrast, is more sexually alluring, especially the turn of her waist and the way her breast appears in silhouette. But she is alluring in a vacuous way, like adolescent fantasies with their props of women seen in magazines or glimpsed on the street. Finally, figure four, with her fleshy solidity, her furrowed and disapproving brow, her intent and confident gaze, is heavy, strong, and matriarchal in my imagination of her. Here too the imagination certainly comes from many memories—uncertain, disconnected, but joined together by this image and bringing their emotions with them. They make her a little disquieting, and inscrutable.

The fact that these final memories relate largely to my own mother suggests that this form of cognitive analysis may have some points of connection with psychoanalysis. Indeed, one could argue reasonably that this cognitive view of emotion and memory is continuous with psychoanalytic approaches, which would simply structure the relevant memories in such a way as to give pride of place to memories from a particular time (childhood, especially the ages of three to five) and regarding particular people (primarily one's parents or, more generally, caretakers). In this way, I believe that one could extend the present discussion productively in a psychoanalytic direction—an idea in keeping with Oatley's incorporative approach to psychological theory. Indeed, such a synthesis could potentially challenge and invigorate principles and practises in both fields, well beyond the issue of literary emotion. However, that is clearly a topic requiring separate treatment.[8]

CHAPTER **7**

From Mind to Matter
Art, Empathy, and the Brain

The main use of neurophysiological research in literary study has been very general (e.g., in debates over whether literature is socially produced).[1] This is unfortunate, as brain studies may bear directly and in detail on any topic treated in the preceding chapters (see, for example, Martindale, "Biological," on creativity). Clearly, I cannot cover all these topics and all the relevant research in a single chapter. At the same time, I do not want to confine the chapter to generalities. I will therefore frame the following discussion in terms of one issue we have been considering, an issue for which recent brain research is, I believe, particularly consequential—literary emotion. I will begin by questioning some conclusions of the preceding chapter, including the conclusions of my own earlier work on emotion and memory. Though this discussion is focused on a particular issue, it should serve to illustrate how neurobiological research may enter into other areas of theory and criticism in literature and the arts.

Problems in Emotion and Literature

In the previous chapter, I presented an account of emotion that has two central components. The first is the ongoing appraisal of changing conditions relative to goals. The second is the activation of episodic memories. In cognitive science today, appraisal and, to a lesser extent, memory are the primary means of explaining emotion. The combination of appraisal and memory theories set out above seems to be well supported by psychological research. Moreover, it makes intuitive sense in relation to our ordinary experience. But it is still not clear that this account successfully explains our emotional response to literature and the arts. Even with the discussion of primed memories and misattribution, one might reasonably wonder if our emotional experience of literature does not still remain somewhat opaque. Do we really misattribute our partially remembered sorrows to the events we merely read about in a novel? Yes, we misattribute emotion in ordinary life, but that is not the norm. We are ordinarily right in our attributions. Could it be that our entire, extended emotional relation to something (e.g., all literature) is based on misattribution? Moreover, in most cases of misattribution the cause we imagine is more plausible, more seemingly relevant, than the real cause. For example, it seems odd to be unhappy due simply to the weather. It seems more reasonable to think that I am unhappy because of something in my life situation. Is this the case with literature? Finally, in reading literature we seem to become genuinely involved in the details of the narrative development, our emotion changing with each small twist in the plot. Is it plausible to think of this as a matter of personal memory and misattribution? In this chapter, I will discuss emotion again, drawing on recent work in neurobiology. In many ways, this work supports the preceding analysis. In other ways, it shows the limits of that analysis and the necessity of reformulating it.

I will frame this discussion by reference to two traditional and notoriously vexing problems in the history of aesthetics. The first, which we have already been considering, might be called "the fictionality problem." Why do we feel literary emotion, even though we know the events in the work are fictional? Why do we sorrow over the fate of Romeo and Juliet when we know there are no such people? There are two subproblems of the fictionality problem. When a theorist articulates a solution to this problem, the solution necessarily predicts a certain amount of agreement or disagreement across readers. The dilemma is that these accounts tend to overpredict one or the other rather strongly. Thus, for some accounts, it is not at all clear why we share emotions. This may be called "the shared emotions problem." In other words, some accounts have no good way of explaining why so many people cry at just the same times when watching *Titanic*. Other accounts face precisely the opposite dilemma. They overpredict similarity rather than difference. Accounts of this sort have difficulty explaining why different people often have such different reactions—why, for example, Jones laughs at a scene where Smith weeps. We may refer to this as "the differing emotions problem."[2]

The other large issue I wish to consider is actually prior to the fictionality problem and more general. This is "the empathy problem." Why do we get so worked up over things that happen to other people, even when those things are not fictional? Why does Jones cry when he hears about some stranger who has lost everything in a flood? Why does Smith feel happy when she reads about some unknown child cured of a fatal disease? Why, in short, do we feel emotions regarding situations that have no bearing on us whatsoever? The fictionality problem is really a compound case of the empathy problem. In the case of fiction, we feel emotions for situations that have no bearing on us—and that never even happened.

A pure appraisal account has fairly obvious difficulties with both the empathy problem and the fictionality problem. Appraisal theories are insistently egocentric. My appraisals bear on *my* goals—not those of Jones or Smith, and certainly not those of Romeo and Juliet who, not being real, don't actually have goals anyway. There does not seem to be any way that this focus on my goals can account for my response to other people.

The memory account of emotion is better able to deal with these issues. Indeed, that is why I drew on Abhinavagupta initially. Moreover, this account is very successful in explaining differences in emotional response. But, of course, that is also its failing. While this account is good at treating emotional differences, it is not so good at treating similarities. Basing literary response on memories would seem to overpredict idiosyncrasy. Again, why do so many people feel sad at precisely the same moments in *Titanic*? Shouldn't their individual memories be so different as to predict a fairly wide range of responses? Indeed, just what is it that triggers particular memories in any given case? No one in the audience has had precisely these experiences (e.g., drowning in the Atlantic). So why do these experiences trigger just the memories and emotions that they do? In addition, there is the problem of how these emotions are activated. It cannot be a matter of remembering the fact that one felt a certain emotion in the past. The whole point is that we feel the emotion now. Remembering the fact that one had an emotion does not necessarily inspire that emotion again. So how and when do memories give rise to emotion?

It is clear that appraisal and memory are crucial parts of emotion. But, at least as we have analyzed them so far, they seem inadequate to account for literary experience and related forms of experience in everyday life. This is one place where brain research may enter in a very consequential way.

Emotions: What Are They Good For?

Before going on to the neurobiological research, however, we need to review some fundamental principles in the cognitive study of emotion. Cognitivists disagree about emotion just as they disagree about other things. However, there are a few common principles that most cognitivists would accept. Put differently, there are a few principles regarding emotion that seem so well established that it is difficult for anyone to deny them. These may be organized into three groups, resulting from three types of analysis: (1) Constituent Analysis. Cognitivists working in a mentalistic framework have isolated a number of components that constitute an emotion. We sketched these in the preceding chapter. (2) Functional Analysis. Cognitivists, working primarily in an evolutionary framework, have explained how emotions serve a positive function, how they "work for us." We touched on this in chapter 6 as well. (3) Causal Analysis. This is where the brain comes in. While the constituent analysis gives us a cognitive architecture that is mentalistic, the algorithmic level has been treated most successfully in terms of brain structures. However, this neurobiological analysis has direct consequences for mentalistic accounts. I will briefly summarize constituent and functional analysis, slightly revising the account given in the preceding chapter, before turning to the brain research, thus the algorithmic level, in the following section.

First, we should reconsider constituent analysis. Intuitively, we tend to think of emotions as feelings—what it is like to be angry, sad, disgusted. However, as we have already seen, from a cognitive perspective, the "phenomenological tone" is only one component of an emotion, and not necessarily the most important one. The first component of an emotion is *eliciting conditions*. These, again, are just what experiences bring on an emotion. A large predator leaping toward one's face with bared teeth, for example, is an eliciting condition for fear. In our intuitive understanding, the next component of an emotion, what follows directly from the eliciting conditions, is the feeling or *phenomenological tone*. Intuitively, we would say that the phenomenological tone is followed by the third component, *expressive outcomes*. Expressive outcomes are immediate physiological manifestations of the emotion. These range from changes in heart rate and perspiration to facial expression and vocalization. Here I am combining the catagories of expression and bodily disturbance from chapter 6. Thus the expressive outcomes of fear would include a racing heart, widened eyes, shrieks, and so on. While our intuition tells us that expressive outcomes follow from feelings, many theorists (e.g., Antonio Damasio) maintain that eliciting conditions generate bodily states—that is, expressive outcomes—and our feelings are actually an experience of those expressive outcomes. Thus our feeling of, say, fear simply is our feeling of an accelerated heart rate, perspiration, and so on. Indeed, this is not confined to the "concealed" part of expression. It is well established that simply making certain facial gestures produces the corresponding feelings in some degree (see Damasio 148–9). In other words, "put on a happy face" really is good advice. It does make us feel a little happy—only a little, but it does have that effect.

There are two other components of emotion. These define practical responses to the eliciting conditions. One involves taking in new information, monitoring the environment. The other is a matter of concrete action aimed at sustaining or altering the environment (e.g., destroying the threat) or one's relation to that environment (e.g., fleeing).[3] The former leads us to our fourth component—*attentional focus*. Particular emotions lead our minds to focus on specific features of the environment that are relevant to that emotion. Thus, in fear, we automatically focus on aspects of the environment that are relevant to fear. Indeed, we not only attend selectively to relevant aspects of the environment. We attend selectively to memories. Fear tends to activate memories relevant to fear.

The final component of emotion, already suggested, is *actional outcomes*. In unemotional, ordinary activity, we may act in any number of ways. The options are countless. However, emotions limit our action automatically. More technically, in ordinary life, we have many procedural schemas that we may activate at any given time. We might sit, stand, walk, ride a bicycle, kick a stone, and so on. Emotions, however, are usually associated with one procedural schema. Depending on the intensity of the emotion, that schema may be activated automatically and we may have no way of overriding it. Thus, when startled, we automatically jerk backward. When we experience certain sorts of fear, we flee.

This leads us to functional analysis. As we have already seen from Oatley's work, emotions are functional in two ways. They are functional *interpersonally* and they are functional *intrapersonally*. As to the former, expressive outcomes serve to communicate emotion from one person to others. Note that this does not simply mean that expressive outcomes signal the presence of an emotion in one person. Rather, the expression of emotion by one person actually inspires emotion in other people. A cry of fear not only tells us that Jones is afraid, it also causes our hearts to beat a little faster, leads us to focus attention on fear-relevant features of the environment, and so on.

But why is that functional? That is functional only if emotion is intrapersonally functional. After all, we would hardly say that irrational hysteria is functional just because it is communicated from one person to another. So why is emotion intrapersonally functional? As we discussed briefly in chapter 6, it is intrapersonally functional because thought is inefficient. In some cases, it is important that we not think about alternatives, but just act. Consider fear. If I spot a lion in the distance, then I should not spend time considering all my options, potentially getting "lost in the byways of . . . calculation" (Damasio 172). I should get away before it sees me. Moreover, I should not have to struggle to keep my attention focused on the lion, as I drift off into Walter Mitty-like fantasies. Rather, my attention should simply be fixed on the lion and related matters. Thus the limitation of procedural schemas and the narrowing of attentional focus are both clearly functional here. Even the phenomenological tone is functional (as we discussed in the preceding chapter). Writers on emotion make a broad distinction between dysphoric and euphoric or negative and positive emotions. We want to put an end to negative emotions. They are painful. We want to continue or intensify positive emotions. They are pleasurable. As such, both provide strong motivational force. In some cases, emotion is so strong that we have no choice. The relevant procedural schema is simply triggered. In other cases, we do have a choice. But the feeling provides a motive for accepting the procedural schema selected by the emotion—thus fleeing, attacking, or whatever.

More exactly, experience is usually complex. It sends us different signals. A single situation might include conditions for many types of action and even many types of emotion, such as anger, fear, and pity. In other words, most situations are to some degree both ambiguous and ambivalent. But our emotional minds, like connectionist networks, usually take this ambivalent input, send it through several cycles, and turn out a much less equivocal feeling. More exactly, a slight advantage in input to a connectionist system often yields a strong advantage in output. In this respect, human emotion fits the connectionist model very well. Ambivalent inputs generally yield "valenced" outputs, outputs that have a distinct, dominant emotional orientation. The advantage of such a system is obvious. In many situations it is crucial that one act in one way or another. Dithering over whether to flee or attack may be more disastrous than either fleeing or attacking. As Ito and Cacioppo explain, "The affect system has evolved to produce bipolar endpoints because they provide both clear bivalent action tendencies and harmonious and stable subjective experiences" (69).

Finally, everyone knows that emotions vary in strength. We have already noted that differences in strength bear on the extent to which the central executive can make decisions regarding procedural schemas cued by an emotion. However, the effects of emotional intensity on the central executive are not merely continuous. They involve stages or thresholds. There appear to be three important thresholds of this sort. We may refer to the first as an "orientation threshold." When an emotion passes this threshold, the result is a narrowing of attentional focus and what has been called "mood-congruent processing" where one is "selectively sensitized to . . . information that agrees" with one's "prevailing emotional state" (Bower and Forgas 108).[4] This stage also has effects on our judgment and may even involve changes in processing *procedures* (not merely the objects we are processing). For example, depending upon our emotional state we may be inclined to assimilate new experiences to preconceptions (i.e., assume that preconceptions are right) or we may be inclined to accommodate our ideas to new experiences (Forgas 18; and Clore, Gasper, and Garvin 131; for discussion, see Fiedler 177–83). In any case, at this stage, we are still able to choose whether or not to act on a particular emotion and we may restrain our expressions of emotion.[5]

The second is the "expressive threshold." Emotional intensity exceeds the expressive threshold when we are not able to control our expression of an emotion—weeping, laughing, and so on. However, we are still able to inhibit actional impulses.

The final threshold is the "control threshold," where we cannot override the actional outcome produced by the emotion-selected procedural schema. Jones knows that freezing in the middle of the road is not a good idea. But he just cannot move.

Aesthetic Thresholds, Emotional Valence, and Literature

This distinction among thresholds has considerable bearing on literary study. For example, it is well known that male readers are less likely than female readers to empathize with characters of the opposite sex (see, for example, Oatley "Emotions, Abstractions" and citations). I imagine that part of the reason for this is that male readers often work against the emotional orientation produced by a literary work about a female protagonist, whereas female readers do not typically work against the emotional orientation produced by a literary work about a male protagonist. (Of course, there is also the problem that this research is all done by interviews and male readers are likely to underreport their identification with a character doing "unmanly" things, whereas female readers may be just as likely to overreport the degree of their compassion.)

Perhaps more interestingly, the division between the orientation threshold and the expressive threshold is to a great extent the division between literature that is considered acceptable as art and literature that is considered popular and sentimental. The mere fact that so many people wept openly while watching *Titanic* was probably enough to assure that it would not be taken seriously by many critics. Of course, there is a distinction by type of emotion here. Mirth, with its expression in laughter, is broadly accepted. However, in keeping with the general depreciation of fully expressed emotion, comedy is widely seen as inferior to tragedy. If we were to make a hierarchy, then, we might say that, at least in the West, canonical literary evaluation has tended to order works in roughly the following manner. At the lowest level, we find melodramas and works of propaganda that pass the expressive threshold for dysphoric emotions, such as sorrow and anger. The middle level is occupied by comedies, especially romantic comedies, that surpass the expressive threshold for euphoric emotions, such as mirth. Perhaps slightly above these, we find works of euphoric emotions (e.g., more serious romances, such as those of Jane Austen) that pass the orientation threshold, but not the expressive threshold. At the very top, we find tragedies that pass the orientation threshold for dysphoric emotions, but not the expressive threshold. Though there are certainly exceptions, this appears to be the general tendency.[6]

Works that do not pass the orientation threshold almost always fall outside this hierarchy. Passing beyond the orientation threshold is literally what keeps our attention. Without that, we drift away, lose interest, and stop reading. Though he does not put it this way, the orientation threshold is in effect what Ed Tan examines in *Emotion and the Structure of Narrative Film*. Tan takes the central emotion of film to be "interest." I believe Tan is mistaken in this formulation. Specifically, I do not believe that interest is properly characterized as an emotion. Interest is the ongoing attentional arousal that accompanies emotions that have passed the orientation threshold. Rather than being an emotion itself, it is a component of orientation level emotions. However, I believe Tan is entirely correct in stressing interest as central to the emotional experience of film.

On the other hand, we do feel emotions below the orientation threshold. We usually refer to these feelings as "moods," though a typical mood is enduring and these feelings may be ephemeral. Moreover, suborientation level emotion does bear on our experience of art. This occurs in contexts where the works in question do not require attentional focus. One case of this sort is background music, which is in some contexts referred to as "mood music." The point of background music is that it can contribute to mood and allow for sporadic attention without demanding continuous attention. The same point holds for decorative arts—including "high art" used as decoration, as when a business office has a painting by Cezanne or a lobby has a work by Monet.[7]

Finally, our tendency to emotional valence has literary implications as well. We noted above that ambivalent inputs cycle through to valent outputs. Again, our emotional systems have developed in this way because, in critical situations, valent outputs usually give a survival advantage over ambivalent outputs. However, in complex social situations, things do not always work the way they should. Indeed, the tendency of emotions to cycle toward valence, and the occasional failure of that cycling, lead to many social conflicts and injustices—as when "the fickle crowd" shifts from one valence to another, all the while based on mere fractional differences in ambivalent inputs. In keeping with this, the issue of emotional valence emerging out of ambivalent inputs is one of the most important themes in literature. For example, one could argue that it is the central concern of Shakespeare's major tragedies. Virtually all these plays could be interpreted as focusing on a conflict between the ambivalence of inputs and the necessity of valent outputs for decisive action. In some cases, the tragedy results from an excessive emphasis on the ambivalent inputs, resulting in a lack of valence in the output, and thus a lack of decisive action. In other cases, it results from an output having a strong valence when the result should have been ambivalence. *Hamlet* is, of course, the obvious example of the former. *Othello* is perhaps the clearest instance of the latter.

Sensitive Brains: Emotion and Neurobiology

But we have yet to consider the precise algorithmic details of emotional processing. Just how does all this work? Precisely what steps are involved in emotion? Probably the most important research on this topic in recent years has been done in neurobiology. One of the most theoretically consequential conclusions of this research is that there are specific emotion centers in the brain. As Joseph LeDoux puts it, "different classes of emotional behavior represent different kinds of functions that take care of different kinds of problems for the animal and have different brain systems devoted to them" (*Emotional* 127). These are evolutionarily developed to reply to specific eliciting conditions by producing certain actional and expressive outcomes and certain associated feelings. They are also designed to stimulate the attention circuits of the brain and to key attention to specific features of the environment (see Adolphs and Damasio 32–3). In other words, these emotion centers fulfill the function of emotions by responding to and/or producing the components of emotions. Though the research is not unequivocal, the amygdala appears to be particularly crucial for emotion.[8] Different parts of the amygdala bear on different emotions, with a broad division into positive and negative. As Adolphs and Damasio explain, "the amygdala circuitry underlying the processing of aversive stimuli depends on the central nucleus of the amygdala, whereas processing of stimuli that are rewarding appears to depend on projections from the basolateral nucleus of the amygdala" (31).[9]

Drawing on a good deal of neurophysiological and mental/phenomenological evidence, LeDoux argues that there are two paths to these centers. He refers to them as the "low road" and the "high road." As LeDoux explains, "information about external stimuli reaches the amygdala by way of direct pathways from the thalamus (the low road) as well as by way of pathways from the thalamus to the cortex to the amygdala" (*Emotional* 164). I will refer to these as "direct" and "cortically mediated"—or, in a mentalistic idiom, "cognitively mediated"—emotion. Note that even cortically mediated emotion is presumably produced by the emotion center. Thus even cortically mediated fear is produced by the amygdala. We will return to this point in a moment.

Emotion centers are sensitive to particular inputs, just the inputs to which they direct attentional focus when aroused. They operate swiftly and, depending upon their intensity, they may preempt other brain functions. Thus, above a certain level (what I just termed the "orientation threshold"), they preempt attention. Above the control threshold, they preempt decisions about action, thus higher cortical (or central executive) operations in that regard. More exactly, the process of direct emotional experience appears to operate in the following way. The emotion centers are innately sensitized to particular environmental features. These features are not complex entities, but fragments or elements of objects and actions.[10] As Damasio puts it, "we are wired to respond with an emotion, in preorganized fashion, when certain features of stimuli in the world or in our bodies are perceived, alone or in combination. Examples of such features include size (as in large animals); large span (as in flying eagles); type of motion (as in reptiles); certain sounds (such as growling)" (131). Our perceptual apparatuses continually take in a quick sketches of the environment. These sketches are rough and fragmentary. They are particularly sensitive to the sorts of feature that bear on the emotion centers. Our perceptual apparatuses also generate fuller, more detailed, and less narrowly focused complexes of information. The rough sketches are sent quickly to the emotion centers (via the "low road"; see LeDoux *Emotional* 169). The more elaborated picture is transmitted to the cortex (via the "high road").

Consider a simple example. I am walking along a path. I glimpse a sinuous shape before me on the path. I immediately jump back, even though I know already when I am jumping that it is just a branch. Someone asks me, "Why did you jump?" I answer, "I thought that was a snake." But, in fact, I never "thought" any such thing. Cortically, I knew that it was a branch from the moment I became aware of it. The detailed information sent from my visual system to my cortex made it clear that this was a branch. However, the preliminary sketch sent to my amygdala was ambiguous. The preliminary sketch included just the sort of information that would set off a fright response. This "first pass" or preliminary information activated the amygdala in such a way as to trigger fear. That activation preempted cognitive decision and led to the jump, over which I had no control. On the other hand, the fuller cognitive information did then go from the cortex to the amygdala. This inhibited further flight as it deactivated the amygdala by altering the input.

Prima facie, it may seem that emotional experience in modern times is so bound up with contemporary situations that it could not possibly have much connection with these primitive fragments. Phobias seem to present particularly striking cases. For example, many people have a phobia of elevators. First, phobias in general seem dysfunctional, thus contrary to the (functional) theory of emotion shared by cognitivists. Second, elevators are a recent invention. An emotive relation to an elevator must be very modern, and very culturally relative. Indeed, this sort of emotion seems to indicate that emotions are thoroughly "culturally constructed." But this is not at all the case. In fact, phobias are in general pathological forms of normal, adaptive emotions. They are, one might say, the hypertrophy of our innate fragmentary sensitivities. We are innately sensitive to enclosed spaces, which is to say, spaces that do not allow escape. Enclosure is something that gets sent to the amygdala in first sketch information. For most of us, the degree and duration of enclosure we experience in an elevator may increase attentional focus. However, they are not enough to stimulate fear. People with a fear of elevators simply have greater sensitivity to enclosure, or to particular sorts of enclosure. Our modern emotions are "culturally constructed" only in the banal sense that cultural developments allow different specifications of innate emotive patterns. In other words, you obviously cannot have a phobia of elevators if your culture has no elevators. But you can have all the sensitivities that would produce such a phobia if your culture acquired elevators.

It is important to point out here that the fragmentary "triggers" in the emotion centers include the spontaneous expressions of emotions. In other words, emotional expressions are not only outcomes, they are also eliciting conditions. Indeed, they are eliciting conditions to which we have particular perceptual sensitivity. This is why shrieks of fear make us fearful. Distinctive features of fearful shrieks are among the elements that are given in first pass information and that activate the fear center. Smiles—as encoded for the particular features to which we are emotionally sensitive—activate the emotion center for joy. Note that this is true for our own expressions as well. As we have already noted, smiling tends to lift one's spirits. Conversely, frowning tends to dampen one's mood. Indeed, an increased heartrate tends to make a person experience one of the emotions associated with an increased heart rate. Anxiety may give rise to indigestion, but indigestion may equally make one feel anxiety.

Finally, there appear to be two sets of variables that govern the degree to which a particular input activates an emotion center. The first concerns the intrinsic nature of the trigger. Someone's smile is a relatively mild stimulant for joy. A predator's growl is a relatively strong stimulant for fear. The second set of variables concerns the environmental situation of the trigger. Variables of this sort include proximity, direction of movement, speed, and so forth. For example, proximity of a trigger tends to intensify the resulting emotion.

The Emotional Low Road in Film and Music

Some of what I have just been discussing has fairly obvious bearing on the experience of visual arts. While literature (apparently) must forego the "low road" of direct emotive stimulation, movies involve subcortical emotive arousal all the time. This is most obvious in genre films. Horror movies make direct use of such fear triggers as enclosed space and limited visibility in darkness. They manipulate such variables as suddenness, speed, and direction of movement. But the use of such triggers is not confined to horror movies. In *Titanic*, the extensive sequence in which Rose saves Jack involves continual reliance on particular fear-triggering fragments. The sudden rush of water down a corridor, the continual narrowing of space as the water rises to the ceiling, the swift movement of the axe in the direction of Jack—these all involve fragmentary triggers of fear. A particularly important trigger here results from their near drowning and their associated expressions of panic. The time Rose and Jack spend under water, and their gasps for air as they surface, can be very distressing for viewers. Perhaps the most potent trigger for panic is suffocation. The representation of their suffocation and panic or near panic—the sounds of their breath, their facial expressions, their voices—help trigger a sense of panic in the viewer.[11]

Of course, fear is not the only emotion triggered in the film. The scene where Jack sketches Rose is clearly designed to expose heterosexual men in the audience to fragmentary triggers of sexual desire. This is true not only of Kate Winslet's body—its features, contours, proportions (e.g., the well-established, cross-cultural preference of men for a 2/3 waist-to-hip ratio [see Pinker *How* 485], which may be part of first sketch information in relevant cases and which seems roughly fitting in this case). It applies also to her reclining position, perhaps even the expression in her eyes. The point, of course, is not simply to arouse male viewers sexually, but to focus their attention and stimulate their interest in the ongoing development of the film.

Here, as elsewhere, the relation of film study to cognitive research need not—indeed should not—proceed all in one direction. As the preceding examples suggest, the study of fragmentary emotion triggers in film could provide valuable evidence for what stimulates different sorts of emotion. In both cases just discussed, the triggers suggested by the film have only been partially studied by neuroscientists—even though fear and sexual desire are the two most widely researched topics in this area. In fact, we have hardly any sense of just what fragments inspire anger, sorrow, affection, and so on. Film provides an obvious starting point for research on these topics because filmmakers have systematically developed ways of triggering all these emotions. Moreover, a research program in film and emotion triggers need not be confined to "contents," but could address film form as well. In this way, the program could treat topics that may not even occur to researchers who confine their work to laboratories. For example, what is it about underlighting that tends to trigger fear? Is it the lighting itself or does the lighting alter our perception of faces in such a way as to exaggerate first sketch signals of hostility? Why does soft focus tend to be associated with affection (not, say, fear or anger)? Moreover, this program of study would bear not only on emotion triggers per se, but on variables also. For example, the variable of proximity is put to use in the close-up, which serves to intensify whatever emotion is at stake at a given moment. One might ask if there are other variables of this sort—relating, for example, to camera movement and the interaction of perception, bodily motion, and feeling.

Many of the same points hold straightforwardly for painting, sculpture, and still photography. Though it may not be obvious at first, the study of emotional triggers has direct bearing on music as well. The emotional effects of music are notoriously difficult to explain. One obvious account is, roughly, mimetic. It begins with some seemingly banal correlations. Sad music tends to be slow, and slow music tends to be sad. Fearful music—or, more exactly, music of tensely fearful anticipation—often involves very short, repetitive notes. Angry music is associated with sharp dynamic variations. Comic music often has with quick tempi. The mimetic account is that musical tempi and dynamics imitate human emotional experience and activity. When sad, we tend to move around slowly. Moreover, sad events are slow. People don't run around or drive quickly at funerals. So music achieves sadness by imitating this slowness. The short, repetitive notes of fearful anticipation mimic our heartbeat in situations of fearful anticipation, and so on. The problem with this explanation is twofold. First, except for tempi, it does not really tell us just what part of an ordinary emotive activity or even what particular emotive activity is being imitated—and tempo seems a fairly crude differentia. Second, it gives no sense of just how this imitation produces its effects.

The cognitive principles just discussed actually make some sense out of this account. They do this by changing it from a mimetic theory to a theory of emotion triggers. Again, innate expressions of emotion are simultaneously triggers of emotion. For example, an increased heart rate is an expressive outcome of different sorts of emotional tension and it tends to induce the emotions that it expresses. Different speeds and types of body movement are also expressive outcomes of different emotions. Insofar as different tempi not only imitate but actually entail these physiological changes, they are likely to foster associated emotions. If a quick tempo leads the listener to engage in swift, if stationary movement (e.g., toe-tapping), this may serve to inspire a mild feeling of the mirth that it partially imitates. Indeed, actual bodily motion is not necessary. A change in respiratory rate may produce the same effects, as may various tensions and relaxations of muscles that usually anticipate or accompany motion. (Jourdain argues that such pre-actional muscular sequences are common in our experience of music [see 325–6].) What is crucial here is that, in this respect, the emotion is directly the result of bodily experiences (due to actions, pre-actional sequences, or whatever.)

It is not a matter of some analogy between the music and those bodily experiences. Precisely what these experiences are and precisely how they occur are topics for future research—research that will benefit not only musicology, but cognitive science in general.

Moreover, these are not the only expressive elements that bear on music. Our auditory apparatus automatically distinguishes different sorts of cry and moan. Different sorts of vocalization express different emotions and, when we hear them, they communicate different sorts of emotion to us. A laugh has a certain rhythm; a cry of fear is marked by a distinctive pitch; a moan of sorrow has a certain contour. We are sensitive to distinctive features of these sounds. We encode them in our first sketch and our emotion centers respond to them. Insofar as music repeats any of these features, the relevant emotion centers will necessarily be affected in the same ways. One might consider a work such as Penderecki's *Threnody to the Victims of Hiroshima* in this context. Its use of tremolos and tone clusters seems to have abstracted and intensified the features that define shrieks of terror and keening cries of sorrow. The effect is particularly obvious in this case. However, similar effects are no doubt produced less overtly and less self-consciously all the time. It seems very likely that the emotional effect, not only of Penderecki's *Threnody*, but of many other pieces results from their repetition of features that activate our emotion centers. In other words, emotion in these cases is not a matter of some broad, mimetic similarity reminding us of, say, sorrow (though that may occur, and indeed does occur in the piece just mentioned). Rather, our emotion centers are sensitive to particular features which are repeated and perhaps even amplified or exaggerated in the music.

On the other hand, this stress on innate triggers returns us to the problems with which we began. Not everyone responds to Penderecki the way that I do. Conversely, most people find Romantic music the most emotionally effective. But I do not find myself particularly drawn to Brahms or Schumann. Thus we face the "differing emotions" problem. Moreover, the account to this point seems to suggest that we will have emotional responses to film, theater, photography, and music—but not to literature. Evidently, we have not fully accounted for emotion in relation to the arts.

Taking the High Road: Appraisal, Memory, and Imagination

Part of the problem is that we have left out the high road. We have treated only the direct perceptual stimulation of emotion centers. The high road of cortical processing is almost exactly what is commonly referred to as appraisal. It seems indisputable that appraisal, thus cortical processing, leads to emotion in the absence of direct perception of emotion triggers. Suppose I get a letter from the IRS announcing that I will be audited. I may have a reaction of fear (accelerated heartbeat, etc.). But the only thing I am perceiving is a letter. And that is not all. As discussed in chapter 6, it seems indisputable that, in other situations, memories generate emotions as well. In short, high road processes do far more than inhibit faulty responses (e.g., assuring the amygdala that the thing in the path is a stick, not a snake). Thus the perception of emotion triggers cannot be all there is to emotion.

Yet it also seems clear that no emotion is generated without the activation of the relevant emotion center, and this activation seems to be a function of the fragmentary inputs just discussed. Indeed, here one might wonder if appraisal per se does in fact trigger emotion. Consider, for example, the fact that people fear air crashes incomparably more than they fear car accidents, even though they know that they are far more likely to be killed in an automobile accident. Cognitive appraisal alone should lead us to fear cars more than planes. There are complications in this case as our appraisal processes are not guided by abstract statistical likelihood, but by the saliency of concrete instances. On the other hand, most of us have seen more automobile accidents than airplane accidents, and most of us have known people killed or injured in automobile accidents, but not in plane crashes. The difference here is not wholly a matter of saliency. In fact, it might be worth considering this example in more detail. Why might we fear plane crashes more than car crashes? Perhaps it has something to do with the precise nature of the accident, and the relation of the accident to fear triggers. It is almost certainly the case that one powerful fear trigger has to do with being in a situation in which one could fall easily. Again, common phobias appear to be hypertrophies of innate sensitivities. Acrophobia presumably develops out of a common fear sensitivity to heights. One form of this development is a fear of flying. We have already noted that enclosure is another fear trigger. Air flights involve this as well. Automobiles may seem to involve enclosure, and they do to a degree. But one can stop a car and get out. In other words, the enclosure is qualified by the possibility of escape. This is not the case in an airplane. Moreover, there does not seem to be any innate fear trigger that would correspond to driving into a wall or into another car. In evolutionary terms, this makes sense. After all, what could correspond to this danger for our ancestors? Running into a tree? Running into another person who is running in the opposite direction? This indicates that our greater fear of planes is at least in part the result of innate fear triggers.

Examples such as this suggest that appraisal alone—or, rather, the pure logic of appraisal—does not give rise to emotions. Rather, emotions are triggered by something about the particular situations one is appraising. That something is, precisely, one of the innate emotion triggers. We may rationally regulate our behavior based on pure appraisal. I put on sunscreen due to an appraisal of the chances of getting skin cancer. But I can hardly be said to feel any fear of skin cancer. When appraisal leads to fear, it is because that appraisal directly involves emotion triggers, such as the sense of enclosure (unmitigated by the possibility of exit) and the sense of a possible fall in the case of airplanes.

But several questions arise at this point. One concerns the specific example of automobiles. Sometimes we do fear cars. Is this inconsistent with the preceding analysis? No. In fact, the cases in which we fear cars fit this analysis perfectly. We fear being run over by a car. This is, of course, a rational fear. However, our response is not always rational. The fear Jones feels when he sees a car coming toward him on the road is not a matter of rational appraisal. It is a matter of a perceptual sensitivity. Our first sketch information includes big entities barreling toward us. This is one of the fragmentary triggers of fear. That is one reason people fear being run over in a way they apparently don't fear driving into a wall. There are also situations in which we fear being in a car. Movies give us a good idea of when we have these fears. Specifically, one common way of evoking fear in movie audiences is to have a passenger in a car suddenly discover that the door handle has been removed so that he/she cannot leave the vehicle. This relies on the trigger of enclosure unmitigated by the cognitive identification of possible escape.

But there is a second problem here. Why would we fear plane flights abstractly? The preceding discussion explains why someone might feel fear when on a plane, but not why he/she would feel fear when just thinking about buying air tickets. Here, there are two reasons. The first has to do with imagination. It is well-established that when we concretely imagine an object, our brains behave in much the same way they do when we actually perceive the object (see Kosslyn 295, 301, 325; Rubin 41–6 and 57–9). Thus it would seem that the imagination of emotion triggers operates in the same general way as the direct perception of those triggers. The intensity may be less. But that no doubt depends on the vivacity of the imagination.[12]

A second reason for the abstract fear of airplanes (or anything else) concerns memory. People who have been on planes and felt fear will remember that experience and the memory will give rise to fear again. Why is this and how does it happen? Here we need to consider another set of important and influential researches in neurobiology. Daniel Schacter and Joseph LeDoux have argued convincingly that episodic memories come in two varieties—explicit or, as I will call them, "representational," and implicit. LeDoux has made a compelling case for "an implicit emotional memory system" in particular (*Emotional* 182). (Implicit memory also includes skill memory.)

Representational memories are what we ordinarily think of as memories. They are stored representations of events or objects—for example, my recollection of posting a letter this morning or my memory of my office. The difference from our ordinary conception is that these memories are fragmentary. As we noted in chapter 6, they are not like little videotapes stored in our heads. Again, our minds reconstruct remembered events in relation to current concerns, experiences, and so on. Thus my recollection of a past event may change significantly, depending on the situation in which I am asked about it (see Schacter 106). The reconstruction of memories is affected by current emotional states as well (Schacter 22, 211, 212). Thus I remember a past event differently if I am now sad than if I am angry, fearful, or whatever. Moreover, it is undoubtedly the case that emotional triggers figure significantly in both initial storage and in recollective synthesis (see LeDoux *Synaptic* 221–9). In other words, features that serve as emotional triggers are particularly prominent among the fragments that are stored in memory (e.g., our fragmentary memory of a predator with bared teeth will include those bared teeth quite prominently). This happens because we encode those features in both first sketch and elaborated perception; we attend to them with particular concentration and purpose when in the relevant emotional states, and so on. Moreover, since we are continually sensitive to emotion-triggering features in new experiences, when new experience operate as probes, they are particularly likely to activate memory fragments with those features—fragments that may, in turn, be integrated into our understanding of and response to new situations. All this bears on our emotional response to current experience (real, literary, or whatever) because emotional triggers in representational memories are likely to activate the relevant emotion centers, at least if those triggers are vividly recalled or elaborated with adequate vividness in the current experience (e.g., in literary imagination).

Perhaps even more importantly, when we have a intense emotional experience, an implicit, "emotional memory" is stored in a different part of the brain from our representational memory. In ordinary brains, whatever activates the representational memory of an experience also triggers the emotional memory of that experience. We are not aware of the emotional memory per se, but our current feeling is more the result of that memory, than of its representational correlate. In a series of fascinating studies, Schacter shows that brain-damaged patients who have lost representational memory of certain events continue to react emotionally to situations that would have evoked those memories (see 171–2). For example, due to temporal lobe damage, some people cannot store new representational memories. In other words, from the time of the damage (e.g., an automobile accident), their representational memories never change. They never remember what has happened to them since the accident. They never recognize their doctor. If they were injured at twenty, each morning they expect to see a twenty-year-old looking back at them in the mirror. But suppose a particular nurse comes in and gives one of these patients a painful shot. The next day, the patient will insist that he/she has never seen the nurse before. And, indeed, the patient has no representational memory of the nurse. However, if the nurse approaches, the patient will withdraw and feel afraid. The approach of the nurse triggers the emotional memory. The patient does not understand why this is the case. But he/she feels the fear no less strongly (see LeDoux *Emotional* 180–93).

Though this phenomenon is most striking in the case of brain damaged patients, it occurs all the time in ordinary people. We feel happy or sad without knowing why. This happens because an emotional memory has been triggered, but we have not reconstructed a coherent representational memory, perhaps because our attentional focus is fixed on something more salient and "attention grabbing." These are among the cases where we are most likely to misattribute our feelings (as discussed in chapter 6).

Emotional memories almost certainly play a major role in literary experience as well. In fact, I now believe the priming of representational episodic memories is not the most important source of literary emotion. Rather, it is the activation of emotional memories. Much as in ordinary life, we misattribute these feelings due to our attentional focus on other (salient and attention-grabbing) events, specifically, the events of the literary work. Note that this misattribution is less mysterious as we are given no direct representational information with the emotion. Again, the emotional memory is "implicit." Our inference to its cause is contingent on the simultaneous activation of a correlated representational memory and our attentional focus on that representational memory. As always, attentional focus is the result of central executive directives or salience of the object. In the case of literature, central executive directives are focusing attention on the literary work, not the representational memories. In addition, the events of the literary work are usually more salient. (This is one result of literary works treating extraordinary events.) Finally, in the case of literature, emotive misattribution is particularly facilitated by our tacit integration of the representational memory fragments into our situation model for the literary work. In this way, the misattribution is, again, partially a correct attribution, for our understanding of the literary events has incorporated part of the relevant memories (as we saw in chapter 6). On the other hand, such misattribution is probably far more common in daily life than we typically imagine, and for basically the same reasons.

More generally, it is clear that emotional memories are an important source of emotional experience, literary and nonliterary. One very consequential aspect of emotional memories is that they are not confined to preset emotion triggers. Emotional memories derive from real sorrows, joys, and so on. Thus they may be completely different from the innate triggers. Someone who had a nearly fatal allergic reaction to honey might experience mild anxiety at the taste of sweetened tea, even if he/she knows that the sweetener is sugar. He/she might feel near panic at a taste that he/she identifies

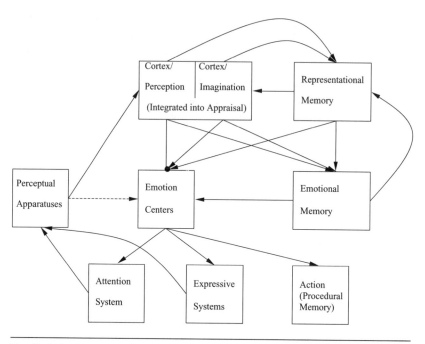

Fig. 6. A simplified schema of emotional response. The dashed line represents the first sketch information. The blunt end indicates that fuller perceptual information inhibits emotional response.

as honey. In this way, new emotional reactions may be added to those that are innate. Indeed, in some cases, they may contradict innate tendencies, as when a panic reaction to the taste of honey overwhelms any pleasure and associated happiness.

The result of all this is the following (see figure 6). We experience emotion when the emotion center is triggered through innate features or through the activation of an emotional memory (which need not involve any innate features and may even overrule such features in cases of conflict). In the former case, the relevant features may be sent to the emotion center through perception (usually in the first sketch information), imagination, or representational memory. One implication of this is that appraisal does not, by its pure logic, give rise to emotion. Instead, appraisal generates emotion through its associated imagery or through its ongoing activation of memories. It is well known that reasoning is often accompanied by visualization or other forms of imagination. When the images have the right features, they will trigger joy, sorrow, fear, or whatever. In addition, Smith and Kirby have presented evidence that appraisal processes rely extensively on the recruitment of memories. These, then, are the routes by which appraisal generates feeling.

The Aesthetician's Dilemmas

We are now, finally, in a position to return to our initial quandaries. We might begin with the two subproblems—the shared emotions problem and the differing emotions problem. The shared emotions problem is solved easily, given these cognitive principles. We all have the same innate emotion triggers, and these are central to our emotional experience. Moreover, the initial encoding of many of our representational and emotional memories has been guided by these triggers. Thus our memories will have a higher proportion of common features than the events they record. Finally, given conditions in the world and given our desires and frailties, at least some of the emotion-eliciting events themselves will be very similar. All this would contribute to considerable commonality of feeling in response to literature and other arts.

What about the converse of this, the differing emotions problem? This too is easy to resolve. The operation of emotional memories, and the possibility of emotional memories overwhelming innate tendencies, provide an obvious way of explaining differences. Though many emotional memories share some common features, the particulars of memories are always different. Moreover, in many cases, even the general features are very different— sometimes to the point of contradicting innate triggers. Indeed, memory helps explain not only individual differences in emotional response, but group differences as well. As we noted in chapter 6, if differences are the result of episodic memories, we would expect some social patterns in literary response where there are social patterns in emotionally consequential experience. Insofar as men and women have different emotional experiences, we would expect them to show patterned differences in literary response. Insofar as people from different cultures have different emotional experiences, we would expect them to have different emotional responses to literature. The same point holds for economic classes, and so on.

But none of this yet responds to the fictionality problem per se. How is it that we respond emotionally to literature at all? It turns out that this too is easy to explain. Our emotional response is a matter of trigger perception, concrete imagination, and emotional memory. The issue of fictionality just does not enter. To know that something is fictional is to make a judgment that it does not exist. But existence judgments are cortical. They have relatively little to do with our emotional response to anything. The intensity of emotional response is affected by a number of variables, as we have noted. These variables include, for example, proximity and speed, vividness, expectedness, and so on. These variables affect our response to literature, film, and other arts just as they affect our response to the natural world. But pure judgments of existence have only limited bearing on any of this. One can see why this would be the case. Our ancestors were not faced with situations where they had to discriminate between real lions and mere illusions. Judgments of existence had no particular value for their survival. Indeed, one might argue that the fictionality problem is backward. The issue is not why we sorrow over Juliet, but why we don't engage in some preventive action during a performance of the play. If existence judgments are entirely irrelevant to our response, shouldn't we simply respond as if the situation were real? Presumably, the emotional excitation surpasses only the threshold of orientation or expression, not that of control. Insofar as it does not surpass the threshold of control, higher cognitive/cortical processes may enter. Thus our judgment about the fictionality of a work does bear on our action (or inaction) in a movie theater. Indeed, it is even possible for cortical processes to have effects beyond orientation and expression. There are many real life cases where cortical processes may inhibit low road emotional responses that are normally compelling, as when I convince myself that a particular snake is safe, lowering the level of fear activation below the threshold of control. There is also a process of habituation whereby our reaction to emotion-triggering features may be dulled, at least in certain contexts. More technically, habituation occurs when "repeated presentation of a stimulus leads to a weakening of a response—you jump the first time you hear a loud noise, but if repeated over and over" without some subsequent harm, "you jump less" (LeDoux *Synaptic* 138). The phenomenon is familiar from animals "overcoming their fear of humans." The same sort of thing happens with, for example, cinema. Early movie-goers apparently were frightened relatively easily by what appeared on screen. However, habituation (due to the recurrence of the trigger without the appropriate outcome—a sort of Hebbian learning) has dulled our responses to the extent that filmmakers require increasingly intense visual effects to foster emotional results. (On the other hand, these visual effects continue to rely on the same basic set of emotion triggering features.)

Finally, we arrive at the encompassing "empathy problem." Empathy is clearly a complex issue that requires fuller, separate treatment. However, at a very basic level, it turns out that this too is a nonproblem. Emotion triggers and variables seem to operate without reference to any calculation of ego-relevance. Indeed, since they operate without calculation of any sort, they could hardly include a calculation of ego-relevance. Of course, some variables do *approximate* ego-relevance, but they do not concern ego-relevance per se. For example, distance is clearly measured by reference to my bodily location. Since I am at my bodily location and most other people are not, the determination of distance is effectively equivalent to a partial determination of ego-relevance. However, the two are not identical, and the difference shows up in important ways. Consider the following scenarios. I am resting my hand on a table. I see a spider on the table. Without thinking, I jerk my arm away, feeling a tinge of fright. I am holding a baby so that his feet rest on a table. I see a spider on the table. Without thinking, I jerk the child away from the table, feeling a tinge of fright. I look down and see a spider crawling up my shirt. Without thinking, I flick it away, feeling a tinge of fright. I am talking with someone in close proximity. I look down and see a spider crawling up his shirt. Without thinking, I flick it away, feeling a tinge of fright. (The last scenario happened to me recently.) In each case, there is hardly any difference in my reaction. In contrast, if I see a spider next to my boot, I may do nothing for a while, looking for a moment before moving my foot. I take these cases to illustrate a basic point about emotions: they are not in and of themselves egocentric. We respond emotionally to triggers. The intensity of our response is governed by a set of variables. In a sense, the entire structure is too crude to allow for egocentrism. It can only approximate egocentrism through such variables as proximity.

Indeed, empathy does not stop there. Not even all cortical processes are egocentric. Some are explicitly nonegocentric, such as imagining oneself in someone else's situation, adopting someone else's point of view. For example, in literature, we must not only imagine the situations and events concretely for the triggers to operate. In some cases, we must imagine the experiences of a protagonist. We must envision ourselves in his/her location and condition. Indeed, this occurs commonly outside literature as well. Perhaps Jones is up on a cliff and sees someone in danger at some distance. Jones feels fear insofar as she imaginatively puts herself in the place of the other person, envisioning the situation as he is experiencing it. (Without imaginatively putting herself in that position, the fear trigger would be too distant to have any effect.) In cases such as this, the generation of emotion is possible only through higher cortical operations. Here too the crucial point is that the emotional response is not egocentric, even though it relies on "high road" processing. It is purely a function of imagination, which gives rise to emotion through the usual triggering features and emotional memories.

In this way, we hardly have to explain empathy at all. Indeed, we have to explain the absence of empathy. Given our emotional constitution, one might expect us to be far more consistently empathic than we are. The enjoyment of cruelty appears as a particular puzzle. Of course, the enjoyment of cruelty relies on a sort of empathic capacity. It involves an ability to share the victim's emotion, but then twists that around to its opposite. Without empathy, we could not share someone's pain. Nor could we feel joy at someone's pain. Just how does our empathic capacity get perverted in this way? I suspect it has something to do with the operation of identity categories and perhaps the relation between moral evaluation and emotional response. Here too we come upon important issues for further study in an ongoing research program.

Your Own Private King Lear: An Informal Study of Student Memories and Emotion Triggers

In chapter 6, I described and tried to explain my emotional response to *Les Demoiselles d'Avignon*. In order to get a broader sense of emotional response, keyed particularly to the themes of this chapter, I would now like to consider a brief questionnaire on *King Lear* that a colleague distributed to her Shakespeare class. Eleven students (out of seventeen) turned in replies. I will conclude with some comments on the results.

The form consisted of six questions. The first asked students to name three emotions they felt when reading the play. The second asked them to name scenes where they felt these emotions. The third asked them to name the scene that they found most emotionally effective and to explain their emotional reaction. The fourth asked them to describe that scene as they imagined it. The fifth question was rather involved. I will discuss it below. The sixth question asked them to name three personal memories that occurred to them in connection with the emotionally effective scene.

In replies to the first question, the most commonly mentioned emotion was pity, followed closely by anger, then disgust/contempt. The explanations of these emotions often involved moral judgments. Some respondents related disgust/contempt to ethically damnable character traits, such as hypocrisy. Anger was often a response to the success of unethical acts. The anger could be directed against the villain (e.g., Edmund) or against someone who was not intrinsically evil, but who allowed evil to succeed because of some nonethical flaw, such as stupidity (as in the case of Lear). Finally, pity tended to be associated with upright characters who suffered undeservedly. The majority of responses focused on the first scene of act one. An average response might have expressed contempt for Goneril and Regan, pity for Cordelia, and anger against Lear. My subjective impression was that these answers showed only limited feeling.

The character of the replies changed noticeably with the question about which scene was most emotionally effective. First, a far smaller percentage of the answers treated the opening act (which seemed to be a sort of default for the initial questions). Second, the students' descriptions of their responses felt more genuinely emotional, at least to me. Finally, their discussions of these responses involved very little moral judgment. Instead, they were more open, personal, and empathic. Rather than addressing hypocrisy or good people suffering, these answers tended to address such topics as family relations. For instance, two students discussed the way Cordelia and Edgar had to witness the disintegration of their fathers. Others talked about Cordelia and Edgar being rejected by their fathers.

Given the responses to questions three and four, it is perhaps unsurprising that, when they answered question six, students presented emotionally significant memories of direct relevance to the scenes they found most affecting. I don't wish to go into the details of these personal memories. However, there are a couple of things worth remarking. First, while students did not choose precisely the same scene as most effective, many of them did choose similar scenes. This may be explained by the fact that they had similar memories—just as we would expect from the preceding account. Thus the repeated focus on the rejection of a child by a parent was related to memories of fights that these students had had with their own parents, and sometimes with incidents of being thrown out of the house. Other scenes and memories related to sibling conflicts and parental favoritism. Of course, not all the scenes and memories were similar and not all were confined to familial conflict. For example, one student found Gloucester's suicide scene the most moving; that student then spoke about a close friend's attempt at suicide.

The correlation between emotional response and personal memory does not mean that there was no issue of innate triggers in these answers. Innate triggers figured importantly. In one case, the student's response seems to have been primarily a matter of emotion triggers, not memories. Specifically, this student found Gloucester's blinding the most emotionally effective scene. He/she insisted that the event did not provoke any particular personal memory. Rather, the emotional effect was the result of the sheer horror of having one's eyes plucked out. Something moving into one's eye is a strong trigger for fright. Moreover, Gloucester's constraint is a clear fear trigger. The student's response based, presumably, on a vivid imagination of the scene nicely illustrates the effect of these triggers. Though this case was perhaps the most obvious, it was not at all the only one in which emotion triggers played an important role. The scenes chosen by other students, including those who stressed personal memories, prominently featured emotion triggers as well. For example, when students described their imagination of the scenes in question, they often emphasized the emotion on a character's face or in his/her tone of voice. Clearly, in their imagination of these scenes—and presumably in their memory of related personal experiences—triggers associated with other people's expressions of emotion were very strong.

The preceding reference to imagination takes us to question five. This question asked students to identify a short passage that expresses a strong emotion but that left them emotionally unaffected. It then asked the students to reread the passage, both silently and aloud, concretely imagining the character's situation and the personal meaning of his/her words. The concluding instruction was "describe what you felt when doing this." Several students did not answer this question. But two-thirds of those who did answer said that the exercise made them feel the emotion expressed in the passage.

Given the design of the questionnaire, and the context in which it was administered, these responses cannot provide evidence for the preceding analysis (that would require far better controls, the establishment of statistical significance, retesting in light of alternative hypotheses, etc.). However, they do illustrate the main points discussed above: the great importance of personal memory and vivid imagination in literary response and the centrality of emotional triggers to that response, both directly (as we experience those triggers in our imagination of the work) and indirectly (as those triggers figure prominently in our memories). The responses also show just the sort of diversity and patterned similarity of response that one would expect from the preceding account. Specifically, they involve reference to universal emotion triggers as well as certain types of personal memories that are not universal, but are common among students of their age and background (e.g., memories of parent/child conflict). At the same time, they manifest some sharp differences due to the necessary diversity of individual experiences.

Finally these responses not only point back to ideas we have already discussed. They also suggest questions for future study. For example, why were the students' initial replies unemotional in comparison with their subsequent answers? Was this simply a result of the artificiality of questionnaires? Or did it have something to do with differences in the nature of the cognitive tasks? In the first two questions, students were asked to engage in a sort of *top-down processing* where they begin with a global judgment, then turn to particulars. In the remaining questions, they were asked to engage in a sort of *bottom-up processing,* where they begin with a particular and then move to at least some abstraction in explaining their emotion (while maintaining "lateral" links with personal memories as well). The difference may suggest something about the nature of emotional cognition, or about the relation between emotion and moral evaluation—which may, in turn, bear on the vexing issue of inhibited empathy. It may also have ramifications for pedagogy or the theory and practice of performance.

In short, here again literary study suggests unique, important paths for further theorization and empirical investigation as part of an ongoing research program in cognitive science. The questions raised even in this informal study bear not only on our response to literature, but on matters ranging from the broad consequences of processing type to the nature and effects of ethical evaluations, perhaps even our fluctuating tendencies toward empathy. In other words, these are not rarified issues of academic literary criticism, but bear instead on highly consequential matters in our ordinary, practical lives.

CHAPTER 8

The Evolutionary Turn

Blindness and Insight in the Explanation
of Art and Mind

After one sets out cognitive architecture and analyzes patterns of mental activity and experience algorithmically in terms of that architecture, one is still left with a question—why are things like this? Why, for example, is the lexicon structured the way it is? Why do we have focused attention in some cases and defocused attention in others? Why did most of us develop constraints on remote associations? Why are there these emotion prototypes and not others? Questions such as these lead us to a different sort of explanation. They lead us from explanation in terms of current cognitive or neurocognitive structures and processes to explanation in terms of origins, of history. Specifically, they lead us to evolution. Within the general field of evolution, one form has been particularly influential among cognitivists, evolutionary psychology. Evolutionary psychology is, as the name suggests, an extension of evolutionary biology to psychology. However, it is not merely a generic term for any evolutionary work that treats the human mind. As developed by theorists such as John Tooby and Leda Cosmides, and extended by writers such as Steven Pinker, it involves specific and controversial doctrines. It is related to sociobiology and shares some of its basic premises—and, in my view, many of its problems.

In this final chapter, I address issues of evolution, cognition, and the arts in four sections. The first section treats the general theory of evolution. The second takes up evolutionary psychology, discussing some problems with this approach. The third section considers different levels of explanation in cognitive science. Specifically, it examines the relation of evolutionary theory to neurobiological, mental, and social accounts, as well as the relation of neurobiological, mental, and social accounts to one another. The final section turns to evolutionary treatments of literature and the arts. It begins with a criticism of some prominent approaches from evolutionary psychology. It then indicates some places where evolutionary theory might prove particularly valuable for literary and artistic study in the future.

What Is Evolution? The Fundamental Principles

At its basis, evolution is a simple process. We begin with some group of organisms that have certain predominant genetic characteristics. There is a change in one or another organism or in the environment. The change has consequences for reproduction. Differences in reproduction rates alter the predominant genetic characteristics of the group. In other words, those with some characteristics reproduce more than those without those characteristics. Because of this, from generation to generation, these characteristics become increasingly predominant in the group as a whole.

Consider the change in organism first. There are many random mutations in genetic pattern. As Ruelle explains, "the hereditary characteristics of animals and plants are transmitted by the DNA in chromosomes. . . . It has been shown that DNA consists of a long chain of elements belonging to four types, which may be represented by the letters A, T, G, C. Heredity therefore consists of long messages written with a four-letter alphabet. When cells divide, these messages are copied, with a few errors made at random; these errors are called *mutations*" (6). Most mutations are not a good thing. Occasionally, however, one is a good thing. Pinker puts the point very well: "Because no copying process is one hundred percent perfect, errors will crop up, and not all of the daughters will be exact duplicates. Most of the copying errors will be changes for the worse, causing a less efficient uptake of energy and materials or a slower rate or lower probability of replication. But by dumb luck a few errors will be changes for the better, and the replicators bearing them will proliferate over the generations. Their descendants will accumulate any subsequent errors that are changes for the better, including ones that assemble protective covers and supports, manipulators, catalysts for useful chemical reactions," and so on (*How* 159).

To say that a mutation is a good thing is to say that it is *adaptive*. This term is often misunderstood, so it is important to explain just how it is used in evolutionary theory. Technically, "adaptive" means "yielding a reproductive advantage." That is all that it means. It does not mean "benefiting the group" or "leading to long term advantage for one's descendants." It does not mean "smarter," "morally superior," or "better." It just means—more likely to produce offspring. Adaptive mutations tend to spread throughout a given population and become dominant simply because (by definition) the organisms that have those mutations reproduce more than everyone else.

There are different ways in which humans become more likely to produce offspring. Obvious possibilities include the following: (1) Living longer—or, rather, having a longer period of potency/fertility. If Jones dies at 15 and Smith dies at 40, then Smith is far more likely to have reproduced. (2) Being more sexually potent/fertile. (3) Having more frequent sex—thus having sex more readily available. (4) Having more partners. (Note that number four is more true for males than females, as is endlessly emphasized in evolutionary discussions. However, if males have different sperm counts, are not always in the mood when the female is fertile, and so on, then the same general principle holds for females.) Those mutations that are adaptive are precisely those mutations that lead to some such consequence (perhaps one of these four, perhaps another). Simple cases are, say, a mutation that yields a stronger heart (thus increased longevity) or one that results in an increased sperm count.

Evolution may also come about through a change in environment. In this case, the alteration in living conditions may change the status of an already existing trait. A particular resistance to hypothermia may be a trait held by a small percentage of the population for accidental reasons. It has no reproductive consequences as long as the climate is temperate. However, if there is a change in climate, that trait may suddenly become adaptive. As the climate alters, those who happen to be more resistant to hypothermia live longer and reproduce more so that, over time, the population as a whole becomes more resistant to hypothermia than it was previously. The same point holds for accidental immunity to a particular sort of illness which suddenly affects the population widely. Note that, initially, these traits resulted from mutations in the genetic code. When they occurred, they produced neither a *selection advantage* (i.e., an advantage in reproduction) nor a selection disadvantage. They were simply neutral and were thus passed on to offspring without systematic extension or loss. It is only when the environment changed that these traits became adaptive. Of course, the opposite can happen as well. Some trait might suddenly become disadvantageous with a change in environment.

Here we might return briefly to emotions. It should be clear how our previous discussion of emotion fits this Darwinian model. Fear is adaptive in the technical sense. By leading us to flee when in danger, it increases our likelihood of survival, thus the likelihood we will reproduce. Similarly, disgust turns us away from putrescent food, even when we are hungry. It thereby decreases the likelihood that we will die from poisoning, and thus increases the likelihood that we will live and reproduce.

Not every evolutionary change in a population is due to adaptation. In some cases, there may simply be a series of accidental occurrences that produce a broad shift in the population with no selection advantage. Thus a random mutation may spread throughout the population, even though it does not contribute to reproduction. This is called "genetic drift" and is usually important only in very small populations. I have not seen it invoked in evolutionary discussions of literature and the arts.

More importantly, some evolutionary traits go along with adaptive traits, but have no adaptive function themselves. These are called *by-products*. One example might be male pattern baldness. Male pattern baldness is the result of male hormones. Male hormones developed through the usual evolutionary mechanisms by producing selection advantages. In other words, the hormones themselves are adaptive. However, baldness does not have any selection advantage. Thus it is not an adaptive trait. Rather, baldness developed as a by-product.

There has been a lively debate as to whether literature is an adaptation or a by-product. The debate seems to me misguided for several reasons. First, literary scholars seem to take offense at the idea that literature is not an adaptation. They take this to be an insult. Again, adaptation simply means that the trait in question offers an advantage in reproduction. It says nothing about the more general value of the trait. In fact, one could argue that most things we truly admire do not yield a selection advantage. For example, altruism—the willingness to sacrifice even one's own life for others with whom one has no personal bond—is perhaps what humans admire most, and it is the actual antithesis of anything adaptive.[1] More importantly, the entire question of whether literature is adaptive seems to me misdirected. We do not ordinarily say that large concatenations of systems or of types of activity are or are not adaptive. We do not consider "society" or "the body" to be adaptive or not adaptive. Rather, we consider specific constituents to be adaptations, by-products, and so on. Literature has a degree of complexity that makes it an inappropriate object for a global judgment in this regard. It is just too big either to be adaptive itself or to be the by-product of some single adaptation (or to have resulted from genetic drift). We need to distinguish its components at the proper level in order to treat this issue.

The debate over whether or not literature is adaptive is part of a broader tendency within evolutionary thought today, what has been called "panadaptationism," "panselectionism," or "ultra-Darwinism." In ordinary scientific practice, we stop seeking explanations once we have an account of all the relevant phenomena and patterns. The elimination of redundant explanatory principles is called "Occam's razor" or the "principle of simplicity." If we have an account of why the baseball traveled to point x, and we have an explanation of why Billy's glove was at point y, we do not need a further explanation of why the ball did not end up in Billy's glove. That result is already explained by the prior explanations that locate the glove and the ball in different places. Similarly, if we have an explanation of whatever goes to make up, say, literature (e.g., if we have an explanation of narrative structure, imagery, poetic line length, our enjoyment of such techniques as assonance, and so on), then it makes no sense to ask for a separate explanation of literature. If we have an account of how the components of literature are either adaptations or by-products, then it makes no sense to ask about whether literature has an adaptive function. Writers with a tendency toward panadaptationism appear to forget the principle of simplicity and ask for evolutionary accounts of a given phenomenon at every level of complexity, no matter how unnecessary this may be.

Finally, before going on to evolutionary psychology it is important to note one further methodological point, one which is, in a sense, the converse of Occam's razor. Just as we need to avoid multiplying explanations beyond what is required to account for all the particulars, we need to carefully fill in explanations for all those particulars. Specifically, an adaptation (or a by-product) has to be explicable at every stage. In other words, there is no divine plan in evolution. There is no goal. Each adaptation must be open to full causal explanation in terms of reproduction at every point along the way. Thus one cannot claim that a particular mutation spread because eventually, after further mutations, it would allow fish to walk. Evidently, a series of mutations led from fins to legs. We may refer to these as mutations $m_1 \ldots m_n$. At m_n, we have a creature with legs, something that can walk. We cannot explain the extension of m_1 or m_2 by reference to this final stage. We cannot say that m_1 extended throughout the population because the organism was developing legs. We have to explain the occurrence and propagation of m_1 solely in terms of the proximate conditions of the relevant organisms at that time—mutations, changes in environment, immediate selection advantages (not selection advantages for descendants in the distant future), and so on. This is related to the use, or misuse, of such terms as "adaptation" and "function." For example, we say that fear "functions" to preserve our lives. This is a perfectly reasonable way of discussing the issue as long as we keep in mind that the "function" does not cause the trait initially. Rather, the function merely explains why the trait is adaptive. It does not name some sort of *purpose* for the trait. Strictly speaking, mutations produce particular mechanisms. It just happens that some of those mechanisms approximate functions (such as preserving life) and thus tend to be reproduced.

Evolutionary Psychology: This Is Not Evolutionary Biology

Biological evolution is pretty straightforward. We often have physical evidence of the precise sequence of developments. Thus we can often map out just what mutation or environmental change occurred when. Moreover, the things we wish to explain are fairly straightforward—things such as birds' wings or people's thumbs. Of course, one can turn evolutionary biology into unscientific nonsense, as did nineteenth century racialism (see Gould, *Mismeasure*, on the ways in which scientific principles were twisted, sometimes crudely, sometimes subtly, in racist and related work). But when pursued honestly, and with genuine scientific constraints, there are no more problems for evolutionary biology than there are for other sciences.

Evolutionary psychology is different. Evolutionary psychology concerns the evolution of mental phenomena, not biological organs, systems, and so forth. Thus, if we explain emotion, marital preferences, or literary practices in evolutionary terms, we are dealing with evolutionary psychology. These are not straightforward objects of study. In fact, we often know distressingly little about them. We claim to know what marital preferences are, what literature is. But usually we do not. For example, we judge marital preferences by surveys, which are notoriously unreliable. To a great extent, surveys report, not facts, but stereotypes. As Cynthia Epstein has pointed out, "individuals report feelings and 'traits' normatively prescribed as appropriate for their sex or group," not necessarily feelings and traits they really have (88). Similarly, Deborah Cameron explains that "people consistently misreport their own behavior when they are asked to describe it. They report usages that owe more to the stereotype than to the truth" (34). (For research directly on marital preference research, see Goode.) At the very least, we do not know nearly as much about human psychology as we know about human physiology; we do not know nearly as much about marital preferences as we do about thumbs. More importantly, we do not have detailed physical evidence that plots out the evolutionary stages of marital preferences the way we have such evidence about thumbs. As LeDoux puts it, "we have no fossil record tracing the evolution of behavioral or mental capacities" (*Synaptic* 6). There simply are no archaeological sites where we can dig up something that shows us how two million years ago early human males preferred mates with such-and-such properties, then a million years later how they had preferences closer to our own, then how a half million years later our own preferences appeared. If we try to explain the human thumb or brow today, we can refer back to a detailed history of stages. If we try to explain marital preferences today, we have nothing to refer back to. Moreover, evolutionary biology may make fairly straightforward use of evidence from related species. One can compare thumbs in apes and humans with relative ease. Things are not that simple in evolutionary psychology. Yes, we might look at mating practices among apes. But interpreting ape psychology is far more difficult and far less clear than interpreting ape thumbs.

Of course, none of this is an objection to pursuing a program in evolutionary psychology. However, these differences from evolutionary biology should lead us to exercise particular caution in developing hypotheses in evolutionary psychology. Unfortunately, this rarely seems to happen. Without much physical evidence, the methodology of evolutionary psychologists too often comes down to thought experiments in which the investigator tries to construct some reproductive advantage that might have led to current ideas, practices, and so on—for example, a reproductive advantage that might have led to current marriage preferences (as determined by surveys). More exactly, evolutionary psychology concentrates on the period when our ancestors were hunters and gatherers. Pinker explains that "For ninety-nine percent of human existence, people lived as foragers in small nomadic bands. Our brains are adapted to that long-vanished way of life" (*How* 42). While some hypotheses of evolutionary psychology are well defended, a distressing number involve attempting to imagine what life would have been like for a hunter/gatherer and then trying to move from there to an explanation of some current phenomenon—which, again, is itself usually not well understood.

A major problem with this method is that there is almost nothing one could not explain in this way. Suppose women like men who are fat. Well, that is because our ancestors who were attracted to fat men were more likely to reproduce because, in times when adequate food is scarce, fat men must have plenty of resources. Suppose women like men who are thin. Well, at a time when it was important to be able to flee predators when on a hunt, thin men had a selection advantage. No matter what we believe the data to be, we can come up with some evolutionary account that not only "explains" the data, but in effect shows a particular outcome to be necessary. This problem becomes even more severe because it more or less allows us to make up the outcomes we want as well.

In sum, we often do not have good evidence that the outcome of evolution is what evolutionary psychologists take it to be, and we often do not have good evidence that the evolutionary process was what they claim it to be. In many cases, all that we have is a self-confirming account that serves to make dubious generalizations into virtual laws about human feeling, thought, desire, and so on.

To make matters worse, the generalizations at issue are often politically consequential.[2] Indeed, the political consequences are not always implicit. As Rose and Rose point out, a number of writers in evolutionary psychology and the related field of sociobiology "claim that their new view of human nature should inform the making of social and public policy" (4). Many humanists—and many scientists—are particularly distressed by all this because the political implications of evolutionary psychology (and sociobiology) are often starkly inegalitarian. In pointing this out, I am not advocating that we reject any claims of evolutionary psychology on political grounds.[3]

My point is simply that many of these claims have very serious practical implications for people's lives. As such, they—like, say, claims about food or drug safety—should be more rigorously evaluated than less consequential scientific claims. They should require compelling evidence. But in fact the standards of evaluation in evolutionary psychology are not particularly rigorous; there is no requirement for compelling evidence, even for claims that have very significant social implications.

Consider, for example, Tooby and Cosmides' discussion of sharing. Their contention is that sharing is beneficial, and thus selected for (in evolution), when chance plays a significant role in the acquisition of goods. In contrast, sharing is detrimental and thus selected against (in evolution) when chance does not play such a role but, instead, skill and effort necessarily bring success. The "rational calculation" aspect of their argument appears plausible. But, as developed, it is very problematic. For instance, through their use of examples, they suggest that the distinction between random and nonrandom distribution is clear and sharp. That is not the case. First, virtually all success is a combination of both skill and luck. Second, in any given case, it is not that easy to tell how much success is due to luck and how much success is due to skill. Moreover, it is not true that the only components in success are skill and, so to speak, current luck in the current undertaking. Perhaps the most common reason for success, at least success in society, is one's prior situation (e.g., familial wealth), which includes one's past luck (e.g., being born in a higher rather than a lower class). Clearly, rational calculation dissuades us from cooperation in cases where past luck puts us in a position of virtually certain future success. In short, the basic opposition in rational calculation is not one between skill and luck, but simply the obvious opposition between likely success (for whatever reason) and uncertain success. Finally, it is not at all evident that the rational calculation argument entails selection pressure anyway. In other words, it is not at all clear that Tooby and Cosmides' arguments have any bearing on heritable traits or increased reproductive rates. Indeed, prima facie, it is very difficult to imagine how decisions about sharing could bear on either. Is Jones's decision not to share his wealth the result of a genetic mutation? Does it then allow him to beget more offspring than others whose genetic make-up leads them to more indiscriminate generosity?

Here, as elsewhere, the problems are important, not only intellectually, but politically. The conclusion drawn by Tooby and Cosmides is that, in cases where distribution is not going to be a result of mere current chance, community-wide "sharing would simply redistribute food from those who expend more effort or are more skilled, to those who expend less effort or are less skilled" ("Cognitive Adaptations" 213). Even a bare recognition of past luck would undermine this conclusion.[4] Note that the tendency against redistribution in these cases is, in their view, selected for through evolution. In consequence, this seems very much like a biological argument against socialism and even against such mildly redistributive programs as affirmative action.[5] In other words, it seems to say that affirmative action is nonadaptive and is incompatible with our biologically determined propensities. Moreover, despite the self-conscious antiracism of Tooby and Cosmides, it seems to imply that the statistical correlation between wealth and race reflects differences in skill and/or exertion. In short, it seems to render current social hierarchies biologically necessary.

Similar examples may be drawn from gender study. An extraordinary number of evolutionary psychological analyses concern supposed male/female differences. As it turns out, these differences are almost entirely in keeping with stereotypes. I suspect this does not mean our stereotypes are right, but rather that the researchers have begun with the stereotypes and simply created the evolutionary tale to fit the stereotype. One of the most common stereotypes in this area is that men are warlike due to millennia of war and women are nurturant due to millennia of raising children. But there are several problems here. Is it actually true that warlike men are more likely to reproduce in a society that values war? Might they not be just the people who get killed? Is it really true that women who are selflessly nurturant have a selection advantage? Are women more likely to reproduce if they sacrifice all for others? It is not clear that selection advantages would actually work in the way presupposed almost universally in this field.

More importantly, it is not clear how these properties could be passed on by sex even if there were such a selection advantage. Everyone who discusses the putative evolution of male and female psychological differences seems to forget that men and women are interbreeding populations. Suppose it really is true that Jane has more offspring because she is more selfless and peaceable. Suppose it really is true that John has more offspring because he is more warlike. Well, then the warlike genes (on the bizarre assumption that there are warlike genes) from John get mixed up with the peaceable genes from Jane. They have two children—Bob and Sally. What reason do we have to believe that Bob will inherit warlike genes from his father, not peaceable genes from his mother, while the precise opposite happens with Sally? Here, as elsewhere, it very much seems that the conclusions are ideologically determined, rather than scientifically determined; that, however unconsciously, the evolutionary account has been developed to conform to prior political beliefs.

The creation of ill-supported evolutionary tales to fit prefabricated conclusions is referred to as the making of "just-so stories." Lumsden, a clear proponent of evolutionary accounts, argues that "Just-so stories, unfortunately, comprise the bulk of what passes for explanatory discourse in evolutionary psychology" (160). Clearly, such stories have neither explanatory nor evidential force. Could they at least serve as reasonable starting points for more rigorous study? I do not believe so. Even as imaginative exercises, these just-so stories are problematic. Imagining oneself back to the time of our hunter/gatherer ancestors is usually a matter of projecting current presuppositions back as well. For example, the bulk of the discussion about selection pressure and reproduction seems to focus on such issues as having multiple sexual partners. Projecting backward from contemporary conditions, it does seem that the people with the most sexual partners are the ones who are most likely to reproduce. But this is because almost everyone—at least almost everyone in the immediate vicinity of evolutionary psychologists—is likely to live past the period of fertility. Thus today longevity is not a primary factor in reproduction. In terms of reproduction, it really does not matter if one lives to seventy-five or ninety-five. But it seems very likely that, for our hunter/gatherer ancestors, longevity was overwhelmingly the most important factor in reproduction. It therefore seems that, even as just-so stories, these are not very good. The men who reproduced more did not reproduce more because they had a tendency to infidelity. They reproduced more just because they lived longer.

The weirdest instance of evolutionary psychological argument is probably the argument that rape is adaptive because, among our hunter/gatherer ancestors, the men who raped had a selection advantage in that they were more likely to impregnate more women. This provides a good illustration of the points we have been considering. First, it begins with a presumption about contemporary society that lacks evidential support and, instead, appears to be based primarily on ideology. Specifically, it begins with the assumption that rape is an innate tendency of men, that it is a result of lust, and that it aims toward and culminates in ejaculation. This may seem quite reasonable. But there are alternative analyses. For example, probably the most common feminist account of rape is that it is an act of aggression, not an act of desire. This fits with the fact, reported by Laura Flanders, that rape leads to ejaculation only 50 percent of the time (11). Beyond this, even if rape were a matter of desire, it is unclear just what the desire is. For example, does rape involve an increase in excitement due to the pain of the victim? If so, then this is something the evolutionary account needs to address.

Moreover, it is not entirely clear just how rape would increase the likelihood of reproduction. First, there is the low ejaculation rate. Second, there is the fact that "victims of rape are often either too young or too old to be fertile" (Rose and Rose, Introduction, 3; this undermines the easy identification of rape with forced sex among scorpion flies, one of the prime examples used to support the rape-as-adaptation thesis—for nonhuman "forced sex . . . always takes place with fertile females" [3]). In addition, there are many important ancillary factors. For instance, sometimes rape leads to murder. It certainly leads to murder far more often than consensual sex leads to murder. This hardly seems adaptive. Moreover, one imagines that rape is less likely to conduce toward a stable family life. If family life is adaptive (i.e., if two parents working together to raise children increases the likelihood of the children surviving and reproducing), then rape would seem to be nonadaptive in this respect as well.

Then there is the question of just how this is passed on. True, women are not physically equipped to rape a man. However, if rape involves, say, excitement over the pain of one's partner, shouldn't this be inherited equally by male and female children. Moreover, rape is simply the most extreme case of the putatively male-only adaptation of promiscuity. But shouldn't women who are open to all sexual advances have a selection advantage even beyond that of rapists? As Fausto-Sterling asks, in relation to the supposed biological determination of male philandering, "Why isn't it just as likely that the females who passed on more genes to the next generation were the ones who hedged their bets and slept with more than one male?" (215). Indeed, Fausto-Sterling makes reference to primate research "refut[ing] the dogmatic assertions that . . . females don't gain from exuberant sexual behavior, and that females do best by choosing their mates prudently and with discrimination" (220). Similarly, Wade cites the argument of Olivia Judson that "a female's interest usually lies in having many lovers . . . to guard against male sterility, to ensure diversity in her offspring, to encourage each male in her group to think that he is the father and protect her children accordingly."

Finally, the rape issue raises one further problematic aspect of much evolutionary psychology. One of the arguments that rape is adaptive is that rape is found universally. It is found across cultures and across time periods. As such, the argument goes, it cannot be cultural and must rather be biological. This is an intellectual argument that seems to make sense, but is in fact false. One can see that it is false simply by exposing one of its tacit premises. For the argument to work, it must be the case that there are no universal principles that arise from interpersonal relations, from group dynamics, or from human interaction with an environment. All universals must be biologically innate. But this is implausible. There are things that happen whenever two people try to interact with one another (e.g., when two people try to raise children). There are things that happen whenever a group of people forms a society or otherwise engages in cooperative activity (e.g., hunting). There are things that happen whenever humans deal with different aspects of the environment (e.g., yearly changes in weather or daily changes in light). In short, the universality of some practice does not, by itself, establish that the practice is biologically determined rather than socially determined. Indeed, as a general rule, if we have a good social explanation of a universal and if that social explanation is based on factors that are undeniable anyway, then it is redundant to look for some further, biological/evolutionary account. It is (yet another) violation of the principle of simplicity or Occam's razor.

In sum, the principle of examining our psychological endowment in evolutionary terms is valid and valuable. It will no doubt contribute significantly to our understanding of literature and the arts. But as the field is currently constituted, evolutionary psychological analyses are often deeply flawed. They routinely begin with unwarranted presumptions about what is biological and what is not. They fabricate just-so stories that provide pseudo-explanations for conclusions that are typically based more on dominant ideology than on rigorous empirical study (which should include the generation and testing of hypotheses that do not conform to common stereotypes, adherence to the principle of simplicity, etc.).

Part of the problem here is that writers in cognitive science and evolutionary psychology do not, in my view, have a very clear idea of the ways in which different levels of explanation—neurobiological, mental, social—are related to one another and how each of these might be related to evolutionary analysis. In the following section, I consider that issue, before turning in the final section to the evolutionary study of literature and the arts.

Orders of Explanation: On Studying the Mind, the Brain, and Evolution

In this section, I would like to outline a simple account of the relations among distinct levels of natural scientific explanation, for many problems in cognitive science and evolutionary psychology arise from lack of clarity about these relations. I should first recall that the standard levels of explanation (along with their associated disciplines) are commonly ordered in the following hierarchy:

Society	Political Economics
Mind	Psychology
Organic Matter	Biology
Inorganic Matter	Physics/Chemistry

Roughly speaking, the elements lower in the hierarchy provide necessary conditions for elements higher in the hierarchy.

My first point is the uncontroversial one that *laws are conserved in the conceptual or explanatory movement from lower or more basic levels to higher levels*. Thus, the laws of physics and chemistry do not cease to operate on organic matter. The laws of biology do not cease to operate with respect to mind. The laws of psychology do not cease to operate in society. To take one example, laws of acoustics do not cease to operate in or bear on the psychological experience of music.

The second point I should like to make is also, I believe, uncontroversial. *Each level is defined by the emergence of some structure that is not accounted for by laws at the lower level.* The emergence of life with organic matter results in patterns that are not captured by the laws of chemistry and physics alone. The patterns of mind are not captured by the laws of biology alone. (As the Nobel laureate Roger Sperry put it, "The events of inner experience, as emergent properties of brain processes, become themselves explanatory causal constructs in their own right, interacting at their own level with their own laws and dynamics" [qtd. in Holland *The Brain* 89]). The patterns of society are not captured by the laws of psychology alone. To advert again to music, the sense of a tonal center is not explained by the laws of hearing, say, or acoustics.

Taken together, these uncontroversial generalities have some controversial implications. Consider, for example, the fact that the mind is clearly contingent upon brain function. When the brain is injured, the mind suffers. Doesn't this show that the mind is really the brain, that it is, in fact, "mind/brain"? No, it does not. The mind is contingent upon the brain in the same way that the brain is contingent upon its own physics. Since more basic laws all continue to apply, any disruption of lower-level constituents will, by that fact, be a disruption of the emergent structure. Lesions to certain parts of the brain will destroy various linguistic capacities, just as the fusion of atoms in the skull will destroy brain capacities. It no more follows that we should understand the mind as the singular "mind/brain" than that we should understand the brain as the singular "brain/collection of atoms in the head."

A final banality before going on: this hierarchy represents not only a logical sequence, but a rough temporal sequence as well. Thus each level not only incorporates the preceding level, it derives from the preceding level. Moreover, these levels themselves are not uniform. They too are hierarchized internally, and the hierarchy is derivational. In the case of organic matter, we commonly explain this derivation by reference to evolution.

More exactly, the relation between any given level and the superior level—call them levels one and two—is something along the following lines. The laws that govern elements of level one constrain the possible patterns that can emerge to form level two. There is some transition principle or set of transition principles—which can be mere chance—that allows some possibilities to be realized and stabilized in continuing patterns. Consider two levels within organic matter—for example, two levels in the evolution of the eye. All lower-level laws (those of physics, chemistry, and biology) operate to constrain the possible emergence of new eye-related structures out of level one. Elements of these possible structures arise through random mutation and natural selection largely determines which options continue (whether directly as adaptations or indirectly as by-products).

Emergent Structures = Primary and Secondary Structures
(Level 2)
↑
Realizations of Possibilities = Primary Structures
↑
←Transition Principles
(e.g., Mutation and Natural Selection)
↑
Field of Possibilities
↑
Conjunction of All Lower-Level Laws
(Level 1)

Fig. 7. A general representation of the relation between basic and emergent structures.

Finally, as the new patterns develop, they will themselves have further consequences that arise, not from the initial rules nor from the transition principle, but from the mere concatenation of realized possibilities. We may refer to the initial set of realized possibilities as "primary structure" and the patterns derived from their conjunction as "secondary structure." Together, they define *emergent structure*.[6] (See figure 7.)

Note that this account greatly constrains the application of the transition principles (e.g., mutation and natural selection). As Lyle Jenkins has argued, following Gould ("Darwinian"), Chomsky (see chapter 6 of *New Horizons* and "Linguistics"), and others, evolutionary psychology has tended to ignore prior constraints on natural selection. These prior constraints are what I am calling "conjunction of all lower-level laws." Moreover, evolutionary psychologists have tended to ignore the difference between primary and secondary structures. (Note that primary structures here include both adaptations and by-products.)

Consider the following example. Studies suggest that women are less likely to desire multiple sexual partners than are men. I will leave aside for the moment the reliability of these studies. (Given prevailing social mores, women have reason to underrepresent their promiscuity while men have reason to overrepresent theirs.) Let's assume that this is simply true. Evolutionary psychologists directly explain data of this sort as the result of natural selection, with evolution producing a situation in which women have an innate tendency toward fidelity and men toward libertinism (see, for example, Pinker *How* 469–82). Given the preceding analysis, three issues arise with respect to this evolutionary account. The first concerns the bottom half of my diagram. Here we might ask such questions as—is this psychological development consistent with the laws of biology? Could traits of promiscuity and fidelity be generated and selected in such a way that they were not passed on willy-nilly to a couple's offspring. In other words, is it biologically plausible that the sons inherit promiscuity from their promiscuous fathers with no relevant inheritance from their faithful mothers, while the reverse occurs with daughters?

The second issue concerns the middle of the diagram, the transition principle. Here, we might ask if it is indeed the case that male promiscuity yields a selection advantage while female promiscuity does not. Again, it seems likely that longevity was overwhelmingly the most important factor in reproduction. Moreover, women who were willing to have multiple partners would appear more likely to get pregnant—especially if their steady partner was routinely out having intercourse with other women and thus not always available at the right times. Then there are the ancillary arguments that, given the high likelihood of childhood mortality, wouldn't a constant, protective male presence—a concomitant of male fidelity, not male promiscuity—help assure the survival of the offspring? Wouldn't male fidelity thereby provide a selection advantage?

The final, and for our present purposes the most important issue here concerns the top of the diagram, the relation between realized possibilities or primary structure and the full set of emergent structures which includes secondary structure. Let us grant that this difference between men and women is part of the emergent structure. The evolutionary account posits specifically that it is part of what I am calling "primary structure." Thus it is innate and not a residue of other innate factors. The difference is important. The question then is, can the difference in male and female preferences regarding number of sexual partners be accounted for by other, uncontroversial primary structures or must it be posited as part of primary structure itself. (Graphically, it is the difference between figures 8 and 9; note that

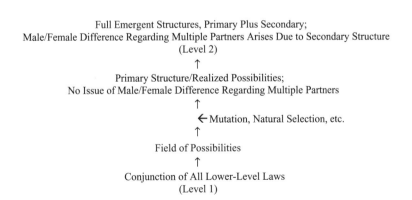

Full Emergent Structures, Primary Plus Secondary;
Male/Female Difference Regarding Multiple Partners Arises Due to Secondary Structure
(Level 2)
↑
Primary Structure/Realized Possibilities;
No Issue of Male/Female Difference Regarding Multiple Partners
↑
← Mutation, Natural Selection, etc.
↑
Field of Possibilities
↑
Conjunction of All Lower-Level Laws
(Level 1)

Fig. 8. A schematic account of gender difference regarding sexual partners as arising in secondary structure, thus not as an innate property.

Full Emergent Structures;
Male/Female Difference Regarding Multiple Partners Is Carried Over
(Level 2)
↑
Primary Structure/Realized Possibilities;
Male/Female Difference Regarding Multiple Partners Arises Here
↑
← Mutation, Natural Selection, etc.;
　　Difference Regarding Multiple Partners
　　Yields Selection Advantages
↑
Field of Possibilities;
Difference Regarding Multiple Partners Fits the Laws of Biology
↑
Conjunction of All Lower-Level Laws
(Level 1)

Fig. 9. A schematic account of gender difference regarding sexual partners as arising in primary structure, thus as an innate property.

the preceding questions about lower level laws and the transition principle apply only to figure 9.)

It is uncontroversially the case that the primary structure includes such things as women being the ones who get pregnant, pregnancy lasting for nine months, pregnancy having a wide range of serious effects on one's physiology, and so on. It includes the physical nature of the sex act, which makes it easier to transmit sexual diseases from men to women than from women to men. That physical nature also makes it possible for women to be subjected to forced intercourse, but not to initiate forced intercourse themselves. What is crucial here is that these and other elements, which clearly appear at the "realized possibilities" level, predict greater caution for women in sexual relations. Moreover, if females are primary caretakers of children—due to the physical nature of feeding (men don't lactate), then there may simply be less time and opportunity for sexual exploration. If these factors are sufficient to explain the male/female difference regarding multiple partners, then the principle of simplicity indicates that positing innate tendencies (i.e., differences in primary structure) is theoretically redundant and should be eschewed. For example, Panksepp discusses the male "hit-and-run" sexual pattern in the following terms: "Males make a smaller biological investment . . . because they do not get pregnant, and so are more likely to depart without establishing long-term commitments than are females, who carry and gestate the fetus" (227). In keeping with this, Panksepp cites cases where the common sexual pattern is reversed: "in many species of fish where external fertilization is the norm, the fathers typically remain to tend and protect the eggs while females depart to entice another receptive male" (246). Of course, there are other relevant data here—data that seem to support innate difference in primary structure; but there are also further emergent structures, especially at the social level, that argue against innatism. The point is that we cannot simply assume that a difference of this sort is part of primary structure—thus biologically innate (with all that this entails socially, politically, and so on)—rather than a contingent feature of secondary structure.

This point is important for those of us interested in cultural study or any other form of inquiry that is incompatible with all-consuming biological accounts. Thus the preceding analysis suggests not only the contingency of emergent structures (specifically, primary structures) on the body of basic laws; it also indicates—to use a Marxist phrase–the partial autonomy of those emergent structures (specifically, secondary structures).

Up to now, I have been speaking about conservation from lower to higher levels. Here, we might ask if higher levels have any consequences for lower levels. I believe they have quite profound consequences. Specifically, while laws are conserved upward, *structures are projected downward*. In other words, the emergent structure is not simply dependent upon lower level structures, but in fact organizes elements of the lower level in its own terms. So, psychological structure does not fix social structure, though the laws of mind place limits on social structure. Rather, patterns that arise at the level of social structure themselves place minds in certain social relations. Neuroanatomy does not fix psychological structure, though the laws of neuroanatomy place limits on psychological structure. Rather, patterns that appear at the level of psychology themselves define certain structural relations in neuroanatomy.

This point is entirely clear when we look at levels that are not contiguous. For example, transportation systems are integrated structures at the social level. It does not matter that they are physically diverse and spatially dispersed. Put differently, facts about pure physical or geographical relations have no direct implications for this social structure (though the structure obviously remains limited by the laws of physics). The social structure of "transportation system" projects down to the physical level, taking diverse bits of matter spread discontinuously across different regions and making them into a single structure.

Similarly, consider the psychological processes by which we hear certain sequences of tones as standing in particular relations with one another, involving quantized pitch intervals (i.e., "rounded off" pitch intervals, as discussed in chapter one), a pattern with a tonal center and other organizational relations (e.g., leading tones), processes by which we cluster tones together into sequences and map them onto other sequences as themes and variations, despite great differences among these sequences (e.g., we may map sequence A onto sequence B despite the fact that it is more similar to sequence C in terms of mere sound—and yet our mapping may be completely correct at the psychological level). This all projects downward to the neurobiology of musical reception or production and to the physics of sound, giving particular patterns to neurobiological processes and acoustic events. Sometimes the treatment of lower-level structures in terms of higher-level structures (e.g., the identification of a particular sort of stimulation of the amygdala as fear) is referred to as "interpretation." Conversely, the treatment of higher-level structures in terms of lower-level structures (e.g., the identification of fear as a particular sort of stimulation of the amygdala) is referred to as "explanation." By the present account, both interpretation and explanation are important and neither is eliminable.

I should emphasize here that I am not saying the higher levels have *causal* consequences for lower levels. Again, causal principles are conserved *upward*. Rather, I am saying that higher levels have *organizational* consequences for lower levels. Several sequences of tones do not form themselves into a set of themes and variations due to their physical properties. Rather, our mentalistic experience of those sequences organizes them in this way. Indeed, that is what separates them out as sequences to begin with. (Needless to say, it does not thereby change the sounds or order of the sounds as physical events; again the relation is not causal). The neurobiological events associated with hearing themes and variations are also isolated as units for consideration, separated from all other aspects of neurobiology, due to this connection with mental events (i.e., with the experience of themes and variations). In other words, the selection and segmentation of brain events is a result of their interpretation in mentalistic terms.

For readers who would like a brain/molecule example, here is one from Joseph LeDoux: "If looked at microscopically, which is to say, molecularly, implicit (unconscious) emotional memory and explicit (conscious) memory of emotion may be indistinguishable. But at the level of neural systems and their functions, these are clearly unique operations of the brain" (*Emotional* 224). I would only add that LeDoux's example presupposes a further, mental level of downward projection, as indicated by his references to consciousness and emotion. Thus, in LeDoux's example, mental structures (e.g., "memory") provide an organizational principle for neural systems, which in turn provide an organizational principle for the subneural or molecular level. Daniel Schacter in effect provides an example of projection from psychology to neurobiology when he organizes data from brain scans by reference to "two levels" of knowledge, "general-event knowledge and event-specific knowledge" (123). The brain scans give us insight into causal principles of the brain. But, at the same time, it is only by reference to the higher-level mentalistic structures that we can interpret the brain scans, organizing them by reference to the mentalistic categories, "general-event knowledge" and "event-specific knowledge."

Downward projection of structure has some significant consequences. One is particularly relevant here. We should know as much as possible about the higher-level structure we are investigating before we go too far with lower-level explanations. Again, the higher-level structure is what organizes the lower level. Without a clear sense of higher-level structure, we cannot even know what there is to be explained. Specifically, cross-level explanation is inseparable from cross-level interpretation. The two necessarily go together (as the example of fear and the amygdala suggests). Interpretation, however, cannot proceed without knowledge of the higher-level structure. After all, the higher-level structure gives us the meaning in terms of which the lower level is interpreted. This may seem to be a rather simple matter when one thinks of emotions such as fear. But it is not at all a simple matter when one is addressing such complex phenomena as language or literature. Thus it was crucial for linguists to learn a great deal about language structure before beginning to examine just what the neurophysiological correlates of language might be and how they may have developed. For the most part, this has not been the case in studies of literature and the arts.

Before going on to treat literature and the arts in more detail, there is one final issue we should address. It concerns the place of intentionality in this structure. The topic bears on a number of important issues, such as the possibility of a purely neurobiological cognitive science, which is to say, a form of physicalism that eliminates intentionality and thus goes directly against Fodor's view of cognitive science as "intentional through and through" (7). (Some writers consider pure neurobiology to be a sort of ideal for cognitive science.) Up to now, I have left something out of our analysis, something that problematizes any encompassing neurobiology or evolutionary psychology of aesthetics—or, for that matter, any objectifying cognitive science of aesthetics: observers. At each level, we have not only an object. We have an observer as well. Thus our initial hierarchy should more properly have appeared as follows:

Observer (political economist) → Society
Observer (psychologist)   → Mind
Observer (biologist)   → Organic Matter
Observer (physicist/chemist)   → Inorganic Matter

There are many arguments that necessitate this, ranging from quantum mechanics to the nature of meaning and the truth conditions for our own assertions (as I have argued in *On Interpretation* [90] and "Structure" [13–4]).

The crucial point is that, though the observer is the human mind, it is a human mind that is solely and entirely subject, a human mind that is not part of what is being explained. Putnam once conjectured that, in von Neumann's view of quantum analysis, "the ultimate observer ... is the Kantian transcendental ego" (251). This is the human mind as pure intentional experience, not as an object at all—not a material object, not a spiritual object. It falls fully outside objectifying description. Rather, it provides a necessary and irreducible condition for all objectal descriptions and for explanations at every level. This is the self of ethics and of empathy as well. It is how we experience ourselves. It is what we imagine for other people when we try to adopt their point of view or when we treat them as ends in themselves. It is also central to our experience of literature. It cannot be treated at the level of neurobiology—nor even at the level of objectified mind. It is on the other side of a fundamental epistemological divide. It is, as Wittgenstein said, not a part of the world, but its limit (5.632). Indeed, it is what makes solipsism and idealism plausible alternatives to physicalism. Put simply, to some extent, the arts will always partake of the left side of our last diagram. My final point here is that this pure subjectivity is necessarily something in the arts—or, indeed, anything else human—that is inaccessible to any program in cognitive neuroscience, evolutionary psychology, or any other objective order of explanation.

Evolutionary Accounts of Literature and the Arts: Past Problems and Future Possibilities

But, of course, to say that there are limits—even a priori limits—on the explanatory possibilities of cognitive neuroscience and evolutionary psychology is not to say that there is nothing for cognitive neuroscience and evolutionary psychology to explain. There is a great deal for them to explain, both in general and with respect to the arts in particular. We discussed the role of neuroscience in the preceding chapter. In this final section, I will consider just what place evolutionary psychology has had in the study of literature and the arts and what place it might have in the future.

Unfortunately, to this point, most evolutionary psychological accounts of literature and the arts have suffered from the problems discussed above.[7] First of all, such accounts have tended to begin without any clear idea of just what is to be explained. Specifically, the most common approach to literature is to ask the very strange question of whether literature is an adaptation or a by-product. As I have already noted, this is not a question that makes much sense. Before even considering such a question, we need a clear idea of just what literature is. But once we begin thinking about what literature is, we realize that we need to be asking much more specific questions about much more specific components of literature.

Consider, for example, Steven Pinker's influential discussion of literature and adaptation. He follows the Horatian view of literature as producing both delight and instruction: "It's helpful to distinguish the delight, perhaps the product of a useless technology for pressing our pleasure buttons, from the instruction, perhaps a product of a cognitive adaptation" (*How* 539). It is difficult to say why the pleasure is not adaptive or just how it arose as a by-product. Here, one suspects that Pinker is simply following the usual prejudice that the pleasure part does not justify literature. Rather, the instruction part justifies literature. Since the pleasure is not a justification, it must not be an adaptation. Since the instruction is a justification, it must be an adaptation. There seems to be an implicit Puritanism here that is not in keeping with evolutionary theory. After all, in general, pleasure is adaptive. Why is sex pleasurable? Because our ancestors who enjoyed sex tended to engage in it and thus to reproduce.

If the nonadaptive nature of aesthetic pleasure is less than fully clear, the connection of instruction with adaptation is, if anything, even harder to figure out. For one thing, it is difficult to say just what instruction literature conveys. The standard view in evolutionary psychology is that, like imagination generally, literature provides a sort of "off line" practice. Literature is a simulation that allows us to hone our skills at difficult actions without any real risk. The instruction one gets from literature is akin to the instruction one gets from one of those driving simulators in driver's education. You can practice speeding down the highway or making left turns without the risk of crashing your car. But is this really a plausible account of literature? If one thinks about the sorts of situation that literature represents, this seems unlikely. After all, one point of literature is to recount things that are not ordinary. The very nonordinariness of literary works would seem radically to reduce their applicability to our ordinary lives. Pinker succinctly states the case for the common evolutionary view of literary instruction, writing that "The intrigues of people in conflict can multiply out in so many ways that no one could possibly play out the consequences of all courses of action in the mind's eye. Fictional narratives supply us with a mental catalogue of the fatal conundrums we might face someday and the outcomes of strategies we could deploy in them" (*How* 543). Initially, this may sound alright. But Pinker's example illustrates the problems with this idea. Alluding to *Hamlet*, Pinker asks, "What are the options if I were to suspect that my uncle killed my father, took his position, and married my mother?" (543). The question is doubly weird. First, how could this particular situation possibly have survival value? How could I possibly increase my likelihood of reproducing simply by learning what to do in these very odd circumstances? Second, *Hamlet* does not actually teach us how to respond in that situation anyway. The very best it could be said to do is to teach us to check someone's identity before killing him (due to the Polonius incident). That is probably good advice for people planning a murder, but hardly a strong argument for this account of literature and adaptation.

Similar points could be made about the arguments of E. O. Wilson, Robert Storey, or John Tooby and Leda Cosmides. For example, Tooby and Cosmides argue that literature answers such questions as "How would I feel if my sister died, and I were responsible?" ("Does Beauty" 23). This may seem to be a better specific example than Pinker's. But is it really plausible that literary works, even literary works dealing with this precise topic, are likely to reduce the rate of sororicide so much that it affects the gene pool? Evidently the idea is that people with sensitivity to literature would read literary works of this sort and not kill their sisters (or not let them die), whereas people without sensitivity to literature would kill their sisters (or let them die). Over time the families of people insensitive to literature would dwindle and literature-sensitive genes would spread throughout the population. This does not seem to be a likely scenario. Finally, there is the serious problem that the literary works in question were all produced well after any significant human evolution ended anyway. As Stephen Jay Gould points out, "*Homo sapiens* has experienced no directional trending for at least 40,000 years" (*Structure* 913).

Tooby and Cosmides' discussion of beauty may have greater prima facie plausibility than any of the arguments we have considered thus far. But it is problematic as well. They begin with an important distinction in modes of neurocognitive adaptation. The first mode is "functional." This is the mode we have been discussing thus far. Functional mode adaptive features directly serve survival or reproduction. The second mode is "organizational." Organizational mode adaptive features facilitate the development of directly functional capacities. For example, language use has direct survival function. Infantile babbling, in contrast, has no direct survival function. However, it aids in the acquisition of language. Thus babbling is an organizational adaptation ("Does Beauty" 16). Tooby and Cosmides maintain that a human aesthetic orientation is an organizational adaptation. This is certainly possible. But their particular account is not compelling.

Specifically, they argue that "A human should find something beautiful because it exhibits cues which, in the environment in which humans evolved, signaled that it would have been advantageous to pay sustained sensory attention to it" (17). Their examples include "everything from members of the opposite sex and game animals to the exhibition by others of intricate skills" (17). First, their examples are overly selective. It is difficult to see how staring into the sky, listening to birdsong, looking at glaciers, or contemplating mountains fits here. Second, even in the cases they name, the explanation does not seem to work. Our sense of human beauty is not at all the same as our sense of physical attraction. For example, facial beauty involves averaging across different facial features we have seen (see Langlois and Roggman) and it is not confined to the opposite sex. There is no clear relation here to propensities that bear on reproduction. As to their second example, we consider some game animals beautiful, but not others (e.g., pigs). Moreover, we consider some predators beautiful, but not others. And we consider some work animals beautiful, but not others. Along similar lines, we consider some birds beautiful—but for the most part these are not birds we eat (e.g., chickens) or watch out for (e.g., vultures). As to "intricate skills," we wonder at acrobats engaging in impractical flips, but not at the actions of sewing. It simply does not seem that Tooby and Cosmides have isolated a pattern here. Moreover, this does not even touch on the issue of whether our awe at people riding a horse while standing on their hands, our delight at a pretty face, our wonder over a strange rock formation or desert landscape, and our pleasure at reading poetry are all experiences of precisely the same type.

The last point brings us back to our initial problem with recent evolutionary attempts to explain art. In addition to the general problems with evolutionary psychology, evolutionary discussions of literature and the arts are particularly hampered by the fact that they begin with an excessively vague idea of their topic. For example, despite a couple of qualifications (see 18), Tooby and Cosmides have a very loose notion of beauty and the response to beauty. Imagine that we began an evolutionary account of "language" without any knowledge of linguistic universals and linguistic variation, the different aspects of syntax, morphology, phonology, semantics, and so on. No theorist, however brilliant, could address the evolution of language successfully with only an intuitive knowledge of language.[8] The same point holds for literature, music, painting, beauty, and so on. All too often, evolutionary psychologists try to explain a higher-level structure (e.g., literature) in terms of a lower-level structure (biology) without first acquiring a detailed understanding of what that higher-level structure is.

How might we overcome this problem? The answer is fairly straightforward. We need to begin with a cognitively well-specified, algorithmic account of particular literary and artistic phenomena. This is precisely what we sought in the preceding chapters. In conclusion, then, I would like to go back through those chapters briefly to consider how these analyses suggest some possible topics for evolutionary research and theorization in the future.

The first chapter analyzes music in terms of standard cognitive architecture. For the most part, then, it does not require an evolutionary account beyond that of the architecture itself. However, there are some specific questions this chapter might raise for evolutionary study. Suppose that the auditory processor does indeed mark incoming sound for relative pitch.

Why is this the case? Is marking of relative pitch adaptive? Perhaps it is functional in the discrimination of different cries. In any case, one might ask here just how the pitches are marked, if there are particular intervals to which we are more sensitive, why this may have arisen, and so on. Note that, even if we decide that relative pitch marking is a by-product, we still have a question as to what it is a by-product of. Other questions from this chapter would include why it is that dissonance is experienced as noise, thus as unpleasant. One could imagine a scenario in which certain sorts of cry are highly dissonant and those who fled from those cries also fled from danger. In other words, one could imagine that this sensitivity has a function comparable to that of dysphoric feelings in emotion. On the other hand, this may simply be a by-product of other developments. (The unpleasantness of cognitive disorientation does not seem to require any special explanation. In general, a clear schematic knowledge of what is happening in one's environment has obvious selection advantages. Our sense of distress at disorientation continues in our experience of music, even if the selection advantage is no longer present in that particular case.)

Chapter 3 raises a number of interesting evolutionary issues. First, consider the difference between having a sharp drop in connection strength among associations and having only a gradual drop. Again, it seems that creativity is in part the result of having only a gradual drop. Any given individual is likely to have a sharper drop in some areas than in others. However, it may be the case that some individuals are on the whole more likely to have a gradual drop while others are more likely to have a sharp drop. If so, one might ask how this comes about. Is it a matter of childhood experience and training, or is there some biological basis for it? If there is a biological source, could this be a case of "disruptive" selection? Most of the time, we think of evolution as pushing everyone in the population toward a particular, shared state. If having an opposable thumb is adaptive, then adaptation pushes everyone in the direction of an opposable thumb. But, in some cases, evolution might push in two different directions. Perhaps fear is a case of that. Perhaps it is adaptive to flee or to freeze. What is not adaptive is to do something in between. If so, then evolution might push in both directions. Of course, due to the interbreeding of populations (freezers and fleers intermarry) these traits are combined. All of us sometimes flee and sometimes freeze. But it might have happened that the traits did not combine. It might have happened that fear was like eye color. We get one eye color from our parents, not a mixture of the two. Thus we might have inherited either freezing or fleeing. Perhaps that is what happens with sharp and gradual drops in connection strength. We might also ask in this context whether both are adaptive in isolation or if one becomes adaptive in the context of a society with division of labor—and, if so, what consequences that might have.

Other issues arise in relation to the representationalist part of this chapter. Clearly, the operation of schemas, prototypes, and exempla is a general issue within evolution. It is not specific to the arts. Moreover, the issue of variations in these structures is general as well. Nonetheless, one might wonder about the particular prominence of cross-domain innovation. Here one might ask not only how it comes about that the mind is structured into particular domains, but how it happens that we draw cross-domain connections at all. Conversely, one might ask how it develops that we draw cross-domain connections so rarely, given that it is apparently the means for producing great artistic and scientific innovations. Of course, in all this, we would need to keep in mind the role played by social organization (e.g., institutionally regulated disciplinary divisions).

Finally, this chapter raises the issue of just how the particular modes of childhood artistic expression arose. Are they instances of more general processes? Can they be analyzed into components? Did these components arise through evolution? To what extent are these modes the result of innate tendencies and to what extent are they the result of universal aspects of childhood experience?

Chapter 4 takes up several sorts of cognitive process. One involves the transfer of lexical information. This is clearly something to be considered in relation to more general (i.e., not purely literary) issues surrounding the evolution of the structures and processes of the lexicon. As to the Lakoff/Turner account of conceptual metaphor, here too we are dealing with such an advanced and complex process that we can hardly address it globally in evolutionary terms. On the other hand, it is clear that eventually followers of Lakoff and Turner would want to consider such issues as the evolutionary development of modeling one set of concepts on another, the primary and secondary structures involved in this, and so forth. They will also want to consider whether particular conceptual metaphors are universal and, if so, whether they have an evolutionary role (or, if not, how they have arisen otherwise). Finally, the broad processes of conceptual blending are almost certainly the product of evolution. But these too are complex. One would need to consider the development of working memory, the development of particular procedural schemas that operate in the selection of information to project to the general workspace, the processes of cognitive identification and differentiation of the particulars being blended, and so on.

Chapter 5 addresses the cognitive reconstruction of story from discourse. This involves precisely the same structures and processes that we use to construct a situation model from our incomplete and discontinuous looks around a room. In this case, there is no special question to ask about the literary activity. Even the treatment of universal story structures appears to reduce to a nonliterary issue—the nature of emotion prototypes. On the

216 · Cognitive Science, Literature, and the Arts

other hand, this section does raise the question of just why these particular emotion prototypes might have arisen. (I have tried to give at least a preliminary account of this in the afterword to *The Mind and Its Stories*.)

Chapter 6 considers emotions as appraisals. Since the theory of emotions as appraisals arose in the context of evolutionary analysis, there is no issue of trying to find an evolutionary account here. This chapter also treats simulation. It does seem that the evolutionary psychologists are right that, in general, simulation allows us to imagine possible scenarios without the risks involved in actually acting out those scenarios. Thus I can imagine what will happen if I decide to teach a summer course (more money, less time) and if I do not (less money, more time). Having imagined those scenarios, I can make a better decision than if I could not imagine them. As such, imagination clearly has an adaptive function, and imagination is clearly put to use in literature. However, this still needs to be worked out in greater algorithmic detail.

The chapter also considers the lexical processes of access and priming and the emotive effects of memories. Lexical access and priming are clearly general features of cognition. Thus an account of their genesis is not peculiar to literary study. Similarly, the emotive effects of memories in literary experience result from the emotive effects of memories generally. These effects have a clear evolutionary function. If I experience danger in a particular place, the fear associated with the memory will provide a disincentive for returning to that place. That disincentive has evident selection advantages.

Chapter 7 also deals with ideas about emotion that arose in the context of evolutionary thinking. Those particular ideas, then, do not require further analysis in evolutionary terms. However, one might still ask about the role of emotion in vivid imagination. This appears to be part of the general adaptive function of simulation. Insofar as simulation functions to encourage self-preserving decisions and discourage non-self-preserving decisions, that function is clearly facilitated by emotion. If I imagine a dangerous situation concretely but feel no fear, I may go into the dangerous situation anyway.

The philosophical problems discussed in chapter 7 also connect with evolutionary concerns. One is the emotional effect of fiction. We noted that salient or vivid images tend to produce emotions and that knowledge about existence does not seem to have much bearing on these emotions. This is a good instance of the difference between mechanism and function. Again, evolution does not produce teleological functions or "designs," though talk about adaptations may sometimes seem to imply this. Rather, evolution produces mechanisms. These mechanisms approximate certain functions and that is why they have survival value. Thus the mechanism of responding to salience or vividness approximates responding to existence.

In other words, if I fear something that is very vivid or salient, I am probably fearing something that exists. That is why responding to vividness or salience is adaptive. It is a simple mechanism that will in most cases produce the same result as a calculation of existence, but it will do so more quickly. The same point may be made about some other variables affecting emotion, such as proximity. We noted that, in general, emotion appears to become more intense as its cause comes closer. Sensitization to proximity is a simple mechanism that approximates ego-relevance. It is clearly adaptive (a similar point is made by LeDoux [*Synaptic* 122]). Though a calculation of proximity is less accurate than a calculation of ego-relevance, it is far easier to perform; thus it is much more likely to arise in the first place and to produce successful results. All this has clear bearing on the issue of empathy as well. What is interesting for the analysis of empathy is that in approximating emotional egocentrism, such evolutionary mechanisms actually avoid emotional egocentrism. The fact that proximity produces the same self-preserving results in critical situations in effect frees emotion from the necessity of egocentrism. The point may have broader implications (e.g., in ethics) and is certainly worth further study, including further evolutionary study.

I have argued in this chapter that there are some severe problems with evolutionary psychology as it has developed in recent years, both generally and in its particular relation to literature and the arts. On the other hand, it seems clear that evolutionary accounts of cognitive structures and processes are crucial. In all likelihood, they will be increasingly important in the coming years, and they will bear increasingly on literary study. This can be a very good thing. But it will be a good thing only if we establish our hypotheses with genuine empirical rigor and develop our explanations algorithmically, not only in terms of a well-specified cognitive architecture, but also in terms of all other relevant levels of explanation. Indeed, it will be a good thing only if we keep in mind the relations among different levels of explanation and the principles that govern these relations. This includes those principles that bear on practical social life and on the human subjectivity that is always implied by, but never captured in, our neurobiology and psychology. After all, it is human experience and human society—the primary fields of arts and humanities—that, in the end, give all the other levels their significance.

Notes

Introduction

1. One book simply cannot treat all four of these areas equally. Painting receives the least coverage. Most obviously, I do not discuss the extensive work on the perceptual psychology of visual art. Readers interested in this might consult Robert Solso's *Cognition and the Visual Arts*. Indeed, I do not give much attention to the perceptual aspects of film or literature. Readers interested in these topics may wish to consult Joseph Anderson's *Reality of Illusion* on film and the work of Reuven Tsur on literature. There is also cognitive work on new and hybrid art forms, such as hypertext (see, for example, Rouet, Levonen, Dillon, and Spiro). For further literary bibliography readers may wish to consult such websites as www2.bc.edu/~richarad/lcb/home.html and cogweb.ucla.edu.

2. I hope that my treatments of Picasso and Coltrane and my briefer references to Joyce, Schoenberg, and others indicate that cognitive approaches to the arts are not incompatible with modernist or postmodernist innovation, despite Steven Pinker's recent contentions (see chapter 20 of *The Blank Slate*) and the claims of cognitive musicologists, such as Jourdain.

Chapter 1

1. A great deal of Lerdahl's and Jackendoff's seminal *Generative Theory of Tonal Music* involves an attempt to articulate the rules governing segmentation. Readers interested in pursuing these issues further may wish to consult their work. One of the most influential distinctions in their book is that between "well-formedness rules" and "preference rules." Various aspects of cognitive processing are governed by absolute rules that determine whether or not a given sequence is "well formed," which is to say, cognitively permissible. Other aspects are governed only by preferences. Thus cognitive processes have to follow certain principles—well-formedness rules—or else they fail. Other principles—preference rules—apply when possible, yielding more fluent or otherwise "better" processing sequences, but they are not necessary. I will not be making any use of this distinction in the following pages, but it is valuable and has been taken up by other writers on the arts, including writers outside music. For literary uses of this and related ideas from Jackendoff, see the works by Spolsky and Jahn.

2. It is difficult to say just how much segmentation and structuring occur in the auditory processor and how much in working memory. I will draw a line here which may put too much into one unit or the other. (For some neurobiological observations that bear on this issue, see Jourdain 28 and 54.) The important point, however, is to illustrate the processing sequence.

3. Here, musical experience and training make a good deal of difference. People trained in music have quite a range of relevant schemas. On the other hand, whatever our training, we all have at least some basic sense of the tonal center. Dowling's experimental research appears to indicate that inexperienced listeners do not schematize for very much tonal structure. But it seems virtually impossible that they do not schematize for tonal structure at all, at least for the tonic itself. For example, Sloboda cites research indicating "the importance of establishing a key, or tonal centre, for memorization of melodic sequences" (*Musical* 180)—and the memorization of melodies (e.g., "My Favorite Things") is hardly confined to musically trained listeners. Sloboda writes that even "a moderate amount of training leads listeners to use an implicit coding scheme based on the familiar major diatonic scale" (124). Tillman, Bharucha, and Bigand go further, maintaining that "explicit learning is unnecessary to exhibit a sensitivity to subtle musical structures." Indeed, "mere exposure to . . . musical pieces suffices to develop implicit but sophisticated knowledge" (906). In any case, it seems safe to say that anyone who actively listens to, say, jazz (rather than passively hearing it as

background music) not only encodes the sequence of notes for relative pitch, but tacitly schematizes it for scalar relations (dominant, leading tone, etc.).

4. In placing this tonal scale encoding in working memory, I am shifting the boundary somewhat from where Dowling places it.

5. Terminology in this area is not entirely fixed. Many writers on jazz distinguish improvisation based on "motifs" from improvisation based on "formulas" (see chapter 6 of Kernfeld *What*; on Coltrane in particular, see his "Two Coltranes"). This division tends to assume that motifs are flexible—open to variation—whereas formulas are relatively fixed. The flexibility of motifs is extremely important. However, I do not distinguish motifs from formulas as I do not see a difference in types of cognitive structure here. Rather, I see a difference in the uses of one type of structure. Thus I would not say that some performers use flexible motifs while others use inflexible formulas. Rather, I would say that some performers—in general, the more artistically successful performers—make use of the flexibility of motifs while others do not make use of that flexibility.

6. Some readers may balk at this use of the word "trill." Fuller does note that "Trills on intervals . . . wider than a major second are occasionally mentioned" (870). However, the important issue is not whether the improvisatory technique fits the technical term. The important issue is isolating the technique and noting its adaptability.

7. Here and throughout, I am transposing from Coan's F# to concert E.

8. Any musical composition is, of course, a cognitive feat. Improvisation, however, is a feat not only in its final product, but in its process, for the nature of improvisation prevents revision. In connection with this, there are some obvious parallels between improvisation and oral composition (e.g., the singing of epics by oral bards), as Sloboda has emphasized (*Musical* 138–50). For this reason, one would expect theories of one to have bearing on the other. In connection with this, it is worth mentioning David Rubin's *Memory in Oral Traditions*. In that work, Rubin argues that poets recite poems through a process of "cuing and constraint." Specifically, the poet learns a complex set of schemas—rhythmic patterns, rhyme schemes, images, and so on. For any given line the poet recites, these schemas (along with the meaning of the line itself) serve to cue memories of events, phrases, or images that might follow, while simultaneously placing constraints on those events, and so on. Rubin takes Homeric epic as an example and explains just what the primary cues and constraints are. From this theoretically simple base, Rubin is able to explain a wide range of data, including the existence and use of epic formulae. Note that cues are necessary or the poet will not have anything to say. But constraints are no less important. Without constraints, the poet would have too many options to choose from. Cues and constraints of some sort undoubtedly operate in jazz improvisation as well.

9. Needless to say, there are noncognitive factors that enter into the success of any piece, including this one. For example, Henry Louis Gates has influentially located Coltrane's "My Favorite Things" in African American cultural traditions (104).

10. Tillman, Bharucha, and Bigand note that "expectations about the 'what' and the 'when' of the events" in a piece of music result "in greater facilitation for expected events that occur at the expected time" (909). That facilitation gives us a sense of orientation, and it is exactly what Coltrane manipulates in these cycles.

11. Porter goes on to maintain that, in Part Four, Coltrane's "saxophone solo is a wordless 'recitation' of the words of the poem," included in the liner, "beginning with the title, 'A Love Supreme'" ("John Coltrane" 442).

Chapter 2

1. This is not precisely true in connectionism or neurobiology, where contents are best thought of as specific circuits of nodes (connectionism) or neurons (neurobiology). On the other hand, most researchers ultimately interpret these circuits in terms of representations. In any case, the reasons for the differences among these approaches will become clear below.

2. For an example of cognitive scientific analysis specified and tested via a computer program, see Johnson-Laird's "Freedom," which deals with jazz improvisation.

3. We will return to this issue in chapter 8. For a modern discussion of Descartes' reasoning and certainty regarding the existence of subjective experience, see Bertrand Russell's *Human Knowledge* 173–81 and *Outline* 129–40.

4. It is worth remarking here that representationalism is most often developed as a form of "functionalism." Functionalists argue that they are isolating structures, processes, and contents that, like software, are not dependent on the specific "hardware" in which they are instantiated. Thus, for functionalists, the rules of Chomskyan grammar could in principle be instantiated in a computer. Other writers dispute this and insist that human cognition is inseparable from the unique biology of the human brain.
5. Though, here as elsewhere, neuroscientists are not in complete agreement (see Holland "Where," 36 and citations).
6. Indeed, synthesis across senses is extremely important, both in life and in arts that make use of more than one sensory mode. For a valuable discussion of the cognitive synthesis of visual and auditory streams in cinema, see chapter 5 of Anderson.
7. Though I do not make much use of the feedback look in the following pages, it is valuable in literary study. Norman Holland in particular has taken up this idea in his important work on literary response (see *The Brain* and *The Critical I*).
8. It is a commonplace of cognitive science that the mental lexicon does not distinguish sharply between definitions and empirical knowledge (i.e., it does not separate dictionary information from encyclopedia information). The feature list may be understood as representing a rough movement from definitional to empirical features, but without any point where there is a decisive change from one to the other.
9. The classic discussion of scripts is Schank and Abelson.
10. To a great extent, influence is a matter of an author's complex cognitive relations to non-prototypical exempla (for discussion, see chapter one of my *Joyce*).
11. Here one might ask where these thresholds, and so forth, come from. They are arbitrary. One assigns a set of thresholds, et cetera, then runs the system, altering the numbers according to specific rules until one gets an output that works. This may seem like a bad thing. But, in fact, the arbitrariness of the initial numbers is a great advantage for it indicates the explanatory robustness of this simple architecture. Starting with arbitrarily assigned thresholds (or connection strengths, which we will discuss below), a connectionist system can arrive at a final set of numbers with great explanatory power. In the connectionist view, this shows, among other things, that vast human learning can take place with minimal innate architecture. Specifically, when we turn from connectionist models to neurobiology, the obvious way of treating nonrandom initial numbers is by assuming that these numbers are innate. The connectionist use of random initial numbers shows that such innatist assumptions are unnecessary.
12. The second half was not part of Hebb's initial formulation. On the addition of this, and other complications, see McLeod, Plunkett, and Rolls 319–20.
13. The preceding examples present cases of simple input and output. One node feeds into a set of nodes and this yields some observable result. However, the real power of connectionism results from the inclusion of intermediate or "hidden" nodes (i.e. nodes between input and output nodes). These hidden nodes often involve cycles of activation and inhibition so that the passage to equilibrium becomes far more complex and far more interesting than in these simplified examples.
14. On the other hand, we are implicitly bringing representationalism into connectionism by speaking as if the nodes ("death," "Hell," and so on) have representational content. Indeed, one might argue that this is always the case with connectionism, for we always treat the activation patterns as interpreted, as having a tacitly representational—and ultimately intentional—meaning.

Chapter 3

1. Of course, not all historical periods and not all cultures have valued innovation equally. In part, this is the result of such things as market conditions (e.g., to what extent the body of past literature is available and thus the degree to which new works must differentiate themselves from past works). In part, it is also a matter of semantic prejudice. Some cultures and periods use "innovation" as a term of praise. In those places and times, the most tired clichés will be advertised as radically novel. In other cultures and periods, "innovation" is a term of blame. In those places and times, radical innovation will present itself as an authentic adherence to tradition. Despite all this, it remains the case cross-culturally that

works most often survive and are admired (against available earlier works) only if they involve basic innovation. Moreover, radical innovation is found cross-culturally as well, from the progressive systematization of musical principles and practices in India to the recuperative borrowings from other traditions in African mask carving. Of course, anything that began as a radical innovation may (and often does) become a stifling convention, but that does not affect its initial creativity or the cognitive principles underlying that creativity.

2. My interpretation of the painting is in keeping with that of critics such as Patricia Leighten. Leighten argues that, for Picasso, prostitutes (such as those represented in the painting) were the "most exploited members of the social order" (85). Moreover, she sees the women on the right as "aggressively challeng[ing]" figures (88). Not all interpreters agree. For example, Butler sees Picasso as taking "revenge" on these women, and suggests that "the imposition of the mask" may be seen as a form of "decapitation" (111).

3. Coltrane is not the only avant-garde musician to rely on this particular childhood link. Schoenberg did so as well, most famously in *Sprechstimme*, a "use of the voice midway between speech and song" (Randel 804). Moreover, Butler notes that, in his *Second Quartet* (which adds a soprano to the fourth movement), "Schoenberg has escaped the logic of traditional tonality, by following another logic, that of the spoken language" (52).

Chapter 4

1. Though see Tsur's work, and the interview by Bradburn, for an alternative view.
2. This is not to say that a connectionist approach to metaphor is entirely missing. For a good example of this approach, see Chandler.
3. As should be obvious, I am to some extent combining representational and PDP accounts. Thus I assume there is a scanning process. But this process operates on a lexical network that is structured or put into a scanning order via parallel circuits of activation. These parallel circuits will give different items different degrees of partial activation, thus allowing us to account for data that do not seem to fit purely serial accounts.
4. It is conventional to print titles for metaphor schemas in capital letters.
5. As J. Hillis Miller put it, in the context of an influential interpretation of this poem, "The critic . . . is a follower who repeats the pattern once again and once again fails to 'get it right,' just as Shelley repeats himself and repeats his precursors. . . . The critic's attempt to untwist the elements in the texts he interprets only twists them up again in another place and leaves always a remnant of opacity, or an added opacity, as yet unraveled" (247). I would not quite go so far as Miller. But the complexity of the poem certainly defies any single interpretation.
6. In considering the remainder of the poem, readers may wish to compare this cognitive approach with prominent deconstructive accounts, such as those of Miller or de Man. The reversals of standard hierarchies and schemas recall deconstructive concerns. Indeed, a cognitive reading of this sort may be said to find difference and deferral within presence itself, at least at certain points in the poem. On the other hand, a cognitive reading sees all these contradictions and reversals as forming a coherent cognitive pattern—a very nondeconstructive idea.

Chapter 5

1. Bordwell's work on cognition and film is not confined to narrative. One of his finest works, *Making Meaning*, is a metatheoretical examination of film interpretation. In this book, Bordwell makes a compelling case that professional film interpretations and theories of interpretation, despite seemingly vast superficial differences, follow a limited set of cognitive procedures. Moreover, Bordwell manages to integrate this cognitive argument with a materialist analysis of the socio-economic conditions in which film theory and interpretation are produced. The work is not only an outstanding piece of cognitive theory, but testimony to the fact that social and cognitive approaches can be integrated productively (a distinction it shares with Holland's *The Brain* [see chapter 6]).
2. Here and below, citations of Bordwell refer to *Narration*, unless otherwise noted.
3. Intuitively, one might be inclined to believe that identity is not constructed at all, but spontaneously recognized. However, the cognitive work involved in identity schematization

becomes evident when the relevant cognitive processes are disrupted. For example, Brothers cites a striking case in which a woman came to believe that the image in her mirror was someone else (3).

4. The following discussion focuses on a work of popular cinema. Readers interested in the application of cognitive principles to avant-garde works may wish to consult Peterson.

5. The Production Code was a set of rules, adopted by the motion picture industry in 1934, to guarantee the moral decency of Hollywood films.

6. For a fuller discussion of perception and our sense of continuity and simultaneity in film, see chapter 6 of Anderson.

7. Cameron paid a great deal of attention to precise details of sound in *Titanic*, yielding subtleties that go well beyond anything we can discuss here (see Kenny).

8. For an elaborate and influential discussion of narrators and narrative schematization, see Branigan (especially chapter 4).

9. One prominent approach—which runs contrary to the prototype-based treatment in this section—is that of "story grammars." Story grammarians seek to establish a set of strict rules that will generate all and only well-formed stories, in the way that the grammar of a language will generate all and only well-formed sentences of that language. Rumelhart is the classic essay. For a more recent, literary account, see Pavel.

10. I am not the only one to treat universals. Pioneering work was done by Kiparsky (following Jakobson) and Brewer ("Story"). More recently, Bordwell has developed an account of universals to treat aspects of film, (see "Convention"). Approaching the issue somewhat differently, Alan Richardson has treated the complexity of the relation between cognitive universals and literary thematics. For some current work, see http://litup.unipd.it.

11. For a more detailed discussion of universals, see Comrie or Croft in linguistics and Brown in anthropology. I will be following the conventions in linguistics.

12. Some readers may find the physical prototype to be less intuitively plausible than the others. It is the least common today. However, for most of our history, the major concern of humankind has been getting enough food. It remains even now the major concern for millions of people.

13. For my evidence and for details of the cognitive analysis, see *The Mind and Its Stories*.

Chapter 6

1. Some critics, prominently Ellen Spolsky, have argued that modularity has significant consequences for literature and the arts, as well as other cultural phenomena.

2. This is not to say that a full list of emotions is quite limited. There are many nonbasic emotions in this account (e.g., envy). These are built up from basic emotions.

3. Oatley's discussion of emotion focuses on "story" or the actual sequence of actions and events. There has also been important cognitive work on the relation of emotion to discourse or the order and manner of presentation (see, for example, Brewer's "Literary Theory," Brewer and Lichtenstein, and Feagin).

4. For a fuller discussion of cognition and identification, see Gaut and citations.

5. Note that Tan's idea of a preferred final outcome does not solve the problems mentioned above regarding our emotional response to literary narrative. It merely restates them. Now the question becomes, "Why do we formulate this preferred final outcome, then care so much about it, when the events are fictional and we have no egocentric involvement in them?"

6. On the complexity and variety of a reader's or viewer's goals, see Currie.

7. Though it is interesting to note that the earliest versions of this figure "originated in Picasso's own self-portrait" (Leighten 85).

8. A number of authors have sought to synthesize psychoanalysis and cognitive science. See, for example, Holland *The I*, as well as *The Brain* 3–6 and citations.

Chapter 7

1. See, for example, the introduction to Crane. One major exception to this is the work of Norman Holland, especially *The Brain*. Holland draws extensively on neurobiological

research in treating both broad patterns in literary cognition and in treating individuality in creation and response.

2. Norman Holland has raised versions of these questions in a neurocognitive context as well (see *The Brain* 154).

3. In positive emotional states, we seek to sustain or intensify the eliciting conditions. In negative emotional states, we seek to eliminate or diminish those conditions.

4. Mood-congruent processing has figured importantly in some cognitive treatments of film. Noël Carroll has discussed the ways in which distinctive emotional orientations guide our response to particular genres. For example, horror movies lead us to focus on fear-relevant features of scenes and characters. Carroll has explored the emotional subtleties of several genres in these terms.

5. Depending on one's purposes, one may wish to distinguish subthresholds here and below. For example, Smith and Kirby distinguish between "activation" and "focal awareness." In the former, the emotion has consequences, though we are not consciously aware of it. In my terms, activation and focal awareness would be two substages within orientation.

6. I should perhaps note that I myself do not agree with this hierarchization. I am merely pointing out that it seems to capture a common pattern in western aesthetic evaluation.

7. This is not to say that mood is irrelevant to more intense emotional experiences. At each threshold or stage, the emotional elements of preceding stages are preserved and, in most cases, extended. For example, attentional focus is at its sharpest when the control threshold has been passed. For an illuminating discussion of the relation between mood and more intense emotions in the experience of film, see Greg Smith.

8. For readers unfamiliar with brain structure and terminology, Brothers presents a simple outline: "The outer layer of the brain is called the cortex. The major components of the brain, going from back to front, are the occipital, parietal, temporal, and frontal lobes, which are paired, one in each hemisphere. Deep within the temporal lobe is a cluster of neurons called the amygdala" (31). The hippocampus, "a memory center that integrates patterns of neural activity for later recall" (58), is also located in the temporal lobe. A more detailed account of brain regions and functions should be readily available in any recent encyclopedia.

9. There is not complete agreement on this. Ito and Cacioppo accept the link between negative emotions and the amygdala, but maintain that the "approach/reward system" is located elsewhere (57).

10. On the other hand, it seems likely that these fragments form the elements of our prototype eliciting conditions for the relevant emotions. Thus the triggers for fear probably combine to form at least part of our prototypically fearful situation—a situation of the sort we see in, for example, horror movies.

11. For a fuller discussion of facial expression and the communication of emotion in film, see Plantinga.

12. In some cases, our imagination of a situation may present the relevant information more vividly than an actual perception. The point is most obvious in literature. Literature is aimed at stimulating the imagination and at developing the details of the situation being imagined. Elaine Scarry's influential *Dreaming by the Book* examines this image-generating function of literature. Specifically, Scarry argues that "a poem or a novel is a set of instructions for mental composition" (244). The instructions lead us to "reproduce the deep structure of perception," leading to unique "vivacity" (9). In this context, it is unsurprising that literature has strong emotional effects.

Chapter 8

1. A number of writers claim that altruism is adaptive. But they are talking about altruism in the very limited sense of self-sacrifice for one's gene-pool (e.g., one's children). Thus Paul Hernadi refers to "the genetically coded call in many animal species for altruistic behavior toward offspring and other close kin" (65). (Hernadi notes that the most influential discussion of this may be found in Dawkins 88–108. On some of the difficulties with Dawkins' theories, which have been very important in evolutionary psychology, see Dover.) I am referring to cases in which the individual has no such personal connection. These are highly admired, and very nonadaptive.

2. The point has been noted by a number of writers on evolutionary psychology and the related field of sociobiology. See, for example, Bruce, et al. (a letter on "The Politics of Sociobiology" from Stephen Jay Gould and others) and Mackenzie.

3. Nor am I saying anything about the political views of individual evolutionary psychologists, which are irrelevant anyway. Indeed, judging from personal conversations, I suspect that Steven Pinker would be one of the most humane people in practical situations. I have the same impression of John Tooby and Leda Cosmides. My arguments here have to do with the content of the theories, not with the personalities of the theorists.

4. There is also the problem that, even in cases where skill is the crucial factor, it is not obvious that the skills at issue are praiseworthy, as one is likely to assume from Tooby and Cosmides' phrasing. For example, one hunter may be the most successful because he/she has the most skill at convincing other people to interfere with the hunting success of any competitors, because he/she is best at lying, because he/she has a talent for stealthily nabbing other hunters' kills. The point is important for the evolutionary account itself and for its social policy consequences.

5. This is not unique to Tooby and Cosmides. Fausto-Sterling cites other evolutionary psychologists whose doubtful arguments have much the same implications (see 211).

6. Though there are some general similarities, emergent structures as discussed here must be distinguished from those treated in conceptual blending theory. The latter are really contents, inferred information of the same general sort as the inputs.

7. There are, of course, exceptions to this. Unsurprisingly, some of the more plausible evolutionary accounts of art stay very close to physiology, especially perception (see, for example, the opening chapters of Anderson or the essay by Anderson and Anderson on visual perception and cinema).

8. In fact, evolutionary psychologists sometimes do discuss language in this way, with the severely inadequate results one would expect (see Jenkins for discussion).

Works Cited

Adolphs, Ralph and Antonio Damasio. "The Relationship Between Affect and Cognition: Fundamental Issues." In *Handbook of Affect and Social Cognition*. Ed. Joseph Forgas. Mahwah, NJ: Lawrence Erlbaum, 2001, 27–49.

Anderson, Joseph D. *The Reality of Illusion: An Ecological Approach to Cognitive Film Theory*. Carbondale and Edwardsville, IL: Southern Illinois UP, 1996.

Anderson, Joseph D. and Barbara Anderson. "The Case for an Ecological Metatheory." In *Post-Theory: Reconstructing Film Studies*. Ed. David Bordwell and Noël Carroll. Madison, WI: U of Wisconsin P, 1996, 347–67.

Anderson, Scott T. "John Coltrane, Avant Garde Jazz, and the Evolution of 'My Favorite Things." http://www.room34.com/coltrane/thesis.html.

Bal, Mieke. *Narratology: Introduction to the Theory of Narrative*. 2nd ed. Toronto: U of Toronto P, 1997.

Bertram, Bruce, et al. "The Politics of Sociobiology." (Letter.) *The New York Review of Books* (May 31, 1979). Http://www.nybooks.com/articles/7782.

Bhartrihari. "Bearing the luster of a full moon." In *Bhartrihari and Bilhana: The Hermit and the Love-Thief*. Ed. and trans. Barbara Stoler Miller. New York: Penguin, 1990, 65.

Bordwell, David. "Convention, Construction, and Cinematic Vision." In *Post-Theory: Reconstructing Film Studies*. Ed. Bordwell and Noël Carroll. Madison, WI: U of Wisconsin P, 1996, 87–107.

———. *Making Meaning: Inference and Rhetoric in the Interpretation of Cinema*. Cambridge, MA: Harvard UP, 1989.

———. *Narration in the Fiction Film*. Madison, WI: U of Wisconsin P, 1985.

Bower, G. H. "Affect and Cognition." *Philosophical Transactions of the Royal Society of London, Series B* 302 (1983): 387–402.

Bower, Gordon and Joseph Forgas. "Affective Influences on the Content of Cognition." In *Handbook of Affect and Social Cognition*. Ed. Forgas. Mahwah, NJ: Lawrence Erlbaum, 2001, 95–120.

Bradburn, Beth. "An Interview with Reuven Tsur." Http://www2.bc.edu/~richarad/lcb/fea/tsurin/tsurmain.html.

Branigan, Edward. *Narrative Comprehension and Film*. New York: Routledge, 1992.

Brewer, William F. "Literary Theory, Rhetoric, and Stylistics: Implications for Psychology." In *Theoretical Issues in Reading Comprehension: Perspectives from Cognitive Psychology, Linguistics, Artificial Intelligence, and Education*. Ed. Rand J. Spiro, Bertram C. Bruce, and William F. Brewer. Hillsdale, NJ: Lawrence Erlbaum, 1980, 221–39.

———. "The Story Schema: Universal and Culture-Specific Properties." In *Literacy, Language, and Learning: The Nature and Consequences of Reading and Writing*. Ed. David R. Olson, Nancy Torrance, and Angela Hildyard. Cambridge: Cambridge UP, 1985, 167–94.

Brewer, William F. and Edward H. Lichtenstein. "Event Schemas, Story Schemas, and Story Grammars." In *Attention and Performance IX*. Ed. John Long and Alan Baddeley. Hillsdale, NJ: Lawrence Erlbaum, 1981, 363–79.

Brockman, John. "A Biological Understanding of Human Nature: A Talk With Steven Pinker." *Edge: The Third Culture* (9 September 02): Http://www.edge.org/3rd_culture/pinker_blank.

Brothers, Leslie. *Friday's Footprint: How Society Shapes the Human Mind*. New York: Oxford UP, 1997.

Brown, Donald. *Human Universals*. Philadelphia, PA: Temple UP, 1991.

Butler, Christopher. *Early Modernism: Literature, Music and Painting in Europe 1900–1916*. Oxford: Clarendon P, 1994.

Cameron, Deborah. *Feminism and Linguistic Theory*. London: Macmillan, 1985.

Cameron, James, dir. *Titanic*. Script by Cameron. Director of Photography, Russell Carpenter. Edited by Conrad Buff, James Cameron, and Richard A. Harris. Produced by James Cameron and Jon Landau. Paramount Pictures, 1997.

Carroll, Noël. "Film, Emotion, and Genre." In Plantinga and Smith, 21–47.

Cech, Thomas R. "Overturning the Dogma: Catalytic RNA." In Pfenninger and Shubik, 5–17.

Chandler, Steven R. "Metaphor Comprehension: A Connectionist Approach to Implications for the Mental Lexicon." *Metaphor and Symbolic Activity* 6.4 (1991): 227–58.

Chomsky, Noam. *Language and Problems of Knowledge: The Managua Lectures.* Cambridge, MA: MIT P, 1988.

———. "Linguistics and Brain Science." Paper no. 500. Series A: General and Theoretical Papers. Essen: UAUD, 1999.

———. *New Horizons in the Study of Language and Mind.* Cambridge: Cambridge UP, 2000.

Clarke, Eric F. "Generative Principles in Music Performance." In *Generative Processes in Music: The Psychology of Performance, Improvisation, and Composition.* Ed. John Sloboda. Oxford: Clarendon P, 1988, 1–26.

Clore, Gerald, Karen Gasper, and Erika Garvin. "Affect as Information." In *Handbook of Affect and Social Cognition.* Ed. Joseph Forgas. Mahwah, NJ: Lawrence Erlbaum, 2001, 121–44.

Coan, Carl, transcriber. *John Coltrane Solos.* Music editing, Ravi Coltrane. Milwaukee, WI: Hal Leonard, 1995.

Coetzee, J. M. *Waiting for the Barbarians.* New York: Penguin, 1980.

Coltrane, John. *A Love Supreme.* John Coltrane, tenor sax. McCoy Tyner, piano. Jimmy Garrison, bass. Elvin Jones, drums. Reissue. Universal City, CA: Verve Music Group, 2000.

———. "My Favorite Things." Melody by Richard Rodgers. John Coltrane, soprano sax. McCoy Tyner, piano. Steve Davis, bass. Elvin Jones, drums. *My Favorite Things.* Reissue. Los Angeles, CA: Rhino Entertainment, 1998.

Comrie, Bernard. *Language Universals and Linguistic Typology: Syntax and Morphology.* Chicago, IL: U of Chicago P, 1981.

Cook, Nicholas. "Perception: A Perspective from Music Theory." In *Musical Perceptions.* Ed. Rita Aiello with John A. Sloboda. New York: Oxford UP, 1994, 64–95.

Crane, Mary Thomas. *Shakespeare's Brain: Reading with Cognitive Theory.* Princeton, NJ: Princeton UP, 2001.

Croft, William. *Typology and Universals.* Cambridge: Cambridge UP, 1990.

Currie, Gregory. "Narrative Desire." In Plantinga and Smith, 183–99.

Daix, Pierre. *Picasso: Life and Art.* Trans. Olivia Emmet. New York: HarperCollins, 1993.

Damasio, Antonio R. *Descartes' Error: Emotion, Reason, and the Human Brain.* New York: Avon, 1994.

Dawkins, Richard. *The Selfish Gene.* Oxford: Oxford UP, 1989.

Dawson, Michael R. W. *Understanding Cognitive Science.* Oxford: Basil Blackwell, 1998.

Dean, Roger T. *New Structures in Jazz and Improvised Music Since 1960.* Buckingham: Open University Press, 1992.

De Man, Paul. "Shelley Disfigured." In *Deconstruction and Criticism.* Ed. Harold Bloom, et al. New York: Seabury P, 1979, 39–73.

Dover, Gabriel. "Anti-Dawkins." In Rose and Rose, 55–77.

Dowling, W. Jay. "Tonal Structure and Children's Early Learning of Music." In *Generative Processes in Music: The Psychology of Performance, Improvisation, and Composition.* Ed. John Sloboda. Oxford: Clarendon P, 1988, 113–28.

Ellis, Michael J. *Why People Play.* Englewood Clifs, N.J: Prentice-Hall, 1973.

Epstein, Cynthia Fuchs. *Deceptive Distinctions: Sex, Gender, and the Social Order.* New Haven: Yale UP and New York: Russell Sage Foundation, 1988.

Fausto-Sterling, Anne. "Beyond Difference: Feminism and Evolutionary Psychology." In Rose and Rose, 209–27.

Feagin, Susan L. "Time and Timing." In Plantinga and Smith, 168–79.

Feldman, David Henry. "The Development of Creativity." In Robert Sternberg: 169–86.

Fiedler, Klaus. "Affective Influences on Social Information Processing." In *Handbook of Affect and Social Cognition.* Ed. Joseph P. Forgas. Mahwah, NJ: Lawrence Erlbaum, 2001, 163–85.

Finke, Ronald A. "Creative Realism." In Smith, Ward, and Finke, *Creative,* 303–26.

Flanders, Laura. "Natural Born Rapists." *In These Times* March 6, 2000: 11.

Fodor, Jerry A. *Concepts: Where Cognitive Science Went Wrong.* Oxford: Clarendon P, 1998.

Ford, John, dir. *Stagecoach*. Script by Dudley Nichols, from the short story "Stage to Lordsburg" by Ernest Haycock. Photographed by Bert Glennon. Edited by Dorothy Spencer and Walter Reynolds. Walter Wanger Productions. United Artists, 1939.

Forgas, Joseph P. "Introduction: Affect and Social Cognition." In *Handbook of Affect and Social Cognition*. Ed. Forgas. Mahwah, NJ: Lawrence Erlbaum, 2001, 1–24.

Freeland, Cynthia A. "The Sublime in Cinema." In Plantinga and Smith, 65–83.

Frijda, Nico. *The Emotions*. Cambridge: Cambridge UP and Paris: Editions de la Maison des Sciences de l'Homme, 1987.

Fuller, David. "Trill." In *The New Harvard Dictionary of Music*. Ed. Don Michael Randel. Cambridge, MA: Belknap P, 1986, 869–73.

Galler, Janina. "The Early Experience." In Pfenninger and Shubik, 101–16.

Gardner, Howard. *Art, Mind, and Brain: A Cognitive Approach to Creativity*. New York: Basic Books, 1982.

Garman, Michael. *Psycholinguistics*. Cambridge: Cambridge UP, 1990.

Gates, Henry Louis, Jr. *The Signifying Monkey: A Theory of African-American Literary Criticism*. New York: Oxford UP, 1988.

Gathercole, Susan E. "Models of Verbal Short-Term Memory." In *Cognitive Models of Memory*. Ed. Martin A. Conway. Cambridge, MA: MIT P, 1997, 13–45.

Gaut, Berys. "Identification and Emotion in Narrative Film." In Plantinga and Smith, 200–16.

Gerrig, Richard J. *Experiencing Narrative Worlds: On the Psychological Activities of Reading*. New Haven: Yale UP, 1993.

Gerrig, Richard J. and Deborah A. Prentice. "Notes on Audience Response." In *Post-Theory: Reconstructing Film Studies*. Ed. David Bordwell and Noël Carroll. Madison, WI: U of Wisconsin P, 1996, 388–403.

Gombrich, E. H. *Art and Illusion: A Study in the Psychology of Pictorial Representation*. Princeton, NJ: Princeton UP, 1969.

Goode, Erica. "Jealous? Maybe It's Genetic. Maybe Not." *New York Times* (8 October 2002): D1, D6.

Gould, Stephen Jay. "Darwinian Fundamentalism." *The New York Review of Books*. June 12, 1997. Http://www.nybooks.com/articles/1151.

———. *The Mismeasure of Man*. New York: W. W. Norton, 1981.

———. *The Structure of Evolutionary Theory*. Cambridge, MA: Belknap P, 2002.

Halász, László. "Effect and reminding in literary text processing." In *Empirical Studies of Literature: Proceedings of the Second IGEL-Conference, Amsterdam 1989*. Ed. Elrud Ibsch, Dick Schram, and Gerard Steen. Amsterdam: Rodopi, 1991, 79–85.

———. "Emotional effect and reminding in literary processing." *Poetics* 20 (1991): 247–72.

Herman, David. "Scripts, Sequences, and Stories: Elements of a Postclassical Narratology." *PMLA* 112.5 (1997): 1046–59.

Hernadi, Paul. "Literature and Evolution." *SubStance: A Review of Theory and Literary Criticism* 94/95 (2001): 55–71.

Hogan, Patrick Colm. *Empire and Poetic Voice: Cognitive and Cultural Studies of Literary Tradition and Colonialism*. Albany, NY: State U of New York P, forthcoming.

———. *Joyce, Milton, and the Theory of Influence*. Gainesville, FL: U P of Florida, 1995.

———. *The Mind and Its Stories: Narrative Universals and Human Emotions*. Cambridge: Cambridge UP and Paris: Editions de la Maison des Sciences de l'Homme, 2003.

———. *On Interpretation: Meaning and Inference in Law, Psychoanalysis, and Literature*. Athens, GA: U of Georgia P, 1996.

———. "Structure and Ambiguity in the Symbolic Order: Some Prolegomena to the Understanding and Criticism of Lacan." In *Criticism and Lacan: Essays and Dialogue on Language, Structure, and the Unconscious*. Ed. Hogan and Lalita Pandit. Athens, GA: U of Georgia P, 1990.

———. "Toward a Cognitive Science of Poetics." *College Literature* 23.1 (1996): 164–78.

Holland, Norman. *The Brain of Robert Frost: A Cognitive Approach to Literature*. New York: Routledge, 1988.

———. *The Critical I*. New York: Columbia UP, 1992.

———. *The I*. New Haven: Yale UP, 1985.

———. "Where is a Text? A Neurological View." *New Literary History* 33 (2002): 21–38.

Honeck, Richard P. *A Proverb in Mind: The Cognitive Science of Proverbial Wit and Wisdom*. Mahwah, NJ: Lawrence Erlbaum Associates, 1997.

Ingarden, Roman. *The Literary Work of Art: An Investigation on the Borderlines of Ontology, Logic, and the Theory of Literature.* Trans George Grabowicz. Evanston, IL: Northwestern UP, 1973.

Iser, Wolfgang. *The Implied Reader: Patterns of Communication in Prose Fiction from Bunyan to Beckett.* Baltimore, MD: Johns Hopkins UP, 1974.

Ito, Tiffany and John Cacioppo. "Affect and Attitudes: A Social Neuroscience Approach." In *Handbook of Affect and Social Cognition.* Ed. Joseph Forgas. Mahwah, NJ: Lawrence Erlbaum, 2001, 50–74.

Jahn, Manfred. "Frames, Preferences, and the Reading of Third-Person Narratives: Towards a Cognitive Narratology." *Poetics Today* 18.4 (1997): 441–68.

———. "Windows of Focalization: Deconstructing and Reconstructing a Narratological Concept." *Style* 30.2 (1996): 341–67.

Jenkins, Lyle. *Biolinguistics: Exploring the Biology of Language.* Cambridge: Cambridge UP, 2000.

Johnson-Laird, Philip N. *The Computer and the Mind: An Introduction to Cognitive Science.* Cambridge, MA: Harvard UP, 1988.

———. "Freedom and Constraint in Creativity." In *The Nature of Creativity: Contemporary Psychological Perspectives.* Cambridge: Cambridge UP, 1988, 202–19.

Johnson-Laird, Philip N. and Keith Oatley. "The Language of Emotions: An Analysis of a Semantic Field." *Cognition and Emotion* 3.2 (1989): 81–123.

Jourdain, Robert. *Music, the Brain, and Ecstasy: How Music Captures Our Imagination.* New York: Quill, 2002.

Kahneman, Daniel and Dale T. Miller. "Norm Theory: Comparing Reality to Its Alternatives." *Psychological Review* 93.2 (1986): 136–53.

Kālidāsa. *Śakuntalā and the Ring of Recollection.* Trans. Barbara Stoler Miller. In *Theater of Memory: The Plays of Kālidāsa.* Ed. Miller. New York: Columbia UP, 1984.

Kenny, Tom. "*Titanic*: Sound Design for James Cameron's Epic Ocean Saga." *Mix Magazine* (Jan. 1998). Http://www.geocities.com/Hollywood/Academy/4394/titanic.htm.

Kernfeld, Barry. "Two Coltranes." In *Annual Review of Jazz Studies 2.* Ed. Dan Morgenstern, Charles Nanry, and David A Cayer. New Brunswick, NJ: Transaction Books, 1983, 7–66.

———. *What to Listen for in Jazz.* New Haven, CT: Yale UP, 1995.

Kiparsky, Paul. "On Theory and Interpretation." In *The Linguistics of Writing: Arguments Between Language and Literature.* Ed. Nigel Fabb, Derek Attridge, Alan Durant, and Colin MacCabe. New York: Methuen, 1987, 185–98.

Kosslyn, Stephen. *Image and Brain: The Resolution of the Imagery Debate.* Cambridge, MA: MIT P, 1994.

Lakoff, George and Mark Turner. *More than Cool Reason: A Field Guide to Poetic Metaphor.* Chicago: U of Chicago P, 1989.

Langlois, J. H and L. A. Roggman. "Attractive Faces Are Only Average." *Psychological Science* 1 (1990): 115–21.

Larsen, Steen, János László, and Uffe Seilman. "Across Time and Place: Cultural-Historical Knowledge and Personal Experience in Appreciation of Literature." In *Empirical Studies of Literature: Proceedings of the Second IGEL-Conference, Amsterdam 1989.* Ed. Elrud Ibsch, Dick Schram and Gerard Steen. Amsterdam: Rodopi, 97–103.

LeDoux, Joseph. *The Emotional Brain: The Mysterious Underpinnings of Emotional Life.* New York: Touchstone, 1996.

———. *Synaptic Self: How Our Brains Become Who We Are.* New York: Viking, 2002.

Leighten, Patricia. *Re-Ordering the Universe: Picasso and Anarchism, 1897–1914.* Princeton, NJ: Princeton UP, 1989.

Lerdahl, Fred. "Cognitive Constraints on Compositional Systems." In *Generative Processes in Music: The Psychology of Performance, Improvisation, and Composition.* Ed. John Sloboda. Oxford: Clarendon P, 1988, 231–59.

Lerdahl, Fred and Ray Jackendoff. *A Generative Theory of Tonal Music.* Cambridge, MA: MIT P, 1983.

Lumsden, Charles J. "Evolving Creative Minds: Stories and Mechanisms." In Robert Sternberg, 153–68.

MacKenzie, Lucas. "The Emperor's New Genes." *Cultural Logic* 4.2 (2002): Http://eserver.org/clogic/4-2/mackenzie.html.

Maltby, Richard. "'A Brief Romantic Interlude': Dick and Jane Go the 3½ Seconds of the Classical Hollywood Cinema." In *Post-Theory: Reconstructing Film Studies*. Ed. David Bordwell and Noël Carroll. Madison, WI: U of Wisconsin P, 1996, 434–59.

Martindale, Colin. "Biological Bases of Creativity." In Robert Sternberg, 137–52.

———. "Creativity and Conectionism." In Smith, Ward, and Finke, *Creative*: 249–68.

McLeod, Peter, Kim Plunkett, and Edmund T. Rolls. *Introduction to Connectionist Modelling of Cognitive Processes*. Oxford: Oxford UP, 1998.

Miller, J. Hillis. "The Critic as Host." In *Deconstruction and Criticism*. Ed. Harold Bloom, et al. New York: Seabury P, 1979, 217–53.

Milton, John. *Paradise Lost*. In *John Milton: Complete Poems and Major Prose*. Ed. Merritt Y. Hughes. Indianapolis, IN: Bobbs-Merrill, 1957.

Nagel, Thomas. "What is it Like to be a Bat?" *Mortal Questions*. Cambridge: Cambridge UP, 1979, 165–80.

Neruda, Pablo. "The Insect." In *The Captain's Verses (Los versos del Capitán)*. Trans. Donald D. Walsh. New York: New Directions, 1972, 53.

Oatley, Keith. *Best Laid Schemes: The Psychology of Emotions*. Cambridge: Cambridge UP and Paris: Editions de la Maison des Sciences de l'Homme, 1992.

———. *Brain Mechanisms and Mind*. New York: Dutton, 1972.

———. *The Case of Emily V*. London: Minerva, 1994.

———. "Emotions, Abstractions, and Some Ways in which Literature Enters Life." *Poetics Today*, forthcoming.

———. "Emotions and the Story Worlds of Fiction." In *Narrative Impact: Social and Cognitive Foundations*. Ed. Melanie Green, Jeffrey Strange, and Timothy Brock. Mahwah, NJ: Erlbaum, 2002: 39–69.

———. *Perceptions and Representations: The Theoretical Bases of Brain Research and Psychology*. London: Methuen, 1978.

———. "Why Fiction May be Twice as True as Fact: Fiction as Cognitive and Emotional Simulation." *Review of General Psychology* 3.2 (1999): 101–17.

Oatley, Keith and P. N. Johnson-Laird. "Toward a Cognitive Theory of Emotions." *Cognition and Emotion* 1.1 (1987): 29–50.

Ortony, Andrew. "Are Emotion Metaphors Conceptual or Lexical?" *Cognition and Emotion* 2 (1988): 95–104.

———. "The Role of Similarity in Similes and Metaphors." In *Metaphor and Thought*. 2nd ed. Ed. Ortony. New York: Cambridge UP, 1993: 342–56.

Ortony, Andrew, Gerald Clore, and Allan Collins. *The Cognitive Structure of the Emotions*. Cambridge: Cambridge UP, 1988.

Owens, T. *Bebop: The Music and its Players*. New York: Oxford UP, 1995.

Palade, George E. "Tides of Genius." In Pfenninger and Shubik, 145–58.

Panksepp, Jaak. *Affective Neuroscience: The Foundations of Human and Animal Emotions*. New York: Oxford UP, 1998.

Pavel, Thomas G. *The Poetics of Plot: The Case of English Renaissance Drama*. Minneapolis, MN: U of Minnesota P, 1985.

Peterson, James. "Is a Cognitive Approach to the Avant-Garde Cinema Perverse?" In *Post-Theory: Reconstructing Film Studies*. Ed. David Bordwell and Noël Carroll. Madison, WI: U of Wisconsin P, 1996, 108–29.

Pfenninger, Karl H. and Valerie R. Shubik, eds. *The Origins of Creativity*. Oxford: Oxford UP, 2001.

Pinker, Steven. *The Blank Slate: The Modern Denial of Human Nature*. New York: Viking, 2002.

———. *How the Mind Works*. New York: Norton, 1997.

Plantinga, Carl. "The Scene of Empathy and the Human Face on Film." In Plantinga and Smith, 239–55.

Plantinga, Carl and Greg M. Smith, eds. *Passionate Views: Film, Cognition, and Emotion*. Baltimore, MD: Johns Hopkins UP, 1999.

Plucker, Jonathan A. and Joseph S. Renzulli. "Psychometric Approaches to the Study of Human Creativity." In Robert Sternberg, 35–61.

Policastro, Emma and Howard Gardner. "From Case Studies to Robust Generalizations: An Approach to the Study of Creativity." In Robert Sternberg, 213–25.

Porter, Lewis. *John Coltrane: His Life and Music*. Ann Arbor, MI: U of Michigan P, 1998.

————. "John Coltrane." In *The Oxford Companion to Jazz*. Ed. Bill Kirchner. Oxford: Oxford UP, 2000, 432–45.

Pratt, Mary Louise. *Toward a Speech Act Theory of Literary Discourse*. Bloomington, IN: Indiana UP, 1977.

Pressing, Jeff. "Improvisation: Methods and Models." In *Generative Processes in Music: The Psychology of Performance, Improvisation, and Composition*. Ed. John Sloboda. Oxford: Clarendon P, 1988, 129–78.

Putnam, Hilary. "Quantum Mechanics and the Observer." *Realism and Reason: Philosophical Papers, Volume 3*. Cambridge: Cambridge UP, 1983: 248–70.

Randel, Don, ed. *The New Harvard Dictionary of Music*. Cambridge, MA: Harvard UP, 1986.

Richardson, Alan. "Rethinking Romantic Incest: Human Universals, Literary Representation, and the Biology of Mind." *New Literary History* 31.3 (2000): 553–72.

Rose, Hilary and Steven Rose, eds. *Alas, Poor Darwin: Arguments Against Evolutionary Psychology*. New York: Harmony Books, 2000.

Rouet, Jean-François, Jarmol J. Levonen, Andrew Dillon, and Rand J. Spiro, eds. *Hypertext and Cognition*. Mahwah, NJ: Lawrence Erlbaum Associates, 1996.

Rubin, David. *Memory in Oral Traditions: The Cognitive Psychology of Epic, Ballads, and Counting-Out Rhymes*. New York: Oxford UP, 1995.

Ruelle, David. *Chance and Chaos*. Princeton, N.J.: Princeton UP, 1991.

Rumelhart, David E. "Notes on a Schema for Stories." In *Representation and Understanding: Studies in Cognitive Science*. Ed. Daniel G. Bobrow and Allan Collins. New York: Academic Press, 1975, 211–36.

Runco, Mark A. and Shawn Okuda Sakamoto. "Experimental Studies of Creativity." In Robert Sternberg: 62–92.

Rushdie, Salman. *Midnight's Children*. New York: Penguin Books, 1980.

Russell, Bertrand. *Human Knowledge: Its Scope and Limits*. New York: Simon and Schuster, 1967.

————. *Outline of Philosophy*. London: George Allen and Unwin, 1927.

Scarry, Elaine. *Dreaming by the Book*. New York: Farrar, Straus, Giroux, 1999.

Schacter, Daniel L. *Searching for Memory: The Brain, the Mind, and the Past*. New York: Basic Books, 1996.

Schank, Roger C. and Robert P. Abelson. *Scripts, Plans, Goals, and Understanding: An Inquiry into Human Knowledge Structures*. Hillsdale, NJ: Lawrence Erlbaum, 1977.

Seilman, S. and S. F. Larsen. "Personal Resonance to Literature: A Study of Remindings While Reading." *Poetics* 18 (1989): 165–77.

Shakespeare, William. *Hamlet*. Ed. Susan Wofford. Boston: Bedford Books, 1994.

————. *King Lear*. Ed. Louis Wright with Virginia LaMar. New York: Washington Square P, 1972.

————. "Sonnets." In *The Riverside Shakespeare*. 2nd ed. Ed. G. Blakemore Evans, with the assistance of J. J. M. Tobin. Boston, MA: Houghton Mifflin, 1997, 1839–1874.

Shelley, Percy Bysshe. "A Defense of Poetry." In *English Romantic Writers*. Ed. David Perkins. New York: Harcourt, Brace and World, 1967.

————. "The Triumph of Life." In *The Norton Anthology of English Literature*. 5th ed. Ed. Abrams, et al. New York: W. W. Norton, 1986, 760–77.

Sloboda, John. *The Musical Mind: The Cognitive Psychology of Music*. Oxford: Clarendon P, 1985.

————. Preface. In *Generative Processes in Music: The Psychology of Performance, Improvisation, and Composition*. Ed. Sloboda. Oxford: Clarendon P, 1988, v–xiii.

Smith, Craig and Leslie Kirby. "Affect and Cognitive Appraisal Processes." In *Handbook of Affect and Social Cognition*. Ed. Joseph Forgas. Mahwah, NJ: Lawrence Erlbaum, 2001, 75–92.

Smith, Greg M. "Local Emotions, Global Moods, and Film Structure." In Plantinga and Smith, 103–26.

Smith, Steven M., Thomas B. Ward, and Ronald A. Finke, eds. *The Creative Cognition Approach*. Cambridge, MA: MIT P, 1995.

————. Preface. In Smith, Ward, and Finke, *Creative*: vii–viii.

————. "Principles, Paradoxes, and Prospects for the Future of Creative Cognition." In Smith, Ward, and Finke, *Creative*, 327–335.

Solso, Robert L. *Cognition and the Visual Arts*. Cambridge, MA: MIT P, 1994.

Spolsky, Ellen. *Gaps in Nature: Literary Interpretation and the Modular Mind*. Albany, NY: SUNY P, 1993.

————. *Satisfying Skepticism: Embodied Knowledge in the Early Modern World.* Burlington, VT: Ashgate, 2001.

Sternberg, Robert J. *Handbook of Creativity.* Cambridge: Cambridge UP, 1999.

Sternberg, Robert J. and Todd I. Lubart. "The Concept of Creativity: Prospects and Paradigms." In Robert Sternberg, 3–15.

Storey, Robert. *Mimesis and the Human Animal: On the Biogenetic Foundations of Literary Representation.* Evanston, IL: Northwestern UP, 1996.

Tan, Ed S. *Emotion and the Structure of Narrative Film: Film as an Emotion Machine.* Trans. Barbara Fasting. Mahwah, NJ: Lawrence Erlbaum Associates, 1996.

Tillman, Barbara, Jamshed J. Bharucha, and Emmanuel Bigand. "Implicit Learning of Tonality: A Self-Organizing Approach." *Psychological Review* 107.4 (2000): 885–913.

Tooby, John and Leda Cosmides. "Cognitive Adaptations for Social Exchange." In *The Adapted Mind: Evolutionary Psychology and the Generation of Culture.* Ed. Jerome H. Barkow, Cosmides, and Tooby. New York: Oxford UP, 1992, 163–228.

————. "Does Beauty Build Adapted Minds? Toward an Evolutionary Theory of Aesthetics, Fiction, and the Arts." *SubStance: A Review of Theory and Literary Criticism* 94/95 (2001): 6–27.

Tsur, Reuven. *Toward a Theory of Cognitive Poetics.* Amsterdam: North Holland, 1992.

————. *What Is Cognitive Poetics?* Tel Aviv: Katz Research Institute for Hebrew Literature, 1983.

Turner, Frederick. *Natural Classicism: Essays on Literature and Science.* New York: Paragon House, 1985.

Turner, Mark. *The Literary Mind.* New York: Oxford UP, 1996.

————. *Reading Minds: The Study of English in the Age of Cognitive Science.* Princeton, NJ: Princeton UP, 1991.

Tversky, A. "Features of Similarity." *Psychological Review* 84 (1977): 327–52.

Wade, Nicholas. "Dr. Tatiana, a Dr. Ruth With Advice for Other Species." *New York Times* (5 November 2002): D3.

Ward, Thomas B. "What's Old about New Ideas?" In Smith, Ward, and Finke, *Creative,* 157–78.

Ward, Thomas B. Steven M. Smith, and Ronald A. Finke. "Creative Cognition." In Robert Sternberg, 189–212.

Weisberg, Robert W. "Creativity and Knowledge: A Challenge to Theories." In Robert Sternberg, 226–50.

Wilson, Edward O. *Consilience: The Unity of Knowledge.* New York: Vintage Books, 1999.

Wittgenstein, Ludwig. *Tractatus Logico-Philosophicus.* Trans. D. F. Pears and B. F. McGuinness. London: Routledge and Kegan Paul, 1961.

Zachary, G. Pascal. "My Favorite Coltrane." *In These Times* (January 7, 2002), 28–9.

Index